Apocalypse
and
Allegiance

APOCALYPSE *and* ALLEGIANCE

Worship, Politics, and Devotion in the **Book of Revelation**

J. Nelson Kraybill

BrazosPress
a division of Baker Publishing Group
Grand Rapids, Michigan

To my daughter Andrea,
visionary artist and
intrepid follower of the Lamb

———————————

© 2010 by J. Nelson Kraybill

Published by Brazos Press
a division of Baker Publishing Group
P.O. Box 6287, Grand Rapids, MI 49516-6287
www.brazospress.com

Printed in the United States of America

Library of Congress Cataloging-in-Publication Data
Kraybill, J. Nelson.
    Apocalypse and allegiance : worship, politics, and devotion in the book of Revelation / J. Nelson Kraybill.
        p.   cm.
    Includes bibliographical references and indexes.
    ISBN 978-1-58743-261-3 (pbk.)
        1. Bible. N.T. Revelation—Criticism, interpretation, etc. Title.
BS2825.52.K73 2010
228'.06—dc22   2009036245

God's reign is already present on our earth in mystery.
When the Lord comes, it will be brought to perfection.
That is the hope that inspires Christians.
We know that every effort to better society,
especially when injustice and sin are so ingrained,
is an effort that God blesses,
that God wants,
that God demands of us.

Words spoken by Archbishop Oscar Romero as he celebrated Eucharist on March 24, 1980, at the chapel of Divine Providence Cancer Hospital in San Salvador. In preceding months Romero had summoned the people of El Salvador to nonviolent resistance against a repressive military regime. As he finished his eucharistic homily, a single bullet from an assassin ended his life (James R. Brockman, *The Church Is All of You: Thoughts of Archbishop Oscar Romero* [Minneapolis: Winston, 1984], 110).

Contents

Illustrations

Acknowledgments

Thirty years ago students at an urban high school in San Juan, Puerto Rico, dared me to teach the book of Revelation. Accepting the challenge, I steeped myself in commentary and history to understand John's vision. When placed in historical and literary context, Revelation began to make sense. By the end of the semester, my students had made a poster-sized cartoon strip of John's vision that encircled the classroom, and I had acquired a lifelong fascination with Revelation. In subsequent years I learned more about the last book of the Bible from teachers, colleagues, and students, including the following:

- Professor Paul Achtemeier, my adviser when I wrote a doctoral dissertation on Revelation at Union Theological Seminary in Virginia. The dissertation was published as *Imperial Cult and Commerce in John's Apocalypse* (Sheffield: Sheffield Academic Press, 1996), and as *Culto e Comércio Imperiais no Apocalipse de João* (São Paulo: Paulinas, 2004).
- Students in my classroom in Uruguay—some of whom had been incarcerated and tortured by a military regime in that country—who helped me understand that modern empire can warp values and allegiances in ways similar to ancient Rome.
- Loren Johns, my faculty colleague at Associated Mennonite Biblical Seminary in Elkhart, Indiana, whose specialties include Lamb Christology. We taught Revelation together and jointly led a study tour to the seven cities of Revelation and Rome.
- People at congregations, denominational assemblies, seminaries, colleges, and universities in the United States, Canada, England, Ireland, Japan, Korea, Spain, and Uruguay who contributed insights when I had the privilege of teaching Revelation in those countries.

In addition to studying Revelation on a scholarly level, I aspire to teach John's vision in ways that are accessible to a general audience. This book grew out of such efforts. It includes photos and graphics throughout, a minimum of footnotes or rehearsal of scholarly debates, and some contemporary application. Associated Mennonite Biblical Seminary generously granted me a summer sabbatical, during which I wrote much of this volume. I took many photos on these pages on the three occasions when I collaborated with Tour-Magination of Waterloo, Ontario, to lead study groups to biblical sites in Israel/Palestine, Turkey, and Italy.

I am grateful to Rodney Clapp of Brazos Press for encouraging me to write this book and for shepherding it through the editorial process. The editorial team of Brazos Press masterfully ironed out theological, historical, and hermeneutical wrinkles throughout the manuscript. Others who contributed by critiquing drafts at various stages include Barbara Nelson Gingerich, Loren Johns, Alan Kreider, Eleanor Kreider, Gene Lackore, Mary Lackore, and Heidi Siemens Rhodes. To each of these generous persons I owe much, with the greatest debt to my wife, Ellen Graber Kraybill, who read this book at several stages and was a constant source of encouragement.

J. Nelson Kraybill
Elkhart, Indiana
Good Friday, 2009

Abbreviations

ANF	*Ante-Nicene Fathers*. Edited by A. Roberts and J. Donaldson. 10 vols. 1885–1896. Reprint, Peabody, MA: Hendrickson Publishers, 1994
CIL	*Corpus inscriptionum latinarum*. Edited by T. Mommsen et al. Berlin-Brandenburg: Deutsche Akademie der Wissenschaften, 1863–
JSNTSup	Journal for the Study of the New Testament: Supplement Series
KJV	King James Version
LCL	Loeb Classical Library
NIV	New International Version
OGIS	*Orientis graecae inscriptiones selectae*. Edited by W. Dittenberger. 2 vols. Leipzig: S. Hirzel, 1903–1905
RSV	Revised Standard Version
WBC	Word Biblical Commentary
WUNT	Wissenschaftliche Untersuchungen zum Neuen Testament

Introduction

Worship Is Political

Not long after the 2001 terrorist attacks in the United States, I received an unsettling letter from Trevor, a college friend whom I had not seen for twenty-five years. In our youth we both were persuaded by Jesus' call to peacemaking and love of enemies. But the church Trevor attended in 2001 was not bound to nonviolence, and people there were reeling from a double loss in the terrorist attacks. Among passengers on the plane that plunged into the Pentagon was the granddaughter of a woman from Trevor's congregation. And Todd Beamer, who helped to organize a passenger revolt on the plane that went down in Pennsylvania, was a friend of the pastor. The trauma of these tragedies and fear of further terrorism triggered a shift in Trevor's ethics and allegiance.

In his letter, Trevor described a worship service at his congregation on the Sunday after the attacks:

> The Christian flag was at the front of the church. As we sang "God Bless America," the newest mother in the congregation brought the US flag forward in a funeral march—one step per two beats. I have not felt that filled with the Holy Spirit nor had tears streaming down my face at any service in my memory as I did during that one. When the US flag joined the Christian flag at the front of the church, it looked exactly right. I vowed not to make an issue of whether the national flag should stand at the front of the church as I had at a previous congregation.

Explaining that he no longer held to the nonviolent ideals of his youth, Trevor wrote:

I have always felt that the "turn the other cheek" lesson of the gospel was a lesson against vengeance. As a Christian, there is no room in my religion for making war to gain vengeance. Making war to prevent the further senseless slaughter of my countrymen is perfectly justified, however. If my identity as an American makes me a target, I have an obligation to defend myself, my family, and my neighbors. By choosing to massively attack innocent people, the perpetrators have lost any right to have their point of view considered by civilized people. Whatever happens to them now is their just due, the morality of which needs no further consideration or soul-searching on my part.

Symbols Help Persuade

Many factors—including anger, fear, and shock—must have played into Trevor's shift of attitude toward violence and political allegiance. But what stands out in events leading to his change of conviction is the significant role of *symbol* at each stage. Terrorists struck the World Trade Center (a symbol of economic might) and the Pentagon (a symbol of military power). The perpetrators had also apparently intended to attack the United States Capitol building (a symbol of political power) but were thwarted by a passenger revolt.

Symbols featured prominently in the worship service Trevor described. A young mother (a symbol of new life) carried the American flag (a symbol of loyalty to nation) through a worshiping congregation and placed it beside the cross (a symbol of Jesus' suffering love; fig. I.1) on a Christian flag.

This array of symbols represents forces of awesome power. There is the power of religious fundamentalism that precipitated the death of three thousand innocent people on September 11. There is the "shock and awe" power of retaliatory wars that brought death to thousands in Afghanistan and Iraq. The Christian flag at Trevor's church carries its own powerful symbol: the cross

Fig. I.1. What does it mean when Christians in the United States fly the Christian flag in a position subordinate to the national flag?

of Jesus, instrument of political execution through which God has brought salvation to the world. From start to finish in this story, people with competing worldviews have used *symbol* or *symbolic acts* to mark allegiance and justify deeds of enormous consequence.

When Trevor rejoiced to see the national flag and the Christian flag joined in worship, was he giving allegiance both to Jesus and to country? Did one loyalty trump the other? Should Christians, citizens of the global kingdom of God, even think of their identity and allegiance in national terms? What larger spiritual forces do these symbols represent?

Revelation Uses Symbol to Build Allegiance

These are important questions, and Christians appropriately turn to Jesus and the early church for guidance in responding. John of Patmos, author of the book of Revelation, provides a constellation of images and narratives that help us understand how ideologies shape the world. Revelation makes abundant use of symbols, and John understands how these forge political and spiritual identity. In particular, Revelation highlights the way worship, with its reliance on symbol, expresses and shapes allegiance. The last book of the Bible is not a catalog of predictions about events that would take place two thousand years later. Rather, it is a projector that casts archetypal images of good and evil onto a cosmic screen. These images first of all speak to realities of the author's era. But Revelation also serves as a primer on how good and evil interact in every generation.

The central political reality in the author's day—the late first century—was the indomitable Roman Empire and its "divine" emperors. The pressing issue for John's readers was how Christians, who gave their highest loyalty to Jesus, should conduct themselves in a world where economic and political structures assumed that everyone would worship the emperor. While no Western nation has outright ruler worship today, we do have political, military, and economic powers to which millions give unquestioned allegiance.

John championed the same hope for Christ's return that animates the church today, but his vision does not predict specific political, cultural, or natural events of the twenty-first century. He received his vision in the first-century Mediterranean context, and symbols in his work relate primarily to realities of that era. But the world he inhabited—the Roman Empire—and the symbolic universe his vision created have uncanny parallels to our circumstances today. Sin and death still work havoc, empires continue to rampage, and with John we await the liberation of all creation, which will obtain when Christ returns. In the meantime, what is the Spirit saying through Revelation to us about faithfulness to Jesus Christ in our world?

Fig. I.2. Emperor Nero, who expected to be venerated as a god.

The World Worships Nero

A spectacle organized by Emperor Nero (fig. I.2) in first-century Rome pro-vides a glimpse of the political environment in which John wrote his vision. In AD 66, two years after Rome suffered a catastrophic fire, the emperor hosted a stupendous celebration. Tiridates, king of Armenia, visited the imperial capital. After journeying nine months by horseback, this wise man from the East[1] approached Rome with an entourage of three thousand Par-thian horsemen.[2]

Rome was master of the world, and Tiridates made the long trek in order to align Armenia with the superpower in Italy. Armenia was contested terri-tory between the dominions of Rome and Parthia (an empire centered in the region called Iran today). Although Tiridates himself was of Parthian blood, he wanted to become a client of Rome. Even before his visit to Italy, Tiridates had ceremonially placed his diadem on an image of Nero,[3] knowing he would receive a crown back from the emperor when he reached Rome.

Nero appreciated the propaganda value of hosting Tiridates well and spent a staggering sum of money on the festivities—rumored to be 300,000 *sesterces* out of an annual imperial budget of 800,000.[4] Tiridates arrived by chariot to find Rome decorated with torches and garlands. On the appointed day,

1. Tiridates was a member of the *magi*, the Zoroastrian priestly class.
2. Dio Cassius, *Roman History* 63.2.1.
3. Ibid. 62.23.3.
4. Edward Champlin, *Nero* (Cambridge, MA: Harvard University Press, 2003), 227. Ancient authors vary in their estimates of the expenditure. Cassius (*Roman History* 63.2.2) says Nero spent 800,000 *sesterces* per day to bring Tiridates to Rome.

Fig. I.3. Ruins of the Roman Forum, where Nero received Tiridates of Armenia.

thousands of spectators pressed into the forum before dawn, dressed in white and carrying laurel branches. As the sun rose, Nero entered the forum (fig. I.3), accompanied by the Senate and the Praetorian Guard. Resplendent in purple, the emperor ascended a platform built for the occasion and took his seat on a throne.

Tiridates and his entourage processed toward the platform between two lines of heavily armed Roman soldiers. As he neared the platform, the Armenian knelt before Nero with hands clasped over his breast. At this gesture the great throng—including many on nearby rooftops—thundered approval so loudly that Tiridates momentarily feared for his life. Then the crowd fell silent, and the visitor addressed Nero:

> Master, I am the descendant of Arsaces,[5] brother of the kings of Vologeses and Pacorus, and your slave. I have come to you, my god, worshiping you as I do [the sun god] Mithra. The destiny you spin for me shall be mine, for you are my Fortune and my Fate.

Nero replied to Tiridates with equal flourish:

> You have done well to come here in person, that meeting me face-to-face you might enjoy my grace. For what neither your father left you nor your brothers gave and preserved for you, this do I grant you. King of Armenia I now declare you, that both you and they may understand that I have power to take away kingdoms and to bestow them.[6]

5. Likely a reference to Artaxias (reigned 190–160 BC), founder of the Artaxiad Dynasty, which ruled the kingdom of Armenia for nearly two centuries.
6. Cassius, *Roman History* 63.5.2–3; in *Dio's Roman History*, trans. Earnest Cary, LCL 32 (Cambridge, MA: Harvard University Press, 1955), 8:143–44. In this and subsequent quotations from English translations of ancient works, archaic forms of pronouns and verbs have been

Fig. I.4. In AD 65 Nero issued this *aureus* coin in anticipation of receiving King Tiridates at Rome, which would mark the end of Rome's territorial dispute with the Parthian empire over Armenia. The reverse of the coin (right) shows the temple of Janus at Rome with doors closed, a symbol that the empire was "at peace." (Used by permission of Classical Numismatic Group, Inc., www.cngcoins.com.)

With these formalities finished, Nero—self-proclaimed king of kings— invited Tiridates to the platform. The Armenian sat at Nero's feet, and the emperor placed a diadem on his head. Nero raised Tiridates with his right hand and kissed him. Festivities then moved to the newly gilded Theater of Pompey, with its purple awning and embroidered image of Nero as the sun god Apollo. From there Nero proceeded to the temple of Janus, where he ceremonially closed the doors, a traditional sign in Rome that warfare had ended (fig. I.4). Even rulers from distant lands worshiped Nero, and the world was at peace.

Our World Is Full of Ritual and Worship

The obsequious behavior of Tiridates before Nero would be distasteful to most people in the modern West. We are grateful that our societies do not treat rulers as divine and that no one must be a slave to political masters. John of Patmos also found the kind of scene that unfolded at the Roman Forum abhorrent. But before we dismiss such idolatry as a relic of the distant past, we might ponder habits and rituals of our own society. Is our culture really as free from idolatrous expressions as we would like to imagine? Or are the gods we worship so embedded within our culture that we fail to recognize them?

Writing a decade before the recent global economic crisis, theologian Harvey Cox declared that economic forces of "The Market" had become god in the West, displacing the role of traditional religions:

> [For] all the religions of the world, however they differ from one another, the religion of The Market has become the most formidable rival, the more so because it is rarely recognized as a religion. The traditional religions and the religion of the global market . . . hold radically different views of nature. In Christianity and Judaism, for example, "the earth is the Lord's and the fullness thereof, the world and all that dwell therein." The Creator appoints human beings as stewards and gardeners but, as it were, retains title to the earth. . . .

rendered in modern English, British spellings have been changed to American, and texts have been made gender inclusive when that, arguably, was the intent of the author.

In The Market religion, however, human beings, more particularly those with money, own anything they buy and—within certain limits—can dispose of anything as they choose.[7]

Even when The Market became beastly, as in the global upheaval starting in 2008, most people submitted with little protest. We accepted poverty and unemployment as part of the free market. Companies that funded our retirement plans made huge profits by selling armaments or cigarettes around the world. Corporate executives earned hundreds of times what individual employees in their factories took home. We treated The Market, Cox said, as omnipotent (possessing all power), omniscient (having all knowledge), and omnipresent (existing everywhere). We learned on a day-to-day basis that The Market was "apprehensive," "relieved," "nervous," or "jubilant."

When The Market showed signs of turning beastly even on the middle class, economics professor and Nobel laureate Paul Krugman described a global "crisis of faith."[8] Banks that backed debt for millions of people failed, and credit crumbled. The word "credit" comes from the Latin *credere*—to believe or to trust—and the crisis pointed to the inadequacy of any credo whose object is other than God.[9]

In their book *The Gods That Failed*, British financial journalists Larry Elliott and Dan Atkinson name twelve "governing spirits" that took the world economy into chaos. Peoples and nations of the world put their faith in deities ranging from globalization and privatization to speculation and excess.[10] In language reminiscent of John's Apocalypse, Elliot and Atkinson describe how the gods of The Market

promised us paradise if only we would obey and pamper their hero-servants and allow their strange titans and monsters to flourish. We did as they asked, and have placidly swallowed the prescriptions of the lavishly rewarded bankers, central bankers, hedge fund managers, and private equity tycoons, while turning a blind eye to the rampaging of the exotic derivatives, the offshore trusts, and the toxic financial instruments. . . . These gods have failed. It is time to live without them.[11]

7. Harvey Cox, "The Market as God," *Atlantic Monthly*, March 1999, 18–23.

8. *New York Times*, February 15, 2008, www.nytimes.com/2008/02/15/opinion/15krugman .html (accessed July 15, 2009).

9. See Adam Hamilton, "Faith, Hope, and the Credit Crisis," *Sojourners*, December 2008, 7.

10. Larry Elliott and Dan Atkinson, *The Gods That Failed: How Blind Faith in Markets Has Cost Us Our Future* (New York: Nation Books, 2009), 12–21. The authors name twelve gods: globalization, communication, liberalization, privatization, competition, financialization, speculation, recklessness, greed, arrogance, oligarchy, and excess.

11. Ibid., 271–72.

In addition to gods that have warped the world economy, we might also consider the spiritual dimension of advertising's obsession with sex, leisure, and retirement security, or the temptation for nations to trust in weapons. We need prophets such as John of Patmos to help us recognize idolatry and injustice and to show us life-giving ways to worship a God of justice and sure salvation.

Jews and Christians Are Voices of Dissent

When Tiridates crossed northern Asia Minor (modern Turkey) on his way to Rome, he probably was unaware of a small Jewish sect whose members had recently begun meeting in halls and homes across the region. Tiridates would have known about Jews, since they were a prominent minority in many cities of Asia Minor and had their own homeland in Palestine. But a generation before Tiridates traveled to Rome, a Jewish teacher named Paul had helped spawn a Jewish splinter group in the East called Christians. The inspiration for this movement was a Galilean peasant who had died on a Roman cross, a form of execution reserved for people foolish enough to threaten or disobey the empire. Christianity was a disconcerting spiritual and political movement that was becoming its own religion, spilling beyond the Jewish populations of eastern Mediterranean cities to penetrate diverse classes and ethnicities.

Judaism and its messianic offshoot, Christianity, sometimes baffled and irritated subjects of Rome. Christians and Jews were monotheists, worshipers of one God in a world that revered many. Conquered peoples in the ancient world were normally expected to make a shift of allegiance by accepting the gods of their new masters, and the Romans in turn incorporated numerous foreign deities into their pantheon. In a world of religious syncretism, Jewish and Christian notions of singular loyalty to one God seemed subversive and antisocial.

Not only did Jews and Christians reject the gods of the nations; they also objected to the growing practice of emperor worship. The emperor when Jesus was born, Caesar Augustus (27 BC–AD 14), was hailed as divine. Emperor worship gained momentum throughout the first century AD, becoming prominent especially in the reigns of Caligula (AD 37–41), Nero (AD 54–68), and Domitian (AD 81–96). The spread of emperor worship coincided with the birth and growth of the Christian church. The entire Mediterranean world—except the obstinate Jews and Christians—worshiped at the feet of the emperor.

If Tiridates of Armenia did not yet know about Christians, Nero certainly did. Not long before receiving Tiridates, Nero had blamed the devastating fire at Rome (AD 64) on followers of Jesus. As we soon will see, Nero apparently contrived the accusation when some of his subjects suspected that Nero himself had torched the city. Christians in Rome learned that Nero was dangerous when he launched a fierce persecution against them as punishment for their alleged arson. It is likely that the apostles Peter and Paul both died in Nero's brief bloodbath.

A Prophet Takes on the Empire

Soon to meet his own violent death, Nero could not have imagined the revolutionary power of the embryonic Christian movement. But at the margin of his empire, a fearless Christian prophet named John would soon receive a vision that lampooned emperor worship and foresaw the collapse of the Roman Empire. The vision would identify allegiance as the defining spiritual issue of the day and condemn worship of the emperor as idolatry.

From his platform on the tiny Island of Patmos—like other islands to which Rome banished troublemakers—John the Seer used pen and parchment to take on the greatest political power of his day. Dismissing Rome as a harlot and its empire as a beast, he proclaims that only God and the Lamb are worthy to receive worship. John condemns popular expressions of allegiance to the empire as blasphemous and gives a glimpse of the true worship that should shape readers' lives:

> Then I looked, and I heard the voice of many angels surrounding the throne and the living creatures and the elders; they numbered myriads of myriads and thousands of thousands, singing with full voice,
>
> > "Worthy is the Lamb that was slaughtered
> > to receive power and wealth and wisdom and might
> > and honor and glory and blessing!"
>
> Then I heard every creature in heaven and on earth and under the earth and in the sea, and all that is in them, singing,
>
> > "To the one seated on the throne and to the Lamb
> > be blessing and honor and glory and might
> > forever and ever!" (Rev. 5:11–13)

Anyone familiar with court ceremonies of the Roman emperors would recognize the subversive subtext of John's vision. Like other early Christians, John calls Jesus "Lord," using the exact title that emperors claimed. Revelation summons readers to life-encompassing worship that is an alternative to worship of emperor and empire. A litany early in John's vision says followers of the Lamb are a kingdom and priests serving our God. That is political language, calling followers of Jesus Christ to alternative allegiance and alternative identity.

Emperor worship and rituals of allegiance to empire pervaded politics, business, family, and social life in the Roman world. The first word of Revelation in the Greek text is *apocalypsis*, which means "unveiling." John's vision unveils the Roman Empire, showing it to have become a violent beast that usurps devotion belonging to God. Revelation also unveils the nature of divine love, made known by a Lamb that was slain. Humanity must choose between allegiance to the beast and allegiance to the Lamb.

Prophecy for the Author's Time—and Ours

Revelation refers to itself as prophecy (Rev. 22:7), which can be confusing because modern English uses the terms "prophecy" and "prediction" interchangeably. But biblical prophecy often has more to do with spiritual insight into the writer's immediate circumstances than with forecasts of the distant future. John's vision gave insight into "what must soon take place," in his era (1:1). The seer knew nothing of global warming, the Internet, or the United Nations. He wrote a scathing critique of political idolatry in the first-century Roman Empire, not an analysis of Al Qaeda or the inequities of modern globalization.

But just as the letters of the apostle Paul have become God's Word for us today when the Holy Spirit breathes through them, so God uses Revelation to illuminate our theological and political landscape. Rather than starting with the expectation that Revelation will forecast events of our time, we should seek to understand the life setting of John and the believers to whom he addressed his book. With that background, we then can listen for what the Spirit is saying to the churches about faithfulness to Jesus Christ today.

There are good commentaries on Revelation that give comprehensive, verse-by-verse analysis of the text. In contrast, the intent of this study is to traverse Revelation quickly. We will identify major landmarks and images that readers today may not readily understand. Along the way we will pause to consider issues such as Christology (theology about Jesus) and God's role in the violence so prominent in Revelation. Our focus throughout will be on worship, with the conviction that study of John's Apocalypse should inspire devotion to the God made known in Jesus today.

Our Tour Will Take a Detour

Instead of touring Revelation in the order its chapters appear in our Bibles, we will take a circuitous route, reading the book in a sequence that most quickly illuminates its historical and theological landscape. We will not give equal attention to all parts of the vision. Rather, we will focus on the theme of worship—worship of the emperor, worship of the Lamb, and worship in our world today. After a brief introduction to the author and his circumstances as presented in Revelation 1, we will turn to Revelation 13, with its nightmare of beasts. The first beast apparently represents the empire, and the second embodies the institutions of emperor worship that put pressure on Christians to align themselves with Rome.

John's first-century audience was keenly aware of the pressure to worship the emperor and would have heard the first half of Revelation with that reality in mind. We modern readers, however, typically do not have the Roman Empire or emperor worship in mind when we first encounter John's vision. So we do well to start with the beastly caricature of empire in Revelation 13, then use what we learn there to illuminate the rest of the book.

English translations of the Bible usually begin individual visions in Revelation with words such as, "Then I saw . . ."[12] That rendering of the Greek is not entirely helpful since most of John's visions actually start with "and" (*kai*): "*And* I saw . . ." or "*And* I looked . . ." John introduces the individual visions without necessarily indicating that there is a strict sequential relationship between them. When we are trying to understand the historical and political context of Revelation, we can examine portions of the book in the order that makes them most comprehensible two thousand years later.

There is, however, a theological trajectory to Revelation that culminates with the new Jerusalem, a symbol of salvation for the world. The book begins with a vision of Jesus, takes a long passage through destructive beasts and plagues, and ends with a glimpse of creation restored. We need to keep the end—the new Jerusalem—in view as we slog through the dark valleys of suffering and chaos.

Revelation Is Art and Poetry

At the beginning of our Bible, Genesis describes the dawn of creation. At the close of our canon, Revelation examines the end of time—and the dawn of a new day. With symbol and poetry, the beginning and end of the Bible make the confessional statement that God is sovereign. These books tell more about *who* is Lord than about *how* the cosmos begins or ends. They guide the reader toward faithful living in the present, speaking truth in language that is more metaphor than science. When Revelation depicts a voracious beast emerging from the sea, or the new Jerusalem descending from heaven, such evocative images should open our eyes to see the reality of structural evil in the world and the certainty that God will restore a fallen creation. What John says is true, but it mostly is not literal. We do not need to summon an astronomer to

12. For example, Rev. 5:1; 6:1; 10:1.

search the heavens for a city hurtling toward earth, or a biologist to determine the genus and species of the beast.

We might think of Revelation as an art gallery filled with colorful paintings, numbered and displayed as the artist chose to arrange them. The exhibit is dynamic and cohesive because all pieces contribute to an overall theme. But each painting also makes its own statement and can stand alone. Just as a good gallery can elicit wonder and nurture the human spirit, the book of Revelation can penetrate the soul in ways other than just through cognitive, rational portals. However perplexing Revelation may be to interpret, it is one of the more artistic books of the Bible.

Many Christians in the West have shut out the book of Revelation after seeing it exploited by cult leaders, pop eschatologists, and end-time fiction writers. Others grew tired of Revelation decades ago when churches split over premillennial, postmillennial, and amillennial interpretations of the book. Those disputes centered on whether Christ will return before or after a thousand-year reign (millennium) on earth—and generally missed the discipleship mandate of the book. We will pay little attention to the millennium, which is all of six verses (20:1–6), and simply underscore the main point of that part of John's vision: in the end evil will face defeat, and Christ will reign.

Use This Book as a Tour Guide

Use this book as a tour guide to John's vision, paying attention to the reading assignments in Revelation at the beginning of each chapter. These readings vary in length since we will linger over certain brief passages and pass swiftly through other long sections. Do the full reading of Revelation in your own Bible, not just the few verses reproduced under chapter headings. The historical and theological commentary will make more sense if you engage the entire text.

At the end of each chapter is a short article on "Living the Vision." These are vignettes of faithful witness by followers of Jesus Christ in centuries since John wrote Revelation. Some stories are from the early church, but most are contemporary or recent. All have parallels to some aspect of circumstances depicted in Revelation. The stories illustrate that followers of the Lamb in every generation wrestle with matters of allegiance, idolatry, violence, witness, and worship.

At the back of this book is a timeline highlighting biblical people and events important to Revelation. There also is a glossary with explanations of people, events, and terminology that may not be familiar to every reader.

John expects that a messenger will read aloud his vision in the context of a congregation (1:3). This suggests that Revelation needs group process and that we may benefit from hearing it read aloud. *Apocalypse and Allegiance* can serve as a guide for group discussion or adult education classes. Fellow Christians can help to identify contemporary parallels to the signs and symbols of John's vision. Questions at the end of each chapter can guide personal or group reflection.

For Reflection

Before going further, take an hour or two to read Revelation from beginning to end. You may want to have pen and paper in hand and make a few notes in answer to these questions:

1. Who or what are the main characters in this drama?
2. What is the emotional or spiritual tone of the vision?
3. What patterns (numerical, visual, or thematic) do you find in Revelation?
4. What riddles and puzzles catch your attention?

1

A Prophet in Trouble

Read Revelation 1:1–20

> I was in the spirit on the Lord's day, and I heard behind me a loud voice like a trumpet saying, "Write in a book what you see and send it to the seven churches, to Ephesus, to Smyrna, to Pergamum, to Thyatira, to Sardis, to Philadelphia, and to Laodicea."
>
> Then I turned to see whose voice it was that spoke to me, and on turning I saw seven golden lampstands, and in the midst of the lampstands I saw one like the Son of Man, clothed with a long robe and with a golden sash across his chest. . . . When I saw him, I fell at his feet as though dead. But he placed his right hand on me, saying, "Do not be afraid; I am the first and the last, and the living one. I was dead, and see, I am alive forever and ever; and I have the keys of Death and of Hades." (1:10–13, 17–18)

Most of what we know about the author of Revelation we must infer from the text of his vision:

> I, John, your brother who share with you in Jesus the persecution and the kingdom and the patient endurance, was on the island called Patmos because of the word of God and the testimony of Jesus. (1:9)

John apparently is in trouble, since he mentions persecution in these words of self-introduction. As his vision unfolds, it becomes evident that he expects that much of the Christian church will soon be in peril as well. One believer at the city of Pergamum—Antipas—has already suffered martyrdom (2:13).

27

Fig. 1.1. The harbor on
the Island of Patmos.

Later, John sees a vast multitude of saints who have come out of a great ordeal (7:9–17). Storm clouds are on the horizon for the whole Christian church.

In these difficult circumstances, the author turns to worship. "I was in the Spirit on the Lord's day," he says, "and I heard behind me a loud voice like a trumpet" (1:10). John's experience of God does not sneak up on him unawares. He is in the Spirit, in an attitude of waiting on God. The fact that his vision comes on the Lord's day (presumably Sunday)[1] suggests that he, like other early Christians, has a weekly rhythm of corporate worship and prayer. There were emerging patterns of worship in the early church, and the Spirit of God moved within that structure.

Worship Is a Spiritual Dance

Like Moses encountering God in the desert (Exod. 3), worship in Revelation unfolds in a kind of spiritual dance, with God and mortal alternating parts. Just as Moses saw a burning bush and turned aside to engage the divine (Exod. 3:3), John hears a voice and turns to engage the Son of Man (Rev. 1:12). When Moses turned toward the mysterious fire, God spoke again and told him to remove his sandals. This alternating initiative between God and Moses continued until Moses received the message and the mandate to confront Pharaoh, greatest ruler in the world known to the people of Israel. Similarly, a voice startles John. He turns, Christ appears, and John falls to the ground. Christ places a hand on John and gives him a message to the churches.

Would we even know about Moses or John if either had ignored the initial signs of God's presence? For both, experience of God happens in a deserted

1. The "Lord's day" could also be an allusion to the "day of the Lord," or appointed time of judgment, as foretold by the Hebrew prophets. See Amos 5:18–20 and Isa. 2:12–21.

Fig. 1.2. This mosaic appears above the entrance to the Monastery of the Apocalypse on the island of Patmos. Legend holds that John received his vision in a cave now enclosed by the monastery. Here John dictates to a scribe what he sees.

place: beyond the wilderness for Moses, and on a remote island for John. These venues suggest escape (from Egypt, for Moses) or abandonment (by God, for John). In each case God visits a person who has reason to feel lonely, angry, or afraid.

John says he is on the island of Patmos (see figs. 1.1; 1.2; 1.3) "on account of the word of God and the testimony of Jesus" (Rev. 1:9 RSV). Although we have no record of the Roman government sending people into exile specifically at Patmos, we know that other small islands nearby in the Aegean Sea were used for this purpose.[2]

Eusebius, a fourth-century church historian, records an early Christian tradition that Emperor Domitian banished John to Patmos in AD 95.[3] As becomes evident in his vision, John communicates the gospel in ways that challenge or offend people who support Roman rule. It is possible that John has gone to Patmos on a preaching mission, but it is more likely that he has fled there to save his life, or has been sent into exile there by the provincial government, which serves at the behest of Rome.

Features within John's vision seem to confirm a late first-century date. Revelation 11 shows the temple at Jerusalem being measured, presumably before its destruction in AD 70. But Revelation also refers to Rome contemptuously as "Babylon," an epithet used by some Jews and Christians after Rome destroyed Jerusalem in AD 70, just as ancient Babylon had done in 586 BC.[4] It is pos-

2. The Roman historian Tacitus (second century AD) mentions three small islands in the Aegean Sea (Gyarus, Donusa, and Amorgus) that were used for political exile. See Tacitus, *Annals* 4.30; 15.71.

3. Eusebius, *Ecclesiastical History* 3.18.1.

4. Other ancient documents that refer to Rome as Babylon include 1 Pet. 5:13 and *Sibylline Oracles* 5.159.

Fig. 1.3. From a hilltop overlooking the harbor of Patmos a visitor can see most of this small island.

sible that John composed parts of his work over a period of years and wove them into one text when he received a vision on Patmos. Regardless of how the text came together, Christians for centuries have known that Revelation is the work of a man who had a profound experience of God.

Who Is John of Patmos?

From early centuries of the church, there is a tradition that the seer was one of Jesus' twelve disciples, the brother of James and the son of Zebedee. This tradition assumes that the same John wrote both Revelation and the Fourth Gospel. But the author of Revelation never says or implies that he is among the twelve disciples, or that he even knew the earthly Jesus of Nazareth. Although Revelation and the Fourth Gospel share some themes, the grammar and writing style are so different that common authorship is unlikely.

The name "John" was not unusual among Jews and Christians in the first century. The author of Revelation probably was an otherwise unknown leader among the seven churches, to whom he directs his writing. John was a "brother" (1:9) to Christians in the western part of the country we today call Turkey, a region the Romans called Asia (often called Asia Minor by modern writers to distinguish it from the continent of Asia).

Calling himself a brother reflects a radical shift of identity that was typical among first-century followers of Jesus. Family was the most important place of belonging in the Roman world. In an era without the welfare-state safety net that we take for granted, family was the primary place of social and economic security. But Roman subjects sometimes ostracized family members who became Christian, and believers might lose employment because of their faith. It was a practical necessity for followers of Jesus to function as sister and brother to one another. Even Jesus, when asked about his relatives, seemed to downplay blood ties and find his deepest kinship with those who shared his passion for obedience to God (Mark 3:31–35).

John Writes to Seven Real Churches

A voice like a trumpet directs John to write down what he sees and send it to his sisters and brothers at seven churches in Ephesus, Smyrna, Pergamum, Thyatira, Sardis, Philadelphia, and Laodicea (Rev. 1:10–11). These were real congregations in real cities, whose ruins we can visit today.

The seven churches in Revelation do not represent seven eras of church history, as interpreters of the "church historical" school suggest. It is hard to imagine why the vision would have been addressed to specific first-century congregations if the primary message were about events that would transpire hundreds or thousands of years later. Imagery in Revelation may seem strange to us, but John understands what he is writing about and expects the small urban congregations he addresses to do the same. The message first of all is about their circumstances in the first-century Roman world.

From the seven letters in chapters 2 and 3, we infer that John was personally familiar with the seven congregations. He knew the spiritual and political circumstances of each and conveyed a pastoral word from Christ to each. Apparently the congregations also knew him, or he could not have expected them to pay attention to his message.

Because John understood Hebrew (9:11; 16:16) and knew the Old Testament well, it is likely that he was Jewish. He never directly quotes the Old Testament, but he does make more than four hundred allusions to it. John wrote Revelation in Greek, which in his day was the lingua franca, the shared common language, of the Roman world. The Romans themselves spoke Latin, but even they had to function in the international language of the Greeks, who had dominated the eastern Mediterranean in previous centuries. All New Testament authors wrote in Greek rather than in the Hebrew or Aramaic of the Jewish and early Christian subculture.

This commitment to common language is a measure of early Christian determination to make the gospel message accessible to the widest audience possible. It also reflects the fact that the early church quickly burst the bounds of nationalism and ethnicity. John seems to have struggled a bit to present his vision in Greek. The text of Revelation contains occasional anomalies of grammar or word order of the sort that happen to persons trying to master a second language.

The vision addresses seven congregations in Asia Minor, listed in the order that a messenger would reach them by following a circular route along public highways (fig. 1.4). The first congregation was in Ephesus, fourth largest city of the Roman Empire and site of extensive mission work by Paul (Acts

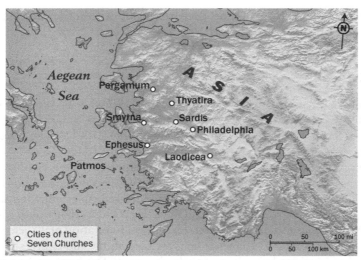

Fig. 1.4. John addressed his vision to seven congregations in the western part of the province of the Roman Empire known as Asia. He wrote from the tiny island of Patmos, fifty miles southwest of Ephesus. The order of cities Revelation addresses (Ephesus, Smyrna, Pergamum, Thyatira, Sardis, Philadelphia, Laodicea) outlines a horseshoe-shaped route a messenger may have traced to deliver John's vision to the seven churches.

18:19–20:1). Because of Paul's ministry at Ephesus, we have more biblical knowledge about that site than about any other city in Asia Minor that the vision names.

John wrote centuries before Christians erected buildings specifically dedicated to worship. The congregations that John knew in Asia Minor almost certainly were house churches, living room–sized clusters of individuals. They were nearly invisible in their cities. Perhaps neighbors became nervous about having members of a strange new religion next door, people who refused to participate in civic rituals of allegiance to the gods and the empire. But aside from occasionally arousing local suspicion, Christian churches played a seemingly insignificant role in the first-century Roman world.

Experience the Vision to Understand It

Revelation is *a book of worship*, not a book about worship. "Blessed is the one who reads aloud the words of the prophecy," John writes (1:3). Since only a small percentage of people in the ancient world were literate, most members of the seven churches would have needed someone to read Revelation to them. This reading would likely have happened in each of the seven cities as the congregations met in private homes to hear John's vision presented in a worship context.

Revelation is meant to be heard, but the unfolding drama involves all of the traditional five senses. John sees flashes of lightning, hears the sound of many waters, worships God in a cloud of incense, comes close to scorching heat, and eats a scroll sweet as honey. Revelation is total immersion drama, meant more to be experienced than analyzed. It is valuable for us today to read the book aloud and occasionally to do so without stopping. We need to feel the flow, absorb the anguish and jubilation, observe the periods of silence, smell the incense, and bow in worship.

The book begins with liturgical blessing: "Grace to you and peace" (1:4). What follows is a blend of politics and religion that permeates the entire vision: Jesus has made us to be a kingdom, priests serving his God (1:6). The word "kingdom" speaks to political identity; "priest" denotes a religious role. Politics and religion converge in acts of worship, and worship shapes allegiance. From start to finish, Revelation gives a resounding call for believers to avoid giving ultimate allegiance to any power other than God and the Lamb.

Symbols Can Point to Sacred Reality

The book of Revelation is a rapidly changing kaleidoscope of imagery: light, dark, crowns, angels, beasts, and much more. This fast-moving visual format is surprisingly appropriate for today's postmodern society, in which advertising, political discourse, and personal communication often take place with quick images and sound bites. Western culture is less literary and more visual than it was a generation ago, and media often convey the essence of an event or concept with visual signs. Consider the impact that images of the collapsing World Trade Center towers have had on the recent course of world events, or the way politicians carefully pick their physical backdrop when announcing a bid for election.

Advertising agencies, politicians, and other communicators use symbol to evoke concepts and feelings deep in the human psyche. "Symbols allow us to express what cannot be expressed in ordinary words," says David L. Barr. "Thus our most cherished convictions—be they religious, political, national— . . . find their expression in symbols: the cross, the yin-yang, Gettysburg, the flag, a bouquet of flowers." Symbols affect us deep down; they "reach out and take hold of us, demand our attention."[5]

Revelation, like modern communication, features signs and symbols. Liturgist Frank C. Senn writes that Christian worship always

> makes ample use of symbolic and metaphorical language simply because sacred reality can only be expressed in images and symbols. This is why we must be on our guard against the Western demotion of symbolic language, as when it is

5. David L. Barr, *Tales of the End: A Narrative Commentary on the Book of Revelation* (Santa Rosa, CA: Polebridge, 1998), 9–10.

said, "This is only a symbol." Western thought has sometimes driven a wedge between "symbol" and "reality." But the language of liturgy, like the language of the Bible, does not know of such a differentiation. Reality is expressed in symbolic language.[6]

Sign Theory Helps Interpret Revelation

Semiotics is the study of how signs work, and this discipline sheds light on the meaning of Christian worship. We will refer to the tools of semiotics because Revelation, more than any other book in the Bible, features signs. Semiotic theory, as articulated by American philosopher Charles Sanders Peirce (1839–1914), places signs—religious or otherwise—into three categories:[7]

1. **Icons** are signs that communicate by having *recognizable similarity* to the object or idea they represent.

   Examples: the recycle bin icon on a computer screen tells us where to dispose of electronic documents, and the curving line on a highway sign indicates a winding road ahead. An observer understands these icons because they look like the function or object they represent.
2. **Indexes** are signs that communicate because they are *affected by* or *changed by* the very phenomenon they register.

   Examples: a weathervane is physically turned as wind moves past it; bloodstains left at a crime scene give evidence of what happened. Both the turning of the weathervane and the bloodstains are caused by the circumstances about which they communicate.
3. **Symbols** are signs that communicate simply because users in a given group or culture have agreed to give them an *arbitrary meaning*.

   Examples: a traffic light communicates at an intersection only because the government has arbitrarily stipulated that red means stop and green means go. In the United States, a donkey represents the Democratic Party and an elephant the Republican Party only because of political conventions in American society.

Icons, Indexes, and Symbols Abound in Revelation

It is possible to place all signs or images in Revelation in one of these three categories. We will limit our analysis to signs that appear in the context of worship:

6. Frank C. Senn, *Christian Liturgy: Catholic and Evangelical* (Minneapolis: Fortress, 1997), 5.

7. The following definitions are adapted from Charles Sanders Peirce, *Peirce on Signs: Writings on Semiotic by Charles Sanders Peirce*, ed. James Hoopes (Chapel Hill: University of North Carolina Press, 1991), 239–40.

1. Examples of icons, signs that have *recognizable similarity* to the objects or persons they represent:

   A vision of the exalted Christ (1:12–20). John "saw one like the Son of Man, clothed with a long robe and with a golden sash across his chest. His head and his hair were white as wool." What John sees is not a literal description of Jesus, since the figure has eyes like flaming fire, and a sword coming from his mouth. Yet John signals that the image he sees has *similarity* to Jesus: "I saw one *like* the Son of Man."

   An image of the beast (13:13–15). The second beast tells people of the earth to "make an image [Greek: *eikōn*] for the beast that had been wounded." The second beast "was allowed to give breath to the image of the [first] beast so that the image of the beast could even speak and cause those who would not worship the image of the beast to be killed." Pictorial or sculptural likenesses of the emperors—who in John's view represent the beast—were common objects of devotion in the first century.

2. Examples of indexes, signs that are evident when worshipers or objects are *affected by* or *changed by* a spiritual encounter:

   Worshipers prostrate themselves before God (4:9–10). Twenty-four elders fall before the one who is seated on the throne and cast their crowns before him, and sing, "You are worthy . . . " Like wind turning a weathervane, the glory of God changes the physical posture of the elders and elicits spontaneous praise.

   People of the earth are awestruck by the beast (13:3–4). One of the heads of the beast "seemed to have received a death-blow, but its mortal wound had been healed. In amazement the whole earth followed the beast. They worshiped the dragon, for he had given his authority to the beast, and they worshiped the beast, saying, 'Who is like the beast, and who can fight against it?'" The beast's apparent resuscitation has such a mesmerizing effect that the whole earth follows after it. Humanity spontaneously cries out that the beast is unstoppable.

3. Examples of symbols, images to which Jews, Christians, or pagan society had assigned meaning:

   A rainbow encircles the throne of God (4:3), reminding John that God will never again destroy the earth by flood (Gen. 9:11–17).

   John sees a great multitude in heaven, "standing before the throne and before the *Lamb*, robed in *white*, with *palm branches* in their hands" (Rev. 7:9, emphasis added). The Lamb symbol has extensive precedent in the Old Testament practice of animal sacrifice. White robes symbolized victory in pagan society, as when throngs dressed in white at Rome to see Tiridates bow before Nero. Palm branches symbolized victory throughout the Mediterranean world and were featured in the Jewish

Feast of Tabernacles, which celebrated deliverance from slavery in Egypt (Lev. 23:39–43).

As often happens with signs, the categories of icon, index, and symbol blur and overlap in Revelation. So, for example, the icon of Jesus as the Son of Man (1:12–19) includes symbols such as a two-edged sword issuing from his mouth. The elders fall on their faces to worship God, an index that includes the symbolic number twenty-four (11:16).

Throughout the rest of this book, we will use the terms *icon, index*, and *symbol* with the semiotic meaning articulated by Peirce. This way of categorizing signs in Revelation will help us analyze their function and better understand the role of signs in our own political and religious contexts.

Modern Readers Struggle with Ancient Symbols

Icons for worship—in Revelation or in Christian artwork through the centuries—usually do not need much explanation. We know what John is talking about when he describes a vision of the exalted Christ or the throne of God. With the cues that John offers, we draw from historical or traditional associations to construct mental images of Christ or God that are familiar to us, even if they have a heavy overlay of symbol.

Indexes that appear in worship in Revelation also are fairly easy for the modern reader to grasp. We generally understand what it means to bow before another person, or to sing in jubilant celebration, or to be dumbstruck by dramatic events. Even people who do not believe in God have experiences of awe or fear that include responses such as singing, silence, or change in bodily posture.

It is the **symbols** in Revelation that are most likely to confound the modern reader, since our culture is far removed from the ancient world that gave those symbols meaning. To unfold the message of John's vision, we have to ask what the symbols meant in the first century. Does a symbol have precedent in the Old Testament? In Jewish or pagan thought of John's day? In practices of the Roman Empire, such as emperor worship? If we fail to ask these questions, we may assign meanings to John's symbols that miss his message.

Political or religious symbols usually penetrate the human psyche below radar, carrying associations and messages of which the receiver is only vaguely aware. Since the unconscious effect of symbols does not necessarily diminish their impact, we do well to consider carefully what symbols we embrace in worship and culture today. We might reflect on church architecture, for example, and what that communicates about our understanding of the body of Christ. We might pay attention to the ideology that stands behind events and heroes featured on currency or postage stamps. We can be alert to symbols and narratives used in advertising and military recruitment, and we can compare their stated or implicit values with the teachings of Jesus.

Revelation Starts with a Vision of Christ

Such sensitivity to symbol is important as we ponder the icon of Jesus in Revelation 1:11–20. We know the figure is the resurrected Christ because he says, "I was dead, and see, I am alive for ever and ever" (1:18). The vision depicts "one like the Son of Man" (1:13), a familiar title for Jesus in the Gospels. To churches in Asia Minor that were numerically insignificant and politically vulnerable, it must have been comforting to know that Christ was standing in their midst.

First-century Christians in Asia Minor would have had reason to think that they might face martyrdom. Prominent leaders of the early church—Stephen, James, Peter, and Paul—already had met violent death. John notes that Antipas, who gave witness to Jesus Christ, was killed at Pergamum, "where Satan lives" (2:13). John writes of an "hour of trial that is coming on the whole world to test the inhabitants of the earth" (3:10). He sees a vision of heaven in which martyred souls are told to rest a little longer while more saints meet martyrdom (6:11; see 20:4).

Despite such grim expectations, Revelation proclaims that neither emperors, provincial authorities, nor any other earthly powers ultimately govern life and death. Believers may lose their mortal bodies, but the Lord who died and rose again is sovereign over the second death (eternal separation from God after physical death) and the book of life (2:11; 3:5). If a life-and-death showdown with the Roman government is approaching, it is reassuring to know that Jesus holds the keys of Death and of Hades (1:18). Like most of early Christianity, Revelation takes a long view of salvation: believers are willing to face physical death with the assurance that eternal life is a gift of God for those who remain faithful.

Propaganda of the Roman Empire reinforced the notion that emperors controlled the world. A coin from the reign of Domitian (AD 81–96), most likely emperor when John wrote Revelation, features an icon of the infant son of the emperor seated on a globe (fig. 1.5). Declared divine by Domitian after an untimely death, the boy appears as the sun god Apollo, surrounded by seven stars. These may represent the sun, the moon, and the five planets known to the ancient world.[8] Revelation subverts the ideology of empire by using similar imagery to elevate Jesus: the risen Christ in John's vision also holds seven stars and has a face like the sun shining with full force (1:16).

8. See Mitchell G. Reddish, *Revelation*, Smyth & Helwys Bible Commentary (Macon, GA: Smyth & Helwys, 2001), 43.

Fig. 1.5. A coin from the reign of Domitian portrays the "divine" son of the emperor seated on a globe, surrounded by seven stars. (Photo courtesy of Harlan J. Berk, Ltd.)

John falls to the ground in fear at this sight (1:17)—a typical response of Bible characters who unexpectedly find themselves in the presence of the divine.[9] As we saw when Tiridates approached Nero, falling to the ground in obeisance also was what first-century people did when they met Roman emperors who claimed to be divine. John's vision underscores that Christians, in offering such gestures or indexes of worship, must choose between Jesus and the emperor.

We Meet God with Reverence and Awe

Few Christians in the West today face anything like the storm clouds of persecution that darkened the horizon for John and his first readers. Perhaps our eyes could be opened to cosmic spiritual struggles today by staying in touch with parts of the world where Christians are in trouble with their government or surrounding society. If we took the radical teachings of Jesus about wealth, power, and violence more seriously, we might feel greater tension with our own culture.

The first vision of John's Apocalypse models the reverence and awe that are appropriate in meeting God. John likely would have little patience for the folksy prayers, feel-good worship, and gospel-of-acculturation sermons that are common in many Western churches today. Such indexes of devotion treat God as an assistant who gives us a little help in coping with the burdens of life. We worship as if we are in control, domesticating the risen Christ by summoning his aid to fix our problems.

We may learn holy reverence for God through the visions of Revelation. John of Patmos encountered the God whose face no one could see and live (Exod. 33:20). He knew the Christ whose transfigured divine presence left awed observers prostrate on the ground (Matt. 17:6). Bible narratives of such encounters usually include the instruction "Do not be afraid," as when Gabriel addressed Mary (Luke 1:30). The Christ who appears as a Lamb in Revelation also takes

9. See, for example, Dan. 8:17; Luke 24:5; Acts 9:4.

John beyond fear. But we are wise to remember that God's grace alone allows sinful mortals to enter the divine presence, to move beyond terror to grace. Our worship should register gratitude that such a miracle is possible.

For Reflection

1. Examine Revelation 1:1–6, identifying the communication links through which John received the vision. Who or what is being revealed? What does that tell you about the purpose of Revelation?
2. Make a list of icons, indexes, and symbols that you see today in politics, business, professions, or religion. Do these have any effect on your attitudes or behavior?
3. Have you heard or seen parts of Revelation presented as theater? What music or artwork does Revelation bring to mind?

LIVING THE VISION

A Chaplain Asks Questions in Texas

In 1991, two weeks before the start of the first Gulf War, a military chaplain at a United States Air Force Base in Texas wrote a letter to the editor of a local newspaper, questioning the wisdom of armed intervention. Although his commanders told him to be silent, Chaplain Garland Robertson persisted in raising ethical questions about the war. The impending attack, he said, could not be justified morally by any Christian tradition. "I cannot be silent while leaders of our nation move dangerously close to beginning an armed conflict with Iraq for which alternatives appear to be the more moral option," he declared.[10]

Chaplain Robertson was reprimanded, and his scheduled transfer to a post in Germany was canceled. The military ordered mental health tests, the first two of which revealed no pathology. On the third test he was deemed to suffer from a "personality disorder which is so severe as to interfere with the normal and customary completion of his duties."[11] He was moved from an office in the base chapel to a windowless storage room next to a noisy runway.

10. Jim Rice, "An Officer and a Pastor," *Sojourners*, April 1994, 12.
11. Ken Sehested, "Loyalty Test: The Case of Chaplain Robertson," *Christian Century*, March 2, 1994, 212–14.

"Are chaplains ministers of the church or ministers of the state?" he asked. "Military chaplaincy is supposed to absolve people for doing things they personally would feel guilty about," he said. "But I called people to make their own discernment, not just to accept the commanders' wishes. Church leaders of many denominations in America had been saying that the war was unjust. I was a pastor representing the church, and I wanted to be faithful to the gospel as I understood it."[12]

Today Robertson is pastor of a congregation in Austin, Texas. In the midst of the second Gulf War, he was among two hundred twenty-two persons arrested for civil disobedience when they gathered for prayer in a restricted zone in front of the White House. This index of loyalty to God got Robertson handcuffed and incarcerated. He refused to give his name, ensuring that he would appear before a judge and have opportunity to explain his allegiance to the way of the Lamb.

12. Garland Robertson, interview by the author, January 12, 2005, Elkhart, Indiana.

2

Stampeding Empires

Read Revelation 12:18–13:10

And the beast that I saw was like a leopard, its feet were like a bear's, and its mouth was like a lion's mouth. And the dragon gave it his power and his throne and great authority. One of its heads seemed to have received a death-blow, but its mortal wound had been healed. In amazement the whole earth followed the beast. They worshiped the dragon, for he had given his authority to the beast, and they worshiped the beast, saying, "Who is like the beast, and who can fight against it?"

The beast was given a mouth uttering haughty and blasphemous words, and it was allowed to exercise authority for forty-two months. It opened its mouth to utter blasphemies against God, blaspheming his name and his dwelling, that is, those who dwell in heaven. Also it was allowed to make war on the saints and to conquer them. It was given authority over every tribe and people and language and nation, and all the inhabitants of the earth will worship it, everyone whose name has not been written from the foundation of the world in the book of life of the Lamb that was slaughtered. (13:2–8)

We now turn to the startling vision of beasts in Revelation 13, because characters in this chapter are central to the message of the entire book. The sight that greets us is fearsome: a seven-headed beast that looks like a leopard, has feet like a bear's, and a mouth like a lion's (Rev. 13:1–10). Bizarre as this monster seems to us, it was recognizable to first-century Jews who knew the Hebrew Scriptures. John uses a beast as the symbol of an empire that has gone beyond its legitimate mandate by demanding idolatrous worship.

In a vision set in the context of Babylon captivity (598–538 BC), the Hebrew prophet Daniel once saw four great beasts come up out of the sea (Dan. 7:2–7). The first was like a lion with eagles' wings, and it stood like a human being. The second was like a bear, with three tusks. It was told to arise and devour many bodies. The third was like a leopard, with four wings and four heads, and dominion was given to it.

Finally, Daniel saw a fourth beast, "terrifying and dreadful and exceedingly strong. It had great iron teeth and was devouring, breaking in pieces, and stamping what was left with its feet. It was different from all the beasts that preceded it, and it had ten horns" (7:7). While Daniel saw four beasts, John of Patmos sees a single beast that combines horrific characteristics of all four creatures in Daniel's nightmare.

Apocalyptic Visions Are Political Cartoons

One way to understand these symbols is to read them like political cartoons. Neither Daniel nor John was trying to be funny. But political cartoons make a serious point by reducing nations or rulers or events to a few symbols or characters.

The adjacent cartoon (fig. 2.1), drawn during World War II, portrays Poland as a combination of Goldilocks and Red Riding Hood. Germany and Russia are in bed together through political alliance, conspiring to devour Poland by carving up that nation between them. No one familiar with the political landscape of Europe in 1940 (and the relevant fairy tales) would misunderstand the ominous meaning of this sketch.

Similar use of symbol occurs in Revelation and in a series of books written first by Jews (and later by Christians) from the second century BC to the second century AD. Eventually called *apocalyptic*—meaning "unveiling"—these works use images of beasts, heavenly beings, and other fantastic symbols to represent political and religious entities. The book of Daniel is among the earliest and most influential of these apocalyptic writings, a prototype for later Jewish and Christian works.

Most Jewish and Christian apocalyptic writings never became part of the Bible familiar to us. But some of these works survive, with titles such as *4 Baruch*, *1 Enoch*, *Testaments of the Twelve Patriarchs*, and *Sibylline Oracles*. Collectively these are known as the Pseudepigrapha (pseudowritings) because they usually attribute their authorship to a prophet or other venerable person who lived centuries before the books were actually written.[1]

The purpose of this ruse was to allow the books to "predict" historical events leading up to the time the actual author lived. Having established a

1. See James H. Charlesworth, ed., *The Old Testament Pseudepigrapha*, 2 vols. (Garden City, NY: Doubleday, 1983–85).

Fig 2.1. Political cartoonists sometimes portray nations or empires as animals. ("Little Goldilocks Riding Hood." A 1939 Herblock Cartoon, © the Herb Block Foundation.)

perfect forecasting record, often related to the rise and fall of political pow-ers, the author then made a few *actual* predictions about the near future for readers of his own day.

Revelation is unusual among Jewish and Christian apocalyptic books in not playing such games with authorship. John of Patmos simply describes himself as "your brother and companion in the suffering and kingdom and patient endurance that are ours in Jesus" (Rev. 1:9 NIV). But John appears to have been familiar both with Daniel and with Jewish apocalyptic books not included in our Bibles. From these works, John takes images and symbols that already have established meaning. For example, a bird or beast in these books probably is an empire. Heads, wings, or horns on such creatures usually represent individual rulers.[2]

Jews Expect God to Intervene in History

Because pagan powers appeared to dominate the world, or because God's people seemed to be unfaithful, apocalyptic authors typically believed that the age in which they lived was irredeemably evil. Things had become so bad

2. The little horn on the fourth beast in Dan. 7:8 almost certainly represents Antiochus IV Epiphanes, the Seleucid despot whose oppressive measures against the Jews triggered the Maccabean Revolt of 167 BC. The great bird in the Eagle Vision of *4 Ezra* (= 2 Esdras) 11–12 just as surely represents the Roman Empire, and its three heads the emperors Vespasian, Titus, and Domitian. Like John, the author of *4 Ezra* sees the beast of empire rising from the sea (2 Esd. 11:1).

FIG. 2.2
FIRST-CENTURY JEWISH APOCALYPTIC VIEW OF HISTORY

that the only recourse was for God to intervene with one or more messiahs (anointed ones) and to end history as mortals know it. God and his messiah(s) would bring the world to judgment and inaugurate an eternal, divine kingdom. Pagan powers and their henchmen would go down in defeat, and saints would reign with God in justice and peace. In the Old Testament, Daniel 7:9–14 is the prime example and prototype of this view of the future.

A schema of history based on Jewish apocalyptic books would look something like the chart in figure 2.2. The actual author of a given book would be located where the X appears, even if the author claims to be Enoch or some other venerable figure who lived centuries earlier. Some—perhaps many—first-century Jews expected the messiah(s) to appear soon to usher in a new era of justice and peace. So it is not surprising that Jesus' announcement that the kingdom of God has come near (Mark 1:15) had an electrifying effect on his listeners. At the end of Revelation, John sees this kingdom descending from heaven as the new Jerusalem (Rev. 21).

Christians Adapt the Apocalyptic Worldview

Christian faith is profoundly apocalyptic, and the gospel of Jesus Christ unveils a seismic shift taking place in history. The gospel builds upon the Jewish apocalyptic view of history as illustrated in figure 2.2, but with a crucial adaptation. Instead of anticipating a clean break between the present evil age and the

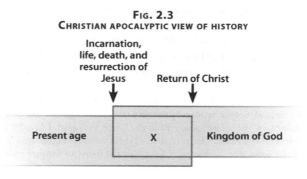

FIG. 2.3
CHRISTIAN APOCALYPTIC VIEW OF HISTORY

kingdom of God, Christian theology understands the two eras as overlapping. John Howard Yoder describes a Christian view of history this way:

> The New Testament sees our present age—the age of the church, extending from Pentecost to the Parousia [return of Christ]—as a period of the overlapping of two eons. These eons are not distinct periods of time, for they exist simultaneously. They differ rather in nature or in direction; one points backward to human history outside of (before) Christ; the other points forward to the fullness of the kingdom of God, of which it is a foretaste. Each eon has a social manifestation: the former in the "world," the latter in the church or the body of Christ.[3]

In a Christian view of history, believers live in the period of overlap between the old and the new, at the place marked X in figure 2.3. The kingdom of God *has already begun to take shape* in the world through the life, death, and resurrection of Jesus—and among people of every nation who claim Jesus as Lord. Empowered by the Holy Spirit, Christians live within the present age as resident aliens (1 Pet. 1:1, 17) and as citizens of the future (Heb. 13:14). We live by the constitution of the kingdom of God as taught and modeled by Jesus, not by patterns of sin and death that often prevail in our world.

Someday Christ will return to bring an end to the powers of darkness that warp creation. In the meantime, forces of violence and greed pull humans back toward an age that is passing away. The love of Christ summons us forward to embrace kingdom standards of justice and reconciliation. As followers of Jesus, we live our lives in tension between the old and the new. Rituals of loyalty and acts of devotion matter a great deal, because these are indexes that reflect and recalibrate our spiritual orientation. Through symbol, icon, and indexes of allegiance, we express and experience what is most essential to us in ways that direct our lives toward God's future.

The purpose of the book of Revelation is to show that the values of Rome (Babylon) and the empire (the beast) reflect patterns of death that will soon pass away. Followers of Jesus will avoid participation in compromising acts of allegiance to persons or institutions not under the lordship of God and the Lamb. Revelation provides a litany of signs primarily related to worship, signs that reorient the soul toward God's future of healing and hope.

Daniel Serves as a Model of Resistance

To understand the origins of apocalyptic thought, we need an overview of the tragic events that precipitated this radical theology. In 586 BC, armies of

3. John Howard Yoder, *The Royal Priesthood: Essays Ecclesiological and Ecumenical*, ed. Michael G. Cartwright (Grand Rapids: Eerdmans, 1994), 9.

Fig. 2.4. As evident in this Christian artwork from the catacombs at Rome, followers of Jesus were inspired by Daniel's courageous resistance to idolatry and empire.

Babylon conquered Jerusalem and destroyed the royal palace of the Jewish monarchs. The invaders also desecrated the temple built by Solomon and reduced it to rubble. They executed the sons of the king of Judah in front of him, then gouged out his eyes and took him in chains to Babylon (2 Kings 24–25).

The book of Daniel is set amid the vortices of politics and worship that followed in the wake of this catastrophe. The Jewish lad Daniel and three fellow exiles become servants at the court of King Nebuchadnezzar in Babylon, where they are exposed to the glamour of world domination (Dan. 1). At the king's court the four young exiles face pressure to eat royal rations that violate dietary restrictions of Jewish law. When the Hebrew youths protest, the Babylonians reluctantly grant them a ten-day trial menu that conforms to Jewish regulations. The four come through the test in fine physical form and gain permission to maintain a kosher diet.

Subsequent trials are more severe. King Nebuchadnezzar makes a gigantic golden icon and demands that his subjects bow before it (Dan. 3). God delivers Daniel and his friends from the executioner's furnace when they refuse to worship the icon. For Nebuchadnezzar's blasphemy, God reduces the king to a state of insanity in which he literally becomes beastly, crawling on all fours to eat grass like an ox (Dan. 4).

The book of Daniel goes on to tell the story of Darius the Mede, a later king who exhibits equally bad judgment. The Medes were allies of the Babylonians, and—according to Daniel—briefly rule Mesopotamia as the Babylonian Empire begins to disintegrate. Darius agrees to a proposal that subjects in his kingdom must pray to him alone (Dan. 6). Daniel disregards the edict, and—as an index of his loyalty to Yahweh—bows three times daily toward Jerusalem in prayer. Thrown to the lions for his insubordination, Daniel is saved when God seals the mouths of the beasts (fig. 2.4).

Stories of Daniel Inspire Later Generations

After returning from captivity starting in 539 BC, the Jewish community apparently told stories of Daniel's faithfulness when persecution arose or the people were tempted to apostasy. The next empire to engulf the Jews came from the west, as Alexander the Great of Macedon conquered Palestine in 333 BC. Ancient tales of Daniel's resistance to pagan culture became particularly relevant between 175 and 164 BC, when a successor to Alexander controlled Palestine. The rogue ruler was the arrogant King Antiochus IV, who added "Epiphanes" ([god] manifest) to his name (fig. 2.5).

The book of 1 Maccabees (1:20–64) relates how Antiochus IV finds willing collaborators among the Jewish people. In Jerusalem he builds a gymnasium, a Greek cultural center of learning where athletes compete in the nude. Antiochus is a rapacious ruler who eventually plunders the temple, exacts heavy taxes, sets Jerusalem on fire, and destroys the city walls. In an attempt to extinguish Jewish religion, Antiochus directs Jews to abandon the religious indexes of circumcision, temple sacrifice to Yahweh, and observance of Jewish holy days. Families who circumcise their baby boys are put to death. Jews are ordered to forget the law of Moses and to sacrifice swine to pagan gods in the temple of Yahweh at Jerusalem.

These outrages trigger a rebellion, the Maccabean Revolt (167–164 BC). Jews wanting to be faithful to the law of Moses succeed in ousting the Greek overlords. They undertake a ritual cleansing of the temple, an event that Jews still celebrate at Hanukkah (1 Macc. 4). The book of Daniel first appeared among Jews in the midst of this crisis, as the people chafed under a pagan oppressor. Stories of the young Jewish men in exile carried a resounding message: be courageous and faithful, and Yahweh will vindicate you as he vindicated Daniel.

Fig. 2.5. Impersonating Zeus, the Seleucid ruler Antiochus IV portrays himself as divine on this *tetradrachm* coin from 169/168 BC. The seated figure holds a small icon of Nike (Victory), and the legend reads, "King Antiochus, god manifest, bearing victory." (Photo courtesy of Freeman & Sear.)

A Parade of Empires Dominates Palestine

The second half of the book of Daniel (chaps. 7–12) contains visions that por-tray the parade of pagan empires, depicted as beasts, that occupied Palestine at the end of the Old Testament era and between the Testaments. In a dream, Daniel learns that the beasts are four kings who will "arise out of the earth" (7:17). These beasts likely represent, sequentially, the empires of Babylonia (Nebuchadnezzar), Media (Darius), Persia (Cyrus), and Greece (Alexander the Great). Each in turn dominated Palestine between the fall of Jerusalem (586 BC) and the beginning of Roman rule in Palestine (63 BC).

The fourth beast of Daniel's vision—the Greek Empire—has ten horns, symbols of rulers who governed the partitioned dominions of Alexander the Great after his death. One of these horns surely represents Antiochus IV. In the Hebrew Scriptures, a horn (*shōfār*) could come from an animal. So a ram's horn could serve as a trumpet to call people to worship, to battle, or to celebration. The book of Psalms warns the wicked, "Do not lift up your horn on high, or speak with insolent neck" (Ps. 75:5). Doing exactly that, the liv-ing horn in Daniel's vision "had eyes and a mouth that spoke arrogantly, and that seemed greater than the others" (Dan. 7:20). The offending horn "made war with the holy ones and was prevailing over them" (7:21). Daniel's vision anticipates divine intervention that will bring judgment on the horn, which will be consumed and utterly destroyed (7:26).

Jesus Is the Son of Man

John of Patmos drew heavily from Daniel and other apocalyptic books for im-agery, and these texts provided icons and symbols that spoke to circumstances facing Christians in the first century. John's vision depicts Christ as one like the Son of Man (Rev. 1:13). This is the same title that appears in Daniel 7:13 to describe a messiah who inaugurates the kingdom of God after the beasts of empire are destroyed:

> I saw in the night visions,
> and behold, with the clouds of heaven
>   there came one like a son of man,
> and he came to the Ancient of Days
>   and was presented before him.
> And to him was given dominion and glory and kingdom,
> that all peoples, nations, and languages
>   should serve him;
> his dominion is an everlasting dominion,
>   which shall not pass away,
> and his kingdom one
>   that shall not be destroyed. (Dan. 7:13–14 RSV)

When Revelation describes Jesus as the Son of Man, it identifies him with the triumphant political figure from Daniel 7 who commands worldwide allegiance to the living God.

The Roman Empire Rises Up from the Sea

Devout Jews who opposed the pagan rule of Palestine were dismayed yet again in 63 BC, when Rome became the next foreign power to capture Jerusalem. Later we will look in some detail at how Rome ruled. For the moment it is enough to say that Rome occupied Palestine in 63 BC and did not leave for centuries. This new empire was so extensive that when Luke wrote about the birth of Jesus, he said, "A decree went out from Emperor Augustus that *all the world* should be registered" (Luke 2:1, emphasis added).

Indeed, to a first-century resident of Palestine, it appeared that Rome wielded universal power. For devout Jews familiar with apocalyptic literature, and for Christians who knew the Old Testament, Rome became identified with the long string of beast-empires that usurped the role of God and sought to dominate the world.

When John depicted the beast of empire rising out of the sea (Rev. 13:1), he may have been referring to Rome and all of Italy geographically rising out

Fig. 2.6. A view looking west toward the harbor from the great theater at Ephesus. In the first century ships could sail directly to the end of Harbor Street—which goes diagonally to the upper center of this photo. Today the harbor is silted up, and the sea is on the far side of the small peaked mountain at the upper left.

of the Mediterranean Sea. Locally in Asia Minor, the symbol of a beast rising from the sea may have pointed to the annual arrival at Ephesus of the proconsul or governor from Rome. Today the ruins of Ephesus are miles from the sea, because the river passing near the ancient city has silted up the bay. But in the first century the sea came right to the edge of Ephesus. The Roman proconsul, whom John must have considered to be an agent of the beast, processed along a boulevard from his ship toward the 24,000-seat theater (fig. 2.6). To citizens of Ephesus, the governor and his entourage appeared to rise out of the sea (see 2 Esd. 11:1).

It was in this theater that a riot ensued when Paul preached the gospel at Ephesus in the middle of the first century (Acts 19:23–41). Two of Paul's traveling companions, Gaius and Aristarchus, were nearly lynched by an angry mob. Despite the danger, and against the advice of other believers, Paul wanted to enter the theater and address the crowd. But Luke reports that "some of the Asiarchs also, who were friends of his, sent to him and begged him not to venture into the theater" (Acts 19:31 RSV). This comment is intriguing because Asiarchs were municipal officials who, among other things, supervised the emperor cult.

John's Imagery Comes from Jewish Tradition

Paul's encounter with the Asiarchs at Ephesus suggests that government officials were alert to the activities of Christians in Asia Minor. It is not difficult to imagine that John, with his caustic view of the Roman Empire, might have been accused of political insubordination by local authorities.

When John finds himself on Patmos and seeks to encourage fellow Christians on the mainland, his eyes are opened to see a spiritual drama with a cast of characters straight out of Jewish history and literature. The cast and set include beasts, angels, the morning star, Babylon, the Ancient of Days, the Son of Man, and much more. By paying attention to the Old Testament and other ancient sources from which John borrows these images, we begin to unravel the mystery of his Apocalypse. In this chapter and the next, we focus primarily on the fact that, for John, a beast represents an empire that rules with violence and usurps allegiance that belongs to God.

Christian Faith Is a Theology of History

We have seen that John's vision makes sense if we place it in the context of a small Jewish nation—and, in John's day, a small Christian community—being stampeded by empires. A minority group of monotheists (believers in one God) felt vulnerable in the face of great political powers that expected allegiance to "divine" rulers and pagan gods.

Christian faith is a theology of history, a conviction that God cares about human affairs and has entered the world in the person of Jesus Christ. History began with God's loving attention at creation, and it will end with God's loving redemption of the world at the return of Christ. In the meantime, followers of the Lamb live in the time between the times, in contested territory between the brokenness of the past and God's restored creation in the future.

We have met the first beast of empire, would-be master of the world. In the next chapter we turn our attention to a second beast, which makes inhabitants of the earth worship the first. Prepare to meet the propaganda machine every empire needs to survive!

For Reflection

1. With what persons or organizations have you heard modern interpreters associate the beast of Revelation 13:1–10? Have any of these associations seemed convincing to you? Why or why not?
2. Name peoples in history or in the present who have rebelled against empire or foreign masters. In what ways did the imperial power or the rebels use religion to advance their cause?
3. What do you infer from Revelation 13:9–10 about John's view of using lethal force to advance a political or religious cause?

LIVING THE VISION

Christian Peacemakers in Palestine

In violation of international agreements, some Israelis in recent years have systematically moved into the Palestinian West Bank to establish dozens of illegal settlements. Israeli soldiers follow to protect the settlers as they occupy land that belonged to Palestinians for generations. Since 1995 a Christian Peacemaker Team (CPT) has lived and worshiped in the West Bank city of Hebron. Israeli settlers and soldiers have occupied the center of historic Hebron in recent years because the tombs of Abraham, Sarah, and other Old Testament patriarchs and matriarchs are there. Scores of Palestinian residents and shopkeepers—Muslims who also cherish the tombs—have left the area because of garbage thrown down on them by settlers in multistory apartment buildings, and other forms of harassment. The CPT members report violence to the international community, escort Palestinian children to school, physically stand in the way of house demolitions, and otherwise find nonviolent ways to work for justice.

Until she herself was deported, Kathleen Kern was part of the Hebron team. "In Hebron we had worship every morning," she says. Worship included hymns, and Kern especially remembers "Abide with Me," with its reference to God as help of the helpless. She says, "We often wept when we sang that verse, because we felt helpless to stop the suffering of innocent people. When we were angry or afraid, we sang stronger, getting more poison out of ourselves. We could mourn with the people of Palestine and hug them. But usually we could not stop their houses from being destroyed."

The poison Kern refers to was simmering anger, and CPT members sometimes threw pillows against the wall to vent their frustration. "We prayed that people's eyes would be opened to see what they were doing," Kern says. Disciplines of prayer steeled the CPT members for witness in dangerous circumstances. "When we saw a house about to be demolished, we climbed onto the roof and were not afraid." The CPT members jumped in front of soldiers about to fire on Palestinians going to mosque during curfew. Kern recalls one Christmas when the CPT group went to church in Bethlehem. "We had to climb over dirt barricades to get there. We arrived at church and sang, 'O come, all ye faithful, joyful and triumphant.'" Not feeling very joyful, they worshiped in tears at the place where the Christ child once was the target of Herod's tyranny.[4]

4. Kathleen Kern, interview by the author, July 15, 2004, South Bend, Indiana.

3

Beastly Worship

Read Revelation 13:11–18

Then I saw another beast that rose out of the earth; it had two horns like a lamb and it spoke like a dragon. It exercises all the authority of the first beast on its behalf, and it makes the earth and its inhabitants worship the first beast, whose mortal wound had been healed. It performs great signs, even making fire come down from heaven to earth in the sight of all; and by the signs that it is allowed to perform on behalf of the beast, it deceives the inhabitants of earth, telling them to make an image for the beast that had been wounded by the sword and yet lived; and it was allowed to give breath to the image of the beast so that the image of the beast could even speak and cause those who would not worship the image of the beast to be killed. Also it causes all, both small and great, both rich and poor, both free and slave, to be marked on the right hand or the forehead, so that no one can buy or sell who does not have the mark, that is, the name of the beast or the number of its name. This calls for wisdom: let anyone with understanding calculate the number of the beast, for it is the number of a person. Its number is six hundred sixty-six.

A second beast lumbers into John's vision, and it "makes the earth and its inhabitants worship the first beast, whose mortal wound had been healed" (Rev. 13:11–12). If the first beast is the Roman Empire, the second beast is some entity that induces people of the world to give loyalty to the empire and its emperors. It appears to represent a web of emperor-worship institutions that orchestrated allegiance to Rome in John's day.

Emperor Worship Grows Out of Gratitude

Emperor worship emerged spontaneously in Asia Minor as the Roman Empire expanded in the first century BC. Initiative for this extravagant expression of allegiance came from people in the conquered territories, not from Rome. Under Caesar Augustus,[1] Rome had gained control of the entire eastern Mediterranean by 31 BC. For a decade before his definitive victory, dueling armies had crisscrossed seas and provinces, leaving destruction and political turmoil in their wake.

When Caesar Augustus succeeded in uniting and pacifying most of the known world, it seemed to many a divine achievement. Poets and politicians hailed the dawn of a new age, which they called the Pax Romana (Roman peace). The Roman poet Virgil (70–19 BC), who had predicted a messianic deliverer for years, wrote these lines after Augustus became emperor:

> This, this is he, whom you so often heard promised to you,
> Augustus Caesar, son of a god,
> Who shall again set up the Golden Age in Latium[2]
> amid the fields where Saturn once reigned,
> and shall spread his empire past Garamant[3] and Indian,
> to a land that lies beyond the stars,
> beyond the paths of the year and the sun.[4]

The Roman poet Horace (65–8 BC), observing that previous heroes often had not received due veneration during their lifetime, wrote these lines to Caesar Augustus:

> Upon you, however, while still among us, we bestow honors in good time, set up altars to swear by in your name, and confess that none like you will hereafter arise or has arisen before now.[5]

At the same time that such extravagant praise sprang from Italy, there were people in the East eager to worship the new emperor.[6] In the years of Roman civil war before Caesar's triumph in 31 BC, leading citizens of Asia Minor

1. The name Caesar Augustus is an honorary title that the new ruler assumed when he formally became emperor in 27 BC. Before then he was known by his given name, Octavian.

2. Latium is the ancient name for the region of Italy in which Rome is situated, essentially the area today called Region Lazio.

3. The Garamantian Empire flourished from about 400 BC to AD 600 in what today is central Libya.

4. Virgil, *Aeneid* 6.791–96; in Virgil, *Aeneid*, vol. 1, trans. H. Rushton Fairclough, rev. ed., LCL 63 (1934; Cambridge, MA: Harvard University Press, 1960), 561–63.

5. Horace, *Epistles* 2.1.15–16; in Horace, *Satires, Epistles, and Ars poetica*, trans. H. Rushton Fairclough, LCL 194 (1926; Cambridge, MA: Harvard University Press, 1961), 397.

6. Egyptians had long considered their pharaohs divine, and Alexander the Great was hailed as the son of Zeus when he conquered Egypt in 332–331 BC. Coins and other state propaganda

Fig. 3.1. The obverse of this *denarius* coin (left) depicts Caesar Augustus (27 BC–AD 14), first Roman emperor and first to be worshiped. The reverse (right) shows the first *temple of emperor worship*, located at Pergamum. The inscription on the pediment of the temple reads *ROM(a) ET AVGVSTVS* (Roma and Augustus). On either side of the temple appear the words *COM ASIAE,* meaning that the coin was issued by the common league of cities in the province of *Asia.* (Used by permission of Classical Numismatic Group, Inc., www.cngcoins.com.)

Fig. 3.2. Ruins of the magnificent complex of Roman temples and government buildings at Pergamum. In 29 BC Pergamum and Nicaea became the first cities in the Roman world to have temples for emperor worship.

made the miscalculation of backing Mark Antony, the contender to the throne whom Caesar ultimately defeated. Afraid of retribution after Caesar emerged victorious, politicians in the region needed a high index of loyalty to display their alignment with the new master of the world. The provincial council of the cities of Asia Minor requested permission from Caesar to set up temples to venerate him as divine.[7]

Romans did not traditionally worship their living rulers, and Caesar Augustus was wary of the proposal. In 29 BC he allowed Romans in the cities

---

proclaiming Alexander's divinity may have helped prepare peoples of the East to accept the worship of Roman rulers.

7. Dio Cassius, *Roman History* 51.20.6; Tacitus, *Annals* 4.37. See Steven J. Friesen, *Imperial Cults and the Apocalypse of John: Reading Revelation in the Ruins* (Oxford and New York: Oxford University Press, 2001, 2006), 27–28.

of Ephesus and Nicaea to erect temples dedicated to the goddess Roma and Julius Caesar (the deceased adoptive father of Caesar Augustus). Then, setting momentous precedent for a living emperor, he authorized Greeks in the cities of Pergamum and Nicomedia to consecrate temples to Roma and himself.[8]

So Pergamum—among the seven cities of Revelation—was one of the two first venues in the Roman world with a temple to a living Roman emperor (figs. 3.1; 3.2). The temple served the entire province of Asia, not just the city of Pergamum. Given John's view of emperor worship as satanic, it is no surprise that his vision refers to Pergamum as the place where Satan's throne is (Rev. 2:13). Nor is it surprising that the goddess Roma, venerated throughout the ancient world as a symbol of the Roman Empire, appears in John's vision as a whore (Rev. 17).

Political Allegiance Becomes Outright Worship

In about 9 BC the provincial government of Asia announced that it would present a golden crown to the individual who proposed the highest honors for Caesar Augustus. An inscription with the winning entry survives, and it proposes that the province organize the calendar around the birthday of Augustus. Language of the winning entry illustrates how far political allegiance had moved toward outright worship:

> [It is difficult to know whether] the birthday of the most divine Caesar is a matter of greater pleasure or greater benefit. We could justly consider that day to be equal to the beginning of all things. He restored the form of all things to usefulness, if not to their natural state, since it had deteriorated and suffered misfortune. He gave a new appearance to the whole world, which would gladly have accepted its own destruction had Caesar not been born for the common good fortune of all. Thus a person could justly consider this to be the beginning of life and of existence. . . .
>
> Therefore, it seems proper to me that the birthday of the most divine Caesar be the one, uniform New Year's day for all the polities [municipal governments]. On that day all [government officials] will take up their local offices, that is, on the ninth day before the Kalends of October. . . . A decree of the *koinon* [provincial council] of Asia should be written encompassing all his virtues, so that the action devised by us for the honor of Augustus should endure forever.[9]

Similar Language Honors Christ and Caesar

Already in this public document, a century before John wrote Revelation, we see veneration of the emperor that is similar to devotion Christians soon

8. Cassius, *Roman History* 51.20.6–8; Suetonius, *Augustus* 52.
9. *OGIS* 458 1.3–30; in Friesen, *Imperial Cults*, 33.

would give to Jesus. The provincial council awarded the prize, reorganized the calendar, and issued a decree that honored providence for

> bringing Augustus, whom she filled with virtue as a benefaction to all humanity; sending to us and to those after us a savior who put an end to war and brought order to all things; . . . the birth of the god was the beginning of good tidings [*euangelion*] to the world through him.[10]

The trend for people in Asia Minor to pledge allegiance to the divine emperor continued, as this 3 BC inscription from the region of Paphlagonia indicates:

> In the third year from the twelfth consulship of the Emperor Caesar Augustus, son of a god, . . . the following oath was taken by the inhabitants of Paphlagonia and the Roman businessmen dwelling among them: "I swear by Jupiter, Earth, Sun, by all the gods and goddesses, and by Augustus himself, that I will be loyal to Caesar Augustus and to his children and descendants all my life in word, in deed, in thought, regarding as friends whomever they so regard, . . . [so] that in defense of their interests I will spare neither body, soul, life, nor children."[11]

Augustus claimed the title "son of a god" because his adoptive father, Julius Caesar, had been declared divine by the Roman senate after he was assassinated in 44 BC. This inscription implies that loyalty to Caesar Augustus took priority over every other consideration, including family and life itself.

Caesar Claims to Bring Peace to the World

Angels near Bethlehem were not the first to say, "Glory to God in the highest heaven, and on earth peace" (Luke 2:14). A few years before the birth of Jesus, an Altar of Peace (*Ara Pacis*) at Rome made similar claims about Caesar Augustus (fig. 3.3). Completed in 9 BC, the altar was authorized by the Roman Senate to celebrate the return of Caesar Augustus to Rome after successful military campaigns in Gaul and Spain. Caesar claimed to have brought peace and stability to the world.

This gleaming Altar of Peace disappeared from history when the Roman Empire fell. Parts were recovered in the sixteenth century. But not until 1938, when Italian dictator Benito Mussolini wanted the ancient monument to garnish his own imperial pretense, did archaeologists put the pieces back together. Now protected in a modern museum, Caesar's Altar of Peace exudes

10. *OGIS* 458 1.30–71; in Friesen, *Imperial Cults,* 34–35.
11. *OGIS* 532; Naphtali Lewis and Meyer Reinhold, eds., *Roman Civilization: Sourcebook 2, The Empire* (New York: Harper & Row, 1966), 34–35.

Fig. 3.3. The *Ara Pacis* (Altar of Peace) as it appears today in a museum at Rome.

the propaganda of empire. Relief sculptures on the front of the altar depict scenes from the founding of Rome. The sides show Caesar Augustus and his entourage processing toward sacrifice to the gods.

The back of the altar features a personification of Peace (fig. 3.4). With her lap full of fruit, Peace holds two children, perhaps nephews of Caesar who were intended heirs to the throne. To the viewer's left is Sky, seated on a bird. To the right is Earth, resting on a sea monster. Situated as she is between Sky and Earth, Peace ostensibly brought by Caesar Augustus has united heaven

Fig. 3.4. Between Sky (on a bird to the left) and Earth (on a sea monster to the right), Peace (personified as a woman) sits with children on her lap. The infants may be nephews of Augustus whom he viewed as possible heirs to the throne.

Fig. 3.5. Opposite the image of Peace, on the back of the *Ara Pacis*, the goddess Roma sits upon the armaments of defeated foes.

and earth. At the feet of Peace are domesticated beasts, giving a peaceable-kingdom aura to the scene.

Opposite Peace on the same side of the altar is the female goddess Roma, symbol of Rome (fig. 3.5). Although little of the original figure survives on this sculpture, archaeologists can readily sketch in the likeness of Roma because her image was so common in the ancient world. Roma embodies the military power of the Roman Empire. With sword in hand, she proudly sits on a pile of armaments. In some other representations, Roma is seductive, with a breast exposed (fig. 8.3).

By pairing the military figure of Roma with the domestic figure of Peace, the altar reveals the truth about empire: the Pax Romana (Roman peace) really was pacification, compliance enforced by threat of arms. The original location of the Altar of Peace was where the army conducted exercises at the edge of Rome—the Field of Mars (Campus Martius), so named for the god of war. Caesar's peace depended on violence.

People in the provinces often experienced Pax Romana as brutal. Writing about Rome subduing parts of Britain in AD 83–84, Tacitus tells of local chieftain Calgacus, who laid this charge against the invaders: "Robbers of the world, now that earth fails their all-devastating hands, they probe even the sea: if their enemy have wealth, they have greed; if their enemy be poor, they are ambitious." Neither "East nor West has glutted them. . . . To plunder, butcher, steal, these things they misname empire: they make a desolation and they call it peace."[12]

12. Tacitus, *Agricola* 30; in Tacitus, *Agricola*, trans. M. Hutton, rev. R. M. Ogilvie, LCL 35 (Cambridge, MA: Harvard University Press, 1970), 81.

Priests and Temples Promote Emperor Worship

In AD 27, Smyrna became the second city in Asia Minor to build a province-wide temple to an emperor. The province dedicated this temple to Emperor Tiberius, who reigned during the ministry of Jesus, and to his mother, Livia. In AD 89–90, near the time John apparently got into trouble with Rome, Ephesus became the third city of the region to build a provincial temple for emperor worship (fig. 3.6). This one was dedicated to the "revered ones" (*sebastoi*), probably a reference to the deceased Emperor Vespasian (AD 69–79) and his two emperor sons, Titus (AD 79–81) and Domitian (AD 81–96).[13] The head of a gigantic statue from this temple survives (fig. 3.7) and perhaps was a primary image of the beast John had in mind when he wrote his vision.

Supporters of the Roman Empire created structures and institutions to express their allegiance to the divine emperor. A new order of religious officials eventually emerged called *augustales* (fig. 3.8), with titles that included high priest and temple keeper. These men were authorized to officiate at ceremonies honoring the emperor throughout the calendar year. Liturgical high points included New Year's Day, the birthday of the reigning emperor (celebrated monthly), and various dates related to deceased emperors and their families. Music was a prime index of praise in the emperor cult. Towns throughout Asia Minor organized *hymnōdes*, male choirs that sang praises and held banquets to honor the emperor.[14] For generations, male choirs had lauded gods such as Apollo or Zeus, but now they praised the emperor. The choirs at first were voluntary, but in the course of the first century AD, they became professional, and municipal or provincial funds covered expenses.

A second-century altar at Pergamum bears an inscription about the choir for emperor worship in that city. The front of the altar reads, "With good fortune. To Emperor Caesar Trajan Hadrian Olympios, Savior and Founder. The male choirs [*hymnōdes*] of god Augustus and goddess Rome [dedicated this]."[15] The inscription gives directions for celebrating birthdays of emperors, living and dead. Crowns, incense, lamps, and sermons (*encōmia*) were part of the ceremonies. The hymn society had its own building and convened about once every three weeks.

The Stage Is Set for a Showdown with Rome

The early church—as reflected in writings of the New Testament—developed icons, indexes, and symbols for Jesus that had close parallels to those used for

13. Steven J. Friesen, "The Beast from the Land," in *Reading the Book of Revelation: A Resource for Students*, ed. David L. Barr (Atlanta: Society of Biblical Literature, 2003), 52.
    14. Ibid., 104–13.
    15. Ibid., 108.

Fig. 3.6. Ruins of the temple of emperor worship built at Ephesus in AD 89–90, shortly before John apparently got into trouble with provincial Roman authorities.

Fig. 3.7. The gigantic head of an emperor (Titus or Domitian) that once was part of a statue in the temple to the emperors built at Ephesus in AD 89–90.

Fig. 3.8. A sculpture on the side of the *Ara Pacis* depicts the imperial family in religious procession. This detail shows men with spindles on their heads. They likely are priests of the emperor cult.

emperor worship. We should not be surprised that such similarities emerged. Symbols and signs do not have meaning in a vacuum; they must somehow relate to what the users already know. The critical issue for Christian discipleship is whether symbols and signs orient believers toward the beast or toward the Lamb. Both the Roman Empire and the church recognized that rituals of worship, in particular, could be powerful indexes that reflect and forge allegiance. If Christians adapted signs and symbols from the Roman Empire and used them in exclusive worship of God and the Lamb, the borrowing was politically subversive.

Rome did not demand exclusive allegiance to the emperor or to the gods. As long as Roman subjects showed due reverence for the gods and the emperors, they were free to also worship Jesus or almost any other deity. But most Christians did not permit such reciprocity within their ranks. For them there was "one Lord, one faith, one baptism, one God and Father of all, who is above all and through all and in all" (Eph. 4:5–6). That radical exclusivity set the stage for a showdown with the empire.

Nero Turns Perverse and Cruel

On July 19 of AD 64, a devastating fire started in Rome. With thousands of people crowded into multistory tenements and little firefighting equipment, the imperial capital was vulnerable to flame. The fire raged for nine days, destroying or seriously damaging two-thirds of the great city. A distraught population sought to lay blame, and the emperor himself soon fell under suspicion. Early hopes that Nero (AD 54–68; fig. 3.9) would be a wise ruler had already faded, as the young emperor increasingly showed himself to be perverse and cruel. When Rome burned, rumors circulated that Nero had ordered less desirable parts of the city to be torched to make room for his grandiose palaces.

Nero was the adopted son of Emperor Claudius (AD 41–54). His birth mother, Agrippina, married Claudius and then joined a conspiracy to murder her new husband in order to put sixteen-year-old Nero on the throne. With such a debut, it is not surprising that the young man became vain and violent. He eventually murdered his mother and ordered his tutor and adviser, the great philosopher Seneca, to commit suicide. Married three times, Nero divorced (and later executed) his first wife, then kicked his second wife to death while she was pregnant. Upon hearing that his stepson sometimes playacted being a general and an emperor, Nero ordered the lad to be drowned so he would not grow up to seize the throne.[16]

16. Suetonius, *Nero* 35.

Fig. 3.9. A sculpture of Nero as a youth, when hopes were high that he would be a wise ruler.

Fig. 3.10. On the obverse of this *as* coin (left) from AD 64 Nero appears with the spiked crown of divinity. Apollo—or Nero impersonating Apollo—plays a harp on the reverse (right). Suetonius refers to this coin in *Nero* 25. (Used by permission of Classical Numismatic Group, Inc., www.cngcoins.com.)

Fancying himself a musician (fig. 3.10), Nero played the harp and sang at musical contests during a tour of Greece. No one was allowed to leave the theater while he performed. There were reports of women going into labor and giving birth at venues where Nero sang, and of men finding the concerts so tedious they feigned death so they could be carried out.[17] An aspiring athlete, Nero also raced chariots and entered athletic competitions in Greece, "winning" every contest. Given to excesses of every sort, the emperor castrated a boy named Sporus and married the lad in a public ceremony.[18]

The Emperor Lives in Luxury

In Revelation 18 and elsewhere, John blasts the waste and debauchery of Babylon/Rome, and some of the city's bad reputation must be traced to Nero. The emperor reportedly "never made a journey with less than a thousand carriages, his mules shod with silver."[19] But no extravagance surpassed Nero's massive building projects in the city of Rome. Most notorious was his Golden House (Domus Aurea), situated near where the Coliseum stands today. A contemporary of Nero wrote:

> Its vestibule was large enough to contain a colossal statue of the emperor a hundred and twenty feet high; and it was so extensive that it had a triple colonnade

17. Ibid. 23.
18. Ibid. 28.
19. Ibid. 30; in *Suetonius*, vol. 2, trans. and ed. J. C. Rolfe, LCL 38 (1913–14; Cambridge MA: Harvard University Press, 1960), 135.

a mile long. . . . In the rest of the house all parts were overlaid with gold and adorned with gems and mother-of-pearl. There were dining-rooms with fretted ceilings of ivory, whose panels could turn and shower down flowers and were fitted with pipes for sprinkling the guests with perfumes. The main banquet hall was circular and constantly revolved day and night, like the heavens.[20]

In the second century, Emperor Trajan (AD 98–117) filled the building to the roof with rubble and built another palace on top. The latter structure has mostly disappeared, but archaeologists have excavated sections of Nero's palace, including the great revolving banquet room.[21] Nero built this three-hundred-room party palace with the forced labor of prisoners from across the empire; he nearly bankrupted the government with the expense.

The one-hundred-twenty-foot statue of Nero that stood in the vestibule of the Golden House illustrates the scale of the emperor's pretense. The giant sculpture portrayed Nero as the sun god Apollo, with a spiked halo of divinity around his head. Offensive even to some pagans in Rome, this icon of Nero must have seemed particularly blasphemous to Jews and Christians. When John speaks of the image of the beast (Rev. 13:14), he probably refers generically to statues and icons across the Roman world. But no image of the emperor was more notorious than the colossus of Nero at the Golden House.

Christians Become Scapegoats

Nero's decision to build the Golden House shortly after the great fire of AD 64 fueled the rumor that he had torched the city as a perverse strategy for urban renewal. The Roman historian Tacitus describes how the emperor, seeking to deflect suspicion from himself,

> substituted as culprits, and punished with the utmost refinements of cruelty, a class of persons, loathed for their vices, whom the crowd styled Christians. . . . They were covered with wild beasts' skins and torn to death by dogs; or they were fastened to crosses, and, when daylight failed were burned to serve as lamps by night. Nero had offered his Gardens for the spectacle, and gave an exhibition in his Circus, mixing with the crowd in the habit of a charioteer, or mounted on his car [chariot]. Hence, in spite of a guilt which had earned the most exemplary punishment, there arose a sentiment of pity [for the Christians], due to the impression that they were being sacrificed not for the welfare of the state but to the ferocity of a single man.[22]

20. Ibid. 31; in Rolfe, *Suetonius*, 2:137.
21. Archaeologists uncovered this fifty-foot diameter room and rotating mechanism in September 2009. See Marta Falconi, "Nero's Rotating Banquet Hall Unveiled in Rome," Washington Post, September 29, 2009.
22. Tacitus, *Annals* 15.44; in Tacitus, *Annals*, trans. John Jackson, LCL 322 (1937; Cambridge, MA: Harvard University Press, 1956), 283–84.

Nero Likely Is One Head of the Beast

Luck ran out for Nero when his own troops in Gaul, Spain, Africa, and Germany revolted. With the stability of the empire at risk, the Roman Senate pronounced Nero a public enemy and directed that he be flogged to death. Nero fled to the suburbs of Rome, where he apparently committed suicide on June 9, 68.

Although despised by Christians and Jews, and by decent people throughout the empire, Nero was a hero to some in the Greek-speaking East. The emperor loved Greek culture and lavished imperial resources upon cities in Greece and Asia Minor. Nero attempted, but never completed, the most ambitious engineering project of the ancient Mediterranean world: a canal across Greece's isthmus at Corinth. During his reign the Roman government built a stadium and dredged the harbor at Ephesus, keeping it navigable for commerce. All of this made Nero popular in parts of the East, and some people there grieved his death.

A myth emerged that Nero had not actually died or that he would come back to life and retake the imperial throne. Ancient pagan and Christian sources mention what came to be called the Nero redivivus (Nero resurrected) legend.[23] This may be what John had in mind when he said of the beast that "one of its heads seemed to have received a death-blow, but its mortal wound had been healed" (Rev. 13:3).

At several points in Revelation, John seems to nudge the reader, as if to say, "You can figure out exactly what I'm talking about with this symbol." Such a cue comes immediately after John talks about the "mark of the beast," which John believes people of the empire will soon be required to wear: "This calls for wisdom: let anyone with understanding calculate the number of the beast, for it is the number of a person. Its number is six hundred sixty-six" (13:18).

This verse has generated mischief through the centuries: interpreters in every generation have applied the 666 cipher to some person or entity of their own era. But John tells his first readers that anyone with understanding will know to whom the number refers. These words point to some villain of the first century, and the prime suspect is Nero.

The Number of the Beast Makes Sense

Greeks, Jews, and other ancient peoples assigned numerical values to letters of their alphabets, a system known as gematria (figs. 3.11; 3.12). The first nine letters of the alphabet represented single digits, the next nine represented tens, and the next nine represented hundreds. By summing the values of individual

---

23. See *Sibylline Oracles* 4.119–24; 5.93–109, 361–80; Suetonius, *Nero* 57; Cassius, *Roman History* 66.19.3.

letters, it was possible to determine the numerical equivalent of any word. These equivalents were fixed and commonly understood in the ancient world; they are not the invention of a modern interpreter!

Greek

α	alpha	1	η	eta	8	ξ	xi	60	υ	upsilon	400
β	beta	2	θ	theta	9	ο	omicron	70	φ	phi	500
γ	gamma	3	ι	iota	10	π	pi	80	χ	chi	600
δ	delta	4	κ	kappa	20	ϙ	koppa	90	ψ	psi	700
ε	epsilon	5	λ	lambda	30	ρ	rho	100	ω	omega	800
ϝ	digamma	6	μ	mu	40	σ	sigma	200	ϡ	sampi	900
ζ	zeta	7	ν	nu	50	τ	tau	300			

Fig. 3.11. Greek letters and their numerical equivalents in the ancient world. Three letters (*digamma, koppa, sampi*) appeared as numerals in the first century but not in standard writing. Example: Jesus (Ἰησοῦς)—*iota, eta, sigma, omicron, upsilon, sigma* = 888.

Hebrew

א	alef	1	ח	khet	8	ס	samek	60	ת	tav	400
ב	bet	2	ט	tet	9	ע	ayin	70	ך	kaf	500
ג	gimel	3	י	yod	10	פ	pe	80	ם	mem	600
ד	dalet	4	כ	kaf	20	צ	tsade	90	ן	nun	700
ה	he	5	ל	lamed	30	ק	qof	100	ף	pe	800
ו	vav	6	מ	mem	40	ר	resh	200	ץ	tsade	900
ז	zayin	7	נ	nun	50	שׁ	shin	300			

Fig. 3.12. Hebrew letters and their numerical equivalents in the ancient world. The last five letters on this table (*kaf* through *tsade*) are alternate forms of the same letters that appear earlier in the chart and are used in standard writing when these letters are at the end of a word. Hebrew reads right to left. Example: Nero Caesar (נרון קסר)—*nun, resh, vav, qof, samek, resh* = 616; Nero(n) Caesar (נרון קסר)—*nun, resh, vav, nun, qof, samek, resh* = 666.

In the ruins of Pompeii, destroyed by volcano in AD 79, archaeologists found a graffito that says, "I love her whose number is 545." Various combinations of letters could add up to that total, so we cannot be certain which girl the admirer adored. A Christian apocalyptic writer from the second century, referring to the "son of the great God," says, "eight units, an equal number of tens in addition to these, and eight hundreds will reveal the name."[24] The gematrial value of "Jesus" (Ἰησοῦς) in Greek is 888.

If we take the Greek form of Nero Caesar, *Nerōn Kaisar* (Νέρων Καῖσαρ), and transliterate it into Hebrew letters (נרון קסר),[25] the gematrial sum is 666. John wrote his vision in Greek—not Hebrew—and the gematrial sum for

24. *Sibylline Oracles* 1.324–29; trans. J. J. Collins in *The Old Testament Pseudepigrapha*, ed. James H. Charlesworth, 2 vols. (Garden City, NY: Doubleday, 1983), 1:342.

25. The name *Nerō(n)* in Hebrew letters can be spelled with or without a final "n," resulting in two different gematrial sums: 666 for Neron Caesar and 616 for Nero Caesar (נרו קסר). Some ancient manuscripts of Revelation have the number of the beast as 616 instead of 666. This is further suggestion—but not proof—that Nero was the object of Revelation's gematrial riddle.

Nerō(n) Kaisar in Greek is *not* 666. But twice in Revelation, John explicitly reveals that he is thinking in both Hebrew and Greek (9:11; 16:16). Apparently he expects believers in the seven churches—many of whom probably are Jewish—to make the linguistic leap from Greek to Hebrew with the 666 riddle.

If indeed John uses gematria to indict Nero, he is not alone. Suetonius reports that anonymous enemies of Nero at Rome publicly posted the following smear that used numbers to accuse the emperor of killing his mother:

> Count the numerical values of the letters of Nero's name,
>   And in "murdered his own mother."
> You will find their sum is the same.[26]

Although it seems likely that John meant 666 to refer to Nero, we should not limit the meaning of the number of the beast or the symbol of the beast to one demented ruler. Structural evil in Revelation is bigger than the reign of Nero; any human entity that usurps allegiance that belongs to God is beastly. It is possible the number six, used three times, simply was an abstract symbol for John. It would stand in contrast to seven, the number of divine completion, as in the seven days of creation (Gen. 1).

Right Hand and Forehead Represent Allegiance

Interpreters who believe Revelation primarily makes predictions about *our* future have long speculated about how the mark of the beast will be placed "on the right hand or the forehead" of people on earth (Rev. 13:16). Recent popular explanations have included computer chips implanted in the forehead, or credit cards, or universal price code bars on merchandise. These solutions to the riddle are unlikely because John appears to be describing some pattern of idolatrous allegiance in his own era.

The book of Deuteronomy contains instructions Moses gave to the children of Israel just before they entered the promised land. A central concern of this teaching is that the Hebrew people not forget the God who delivered them from bondage in Egypt. They must not dilute worship of Yahweh by revering other gods. As a Jew, John of Patmos would have often recited a passage from Deuteronomy called the *Shema* (*shĕ-MAH*), a word that translates as "Hear!" or "Listen!"

26. Suetonius, *The Twelve Caesars*, trans. Robert Graves, rev. Michael Grant (Harmondsworth: Penguin Books, 1987), 236. Rolfe (*Suetonius*, 2:158–59) gives a strictly literal translation in which the gematrial allusion is more subtle: "A calculation new: Nero his mother slew." The point in either case is that the Greek gematrial value for both "Nero" (Νέρων) and "his mother slew" (ἰδίαν μητέρα ἀπέκτεινε) is 1,005.

Fig. 3.13. Jewish men pray at the Western Wall in Jerusalem. The worshiper on the right wears a phylactery—a small box containing texts from Exodus and Deuteronomy—on his forehead. He similarly has scripture bound to his hand with a strap

Hear, O Israel: The LORD [Yahweh] is our God, the LORD alone. You shall love the LORD your God with all your heart, and with all your soul, and with all your might. Keep these words that I am commanding you today in your heart. Recite them to your children and talk about them when you are at home and when you are away, when you lie down and when you rise. Bind them as a sign on your hand, fix them as an emblem on your forehead, and write them on the doorposts of your house and on your gates. (Deut. 6:4–9)

Some Jews to this day literally place the words "The LORD is our God, the LORD alone . . ." in little boxes called phylacteries fastened on their hands and foreheads (fig. 3.13; see Matt. 23:5). These are symbols of devotion to God. Deuteronomy teaches the people of Israel always to make allegiance to God front and center—as we might say. Worship should govern every thought and action as completely as if God's name were bound to our hands and affixed to our foreheads.

Just as reverence for God should be first in the mind of every Jew and Christian, so allegiance to the beast also is the controlling factor for people beholden to the empire. As we soon will see, worship of emperor and empire so saturated the economy of the Roman world that it became impossible to buy or sell (Rev. 13:17) without participating in beastly worship. Behind this entire system John sees yet another creature—the dragon, symbol of Satan, whose origin and character we consider next.

For Reflection

1. What modern popular interpretations of the beast or its number (666) do you know about? What political or religious agenda accompanies these interpretations?
2. What are the symbols and icons of ideological allegiance in your society? Who are the historical persons or historical events that shape the collective memory of your culture or nation? What do these communicate about beliefs, values, and priorities?
3. In what ways does your society put grassroots social or political pressure on people to support all policies of the government without question? When and where do you feel heat if you disagree with certain agendas of the government or the majority of citizens?

LIVING THE VISION
Poet and Prophet in Japan

As a child in Japan during World War II, Yorifumi Yaguchi stood with other schoolchildren, turned toward a picture of the emperor seated on a white horse, and sang the national anthem:

> May your reign continue for a thousand, eight
> thousand generations,
> Until the pebbles grow into boulders lush with moss.

Many persons in Japan considered the emperor to be divine, the descendant of a sun goddess. When Yaguchi became a Christian as a young adult, he, like many other followers of Jesus, refused to sing the national anthem. "The anthem was associated with militarism," he explains. "And if we sang it, it meant we worshiped the emperor and his eternal reign."[27] Yaguchi became a university professor, a pastor, and a nationally honored poet in Japan. In a recent essay he wrote about those who dropped the atomic bomb:

27. Yorifumi Yaguchi, interview by the author, November 24, 2007, Sapporo, Japan.

When the Enola Gay left for the skies of Hiroshima, a chaplain prayed for the crew's safe flight and successful bombing of the city. . . . They must have believed that the dropping of the atomic bomb on Hiroshima was the will of God. But how did they feel at the sight of Hiroshima agonizing in the terrible whirlwind of destroying flames? More than 140,000 people died within a few months. Many were burnt in an instant, and far more people started to suffer from radiation disease for the rest of their lives. Was the crew pleased with this? . . . I imagine they were cheered by their seniors and comrades. They were told that the bomb was needed to end the war and that if they didn't use it, far more war dead would have accrued. And they believed it. But what kind of god was he who was pleased with such terrible carnage? He is none other than the God of War. He must have been more than happy to see such colossal misery brought to the city and to human history. He is certainly different from the God who created human beings and who loved the world so much that He gave his only Son.[28]

In the following poem Yaguchi reflects on the powerful tug of nationalism:

                    Usually
I love peace
but when I wear a soldier's uniform
I begin to wish a war would happen
and to feel like killing
as many enemies as possible
by raiding them, if so ordered,
and dying willingly
for the sake of the Emperor
and our country.[29]

28. Yorifumi Yaguchi, "Isn't this world under the control of the God of War?" in *Poems of War and Peace: Voices from Contemporary Japanese Poets*, ed. Noriko Mizusaki and Mayumi Sako (Osaka: Chikurinkan, 2007), 119–24; used by permission.

29. Reprinted from *The Poetry of Yorifumi Yaguchi: A Japanese Voice in English*, ed. Wilbur J. Birky (Intercourse, PA: Good Books, 2006), 67. Copyright by Good Books (www.GoodBooks .com). Used by permission. All rights reserved.

4

Accuser of Our Comrades

Read Revelation 12:1–17

Then I heard a loud voice in heaven, proclaiming,

> "Now have come the salvation and the power
>   and the kingdom of our God
>   and the authority of his Messiah,
> for the accuser of our comrades has been thrown down,
>   who accuses them day and night before our God.
> But they have conquered him by the blood of the Lamb
>   and by the word of their testimony,
> for they did not cling to life even in the face of death.
> Rejoice then, you heavens
>   and those who dwell in them!
> But woe to the earth and the sea,
>   for the devil has come down to you with great wrath,
>   because he knows that his time is short!" (12:10–12)

It is likely that both Peter and Paul (fig. 4.1) died in Nero's brief fierce attack on the church at Rome. A letter in our Bibles attributed to Peter was written from "Babylon" (1 Pet. 5:13), the same derisive epithet that Revelation hurls against Rome (Rev. 18). The letter mentions a "fiery ordeal" taking place among Christians (1 Pet. 4:12), perhaps an allusion to the great fire and subsequent persecution at Rome. Likewise the letter of *1 Clement*, written in the imperial capital late in the first century, refers to "the sudden

Fig. 4.1. Peter and Paul both disappear from history near the end of Nero's reign, and it is likely that they died in the persecution at Rome that followed the great fire of AD 64. This image of Peter and Paul, made centuries later, comes from the Christian catacombs at Rome.

and repeated misfortunes which have befallen us" (1.1). The author mentions that "the greatest and most righteous pillars of the Church were persecuted and contended unto death," apparently meaning Peter and Paul, who are named in later verses (5.2–7).

The last we hear of Paul in the New Testament, he is under house arrest in Rome during the reign of Nero (Acts 28:16, 30). This valiant apostle has written to Christians at Rome that "rulers are not a terror to good conduct, but to bad" (Rom. 13:3). When arrested for disturbing the peace in Jerusalem, Paul has appealed his case to none other than Emperor Nero. Apparently he still has hope that Nero will act responsibly and perhaps even embrace the gospel. But Paul and Peter both disappear from history during the last years of Nero's regime, probably victims of the emperor's brutality.

John of Patmos sees the world singing praises to a beast of empire that was blaspheming God and slaughtering followers of Jesus. He presumably feels the hot breath of the second beast, the ideology and institutions of emperor worship that monitor allegiance to rulers John will not revere. His vision speaks to questions that people of faith have struggled with in every generation: If God is good and powerful, how can such evil exist? Are there *two* deities, one evil and one good, locked in mortal combat for control of the world?

A Male Child Will Rule the Nations

Revelation addresses these questions by telling the story, in symbolic language, of why Satan sought to destroy Jesus. John sees a woman "clothed with the sun, with the moon under her feet, and on her head a crown of twelve stars" (Rev. 12:1). She is pregnant and experiencing the pain of childbirth.

Fig. 4.2. With laureate head symbolizing victory, the icon of Vespasian on the obverse of this *denarius* coin from AD 70 (left) proclaims to the world Roman victory over the Jews. The reverse (right) portrays the Jewish nation as a defeated and humiliated woman. She sits in front of a *trophy*, a ceremonial tree or pole on which the ancient Greeks and Romans fastened captured weapons of defeated foes in the semblance of a human figure. (Courtesy of Classical Numismatic Group, Inc.)

On one level, this is an icon of Mary in labor before the birth of Jesus. The male child she delivers is to "rule all the nations with a rod of iron" (12:5). The early church understood this citation of Psalm 2:8–9 as pointing to Christ. But in addition to representing Mary, the woman likely is a symbol of the whole people of God. The entire Jewish nation was in anguish, having suffered exile in Babylon and conquest by a series of pagan empires after returning from exile. After Rome brutally suppressed the Jewish War in AD 70, imperial coins used the image of a woman seated in submission to portray a humiliated Jewish nation (figs. 4.2; 5.8).

If the woman clothed with the sun in Revelation represents the people of God, it is significant that she is standing on the moon (Rev. 12:1). Among other roles, the deity Artemis (Diana) at Ephesus (Acts 19:23–41) was a moon goddess. Roman coins in the second and third centuries sometimes included a crescent moon under an image of the wife of the emperor, signaling her divine affiliation. Other such coins featured an icon of the moon goddess Luna (Roman) or Selene (Greek) on the reverse.[1] The woman seen by John of Patmos stands on the moon, symbolizing the victory of God's people over goddess religion and imperial blasphemy.

Drama attends the moment of childbirth for the woman clothed with the sun. A great red dragon with seven heads and ten horns hovers nearby to devour the newborn. This imagery is reminiscent of Herod killing infants at Bethlehem in an effort to eliminate the Christ child (Matt. 2:16–18). It also reminds us of Pontius Pilate and Caiaphas arranging the death of Jesus (John 18:1–24, 28).

Before the red dragon can seize his prey, however, the newborn is "snatched away and taken to God and to his throne" (Rev. 12:5). Again the imagery works on multiple levels. Herod the Great thought he had destroyed the king born in Bethlehem, but Joseph and Mary, prompted by God, had whisked Jesus to safety in Egypt. Herod Antipas had every reason to think that crucifixion was the end of the teacher from Galilee. But God has raised Jesus from the grave and elevated him to a throne of glory.

1. David R. Sear, *Roman Coins and Their Values*, vol. 1, *The Republic and the Twelve Caesars*, 280 BC–AD 96 (London: Spink, 2000), 13, 31.

Good and Evil Vie for Supremacy

Awful as evil may be in our world today, nothing matches the depravity of an attempt to destroy the Son of God. Explanation for the source of such evil emerges as John sees a vision of war in heaven. The red dragon, it turns out, is not an independent source of power or a second deity. The red dragon began as a member of the heavenly court! Once part of God's created order, the dragon leads an insurrection against the God who made him.

A terrific battle ensues as forces of obedience and forces of rebellion duke it out in the spiritual realm. Michael, the archangel who serves as protector of the Jewish nation (Dan. 12:1; Jude 9), marshals the hosts of heaven to oust the rebels from the presence of God. The dragon, now identified as Satan, is thrown down to earth, along with one-third of the heavenly court (Rev. 12:4, 9). The voice of a worship leader cries loudly at this triumph of good over evil:

> Now have come the salvation and the power
>   and the kingdom of our God
>   and the authority of his Messiah,
> for the accuser of our comrades has been thrown down,
>   who accuses them day and night before our God. . . .
> Rejoice then, you heavens and those who dwell in them! (12:10, 12)

Satan is called the "accuser of our comrades" rather than the persecutor. "Satan" in Hebrew is a title that means something approximately equivalent to "prosecuting attorney." Satan undermines and destroys by accusing, by inducing us humans to think we are worthless and rejected by God.

Summarily expelled from the presence of God, a wounded and dangerous Satan prowls the earth. "Woe to the earth and the sea, / for the devil has come down to you with great wrath, / because he knows that his time is short!" (12:12). Having failed to destroy the newborn Christ, the dragon now pursues the woman, who is a symbol of the people of God.

Like Christians at Jerusalem who fled across the Jordan River to Pella when the Jewish War was about to begin in AD 66,[2] the woman in John's vision is carried to the wilderness. She enjoys divine protection, nourished by God and protected from a torrent of water that the dragon belches after her. This deluge recalls the watery void at the dawn of creation. It is an attempt by the dragon to return the world to the primordial chaos of Genesis 1:2. Furious that the woman escapes, the dragon sets out to "make war on the rest of her children, those who keep the commandments of God and hold the testimony of Jesus" (Rev. 12:17). These are the followers of Jesus.

---

2. Eusebius, *Ecclesiastical History* 3.5; Epiphanius, *Panarion* (*Adversus Haereses*) 29.7.7–7.8; 30.2.7. Some scholars dispute the historicity of the Christian flight to Pella. See also Luke 21:20–22.

Fig. 4.3. Emperor Trajan (AD 98–117) was the recipient of Pliny's famous letter about Christians.

Governor Pliny Questions Christians

From a letter written by a Roman governor about AD 112, we catch a glimpse of what war on the Christian church looked like in the late first and early second centuries. This is the oldest surviving Roman record of what an imperial official understood Christian worship to be.

Most of the time during the first several centuries of the church, the Roman government did *not* persecute Christians. There is not much reason even to believe that John wrote Revelation at a time of widespread persecution, although he clearly expects major persecution in the near future. Christians were despised and socially ostracized, but Roman officials apparently did little to harass the church in the provinces until local people demanded that the government act. There was more peer pressure from friends and neighbors to participate in emperor worship than there was government policy or coercion to do so.

Pliny the Younger was a Roman lawyer, senator, and governor who did prosecute Christians in Asia Minor a few years after John wrote Revelation. In AD 111 Emperor Trajan (fig. 4.3) sent him to serve as governor of Bithynia, a province north of the seven churches of Revelation; there Pliny served as judge for certain capital cases that came to the courtroom. In a letter Pliny wrote to Trajan, we have the first recorded mention of Christians in Roman imperial records.

Pliny asks the emperor for advice on how to handle cases where citizens have pressed charges against individuals suspected of being Christians. His query illuminates the kind of suspicion that surrounded Christianity and gives an extraordinary window into early Christian worship. Pliny writes:

I have never been present at an examination of Christians. Consequently, I do not know the nature or the extent of the punishments usually meted out to them, nor the grounds for starting an investigation and how far it should be pressed. Nor am I at all sure whether any distinction should be made between them on the grounds of age, or if young people and adults should be treated alike; whether a pardon ought to be granted to anyone retracting their beliefs, or if they have once professed Christianity, they shall gain nothing by renouncing it; and whether it is the mere name Christian which is punishable, even if innocent of crime, or rather the crimes associated with the name.

For the moment this is the line I have taken with all persons brought before me on the charge of being Christians. I have asked them in person if they are Christians, and if they admit it, I repeat the question a second and third time, with a warning of the punishment awaiting them. If they persist, I order them to be led away for execution; for, whatever the nature of their admission, I am convinced that their stubbornness and unshakable obstinacy ought not to go unpunished. There have been others similarly fanatical who are Roman citizens. I have entered them on the list of persons to be sent to Rome for trial.[3]

From the beginning of Pliny's letter, we gather that Christians still were largely unknown to Roman government officials. Pliny previously had served for decades as a lawyer and senator in Rome, but he had never been present at the trial of a Christian. He was uncertain whether Christians were prosecuted simply for being members of a suspect religion, or if there were specific criminal acts that Christians were reputed to commit.

Christians Face Anonymous Accusations

In any case, Pliny knew that it was standard procedure to execute Christians who did not recant—unless they were Roman citizens, in which case they were remanded to Rome, as happened to Paul (Acts 25:11–12). The governor viewed Christians as deluded and stubborn. His letter goes on to explain that complaints against Christians have spontaneously come to his court from unnamed sources:

An anonymous pamphlet has been circulated which contains the names of a number of accused persons. Among these I considered that I should dismiss any who denied that they were or ever had been Christians when they had repeated after me a formula of invocation to the gods and had made offerings of wine and incense to your statue (which I had ordered to be brought into court for this purpose along with the images of the gods), and furthermore had reviled

3. Pliny the Younger, *Letters* 10.96.1–4; in Pliny the Younger, *Letters and Panegyricus*, vol. 2, trans. Betty Radice, LCL 59 (Cambridge, MA: Harvard University Press, 1969), 285–87.

the name of Christ: none of which things, I understand, any genuine Christian can be induced to do.[4]

Whom Christians worshiped was a decisive factor in determining guilt. Pliny released defendants who were willing to worship both the emperor and the gods of Rome, so long as they also reviled Christ. The letter then mentions people appearing in Pliny's courtroom who had abandoned Christian faith years earlier: "Others, whose names were given to me by an informer, first admitted the charge and then denied it; they said that they had ceased to be Christians two or more years ago, and some of them even twenty years ago. They all did reverence to your statue and the images of the gods in the same way as others, and reviled the name of Christ."[5] The reference to twenty years earlier reaches back into the reign of Domitian, to what may have been a spate of persecution in Asia Minor at the time John wrote Revelation.

The Church Is a Political Association

Pliny's letter gives a valuable glimpse of how early Christians worshiped, or at least how a Roman ruler understood their worship:

> They also declared that the sum total of their guilt or error amounted to no more than this: they had met regularly before dawn on a fixed day to chant verses alternately among themselves in honor of Christ as if to a god, and also to bind themselves by an oath [*sacramentum*], not for any criminal purpose, but to abstain from theft, robbery and adultery, to commit no breach of trust and not to deny a deposit when called upon to restore it.
>
> After this ceremony it had been their custom to disperse and reassemble later to take food of an ordinary, harmless kind; but they had in fact given up this practice since my edict, issued on your instructions, which banned all political societies. This made me decide it was all the more necessary to extract the truth by torture from two slave women, whom they call deaconesses. I found nothing but a degenerate sort of cult carried to extravagant lengths.[6]

Since there was no common day of rest in the weekly calendar of Roman society, Christians simply chose to gather for worship before dawn on a given day—probably Sunday, the day of Jesus' resurrection. At that early hour they antiphonally spoke or sang a liturgy of worship to Christ. To his surprise, Pliny has learned that these acts of corporate devotion result in the index of ethical behavior.

4. Ibid. 10.96.5; in Radice, *Letters*, 2:287–89.
5. Ibid. 10.96.6; in Radice, *Letters*, 2:289.
6. Ibid. 10.96.7–8; in Radice, *Letters*, 2:289.

After worship, Christians gathered again—perhaps in the evening—but to eat ordinary food, not babies! Pliny probably highlights that Christians ate harmless meals because rumors circulated in the ancient world that followers of Jesus were sexually promiscuous cannibals.[7] The governor reports that Christians had taken an oath not to commit theft, robbery, or adultery. They vowed to tell the truth and to operate with integrity in financial matters.

In discussing the oath, Pliny uses the Latin word *sacramentum*, a term the Roman army used for the oath of allegiance to the emperor. By the end of the second century, and perhaps sooner, the early church also used *sacramentum* to mean baptismal vows. At their initiation into the church by baptism, believers pledged allegiance to Jesus Christ and to the high ethical standards of the gospel. Joining the church was every bit as comprehensive a commitment as joining the army of Caesar.

An imperial edict against clubs of any kind, previously issued by Emperor Trajan to prevent subversive political associations, provided grounds for Pliny to forbid Christians from gathering for worship. Although worship was a political act in the governor's view, he did not seem unduly alarmed. Investigation convinced Pliny that Christianity was nothing more than a vulgar superstition.

The letter ends with Pliny congratulating himself for having successfully checked the spread of Christianity. He laments that people from every age and class and of both sexes have become caught up in the movement. The Christian scourge has afflicted not only cities, where one expects strange things, but also villages and the countryside. Now that he has so wisely addressed the problem, however, Pliny declares that the local economy and the familiar indexes of pagan religious practice are returning to normal:

> There is no doubt that people have begun to throng the temples which had been almost entirely deserted for a long time; the sacred rites which had been allowed to lapse are being performed again, and flesh of sacrificial victims is on sale everywhere, though up till recently scarcely anyone could be found to buy it. It is easy to infer from this that a great many people could be reformed if they were given an opportunity to repent.[8]

In his reply to Pliny's letter,[9] Emperor Trajan affirms the governor's handling of the Christians and says there is no general rule for how to treat them. This comment suggests that there was no formal legislation making the practice of Christian faith illegal. Trajan further directs that Christians should not be sought out for prosecution. If they were denounced, Pliny was to prosecute, but he should ignore anonymous accusations.

7. Minucius Felix, a Roman lawyer and Christian apologist who wrote a century after Pliny the Younger, describes such charges. See Minucius Felix, *Octavius* 9.1–7.

8. Pliny the Younger, *Letters* 10.96.10; in Radice, *Letters*, 2:291.

9. *Letters* 10.97.

Christian Worship Builds Self-Esteem

In this chapter we met the dragon, a personification of rebellion against God. It is ironic that the agent of rebellion is also the accuser (Rev. 12:10). There is legitimate reason for mortals to feel guilt in the divine presence, "since all have sinned and fall short of the glory of God" (Rom. 3:23). But it is part of Satan's twisted design to make even those whom the Lamb has forgiven feel guilty and worthless. For this reason confession of sin *and* proclamation of forgiveness need to be regular features of Christian worship. If we do not acknowledge our sin, we start functioning like little gods who make independent moral choices. If we do not celebrate the forgiveness we receive in Christ, we carry a weight of shame and guilt.

Revelation underscores the value of the individual in God's sight by stating that followers of Jesus dress in white, for they are worthy (3:4). Forgiven sinners are not an exclusive group. Twenty-four elders before the throne of God worship the Lamb, who has "ransomed for God saints from every tribe and language and people and nation" (5:9). John's vision of an innumerable multitude (7:9) emphasizes the enormous scope of God's grace.

After John observes "the accuser of our comrades" being thrown out of heaven (12:9, 10), a loud voice proclaims that they have conquered him by the blood of the Lamb and by the word of their testimony (12:11). By aligning with Jesus, believers receive power to conquer even Satan. The recurrence of jubilant worship in Revelation reflects the joy and freedom of forgiven people. Believers prepare to meet Christ with the expectation of a resplendent bride (19:7–8).

As we saw in the Pliny account, Christians whom the government put on trial in the second century were objects of hatred and contempt for their "degenerate" and "excessive" faith. The apparent power brokers in every generation—whether in government, social circles, religious institutions, or professional guilds—sometimes ostracize or slander followers of the Lamb. In such circumstances, worship becomes a vital activity that restores a sense of confidence and self-worth in believers. Powerful as human rulers and institutions seem to be, they shrink to insignificance before the living God. In the next portion of our study we accompany John as he dares to stand in God's presence in the court of heaven.

For Reflection

1. What is your understanding of Satan and the source of evil? Does it make sense that Satan once was part of the heavenly court? Can you name examples of evil warping something good that God created?

2. Try to infer from the letters quoted in this chapter what motivated Governor Pliny and Emperor Trajan to take the actions they did against

Christians. Are there modern examples of rulers receiving public support for harsh treatment of prisoners who may be innocent?

3. In what ways are Christians honored or respected in your culture today? In what ways are Christians marginalized or lampooned? Do we Christians deserve the reputation we have today?

LIVING THE VISION
Confessing Christ in the Roman Army

In AD 298, enemies of Rome threatened the empire on several fronts. For reasons of state security, the government increased pressure on soldiers to demonstrate allegiance by regular participation in emperor worship. In the country today called Morocco, a centurion named Marcellus was expected to lead his soldiers in worship of the Roman gods and emperors. Instead, in a startling index of new loyalty, Marcellus threw down his soldier's belt—which carried his weapons—in front of the legionary standards. In a loud voice he declared, "I am a soldier of Jesus Christ, the eternal king. From now I cease to serve your emperors and I despise the worship of your gods of wood and stone, for they are deaf and dumb images." An ancient account of his trial and execution on October 30, 298, records the following exchange between judge Agricolanus and defendant Marcellus:[10]

Agricolanus: Did you say the things that are recorded in the prefect's report?
Marcellus: Yes, I did.
Agricolanus: You held the military rank of centurion, first class?
Marcellus: Yes.
Agricolanus: What madness possessed you to throw down the symbols of your military oath and to say the things you did?
Marcellus: No madness possesses those who fear the Lord.
Agricolanus: Then you did say all of those things that are set down in the prefect's report?
Marcellus: Yes, I said them.
Agricolanus: You threw down your weapons?

10. Adapted from Herbert Musurillo, trans., *The Acts of the Christian Martyrs* (Oxford: Clarendon, 1972), 250–59.

Marcellus: Yes, I did. For it is not fitting that a Christian, who fights for Christ his Lord, should fight for the armies of this world.

Agricolanus: What Marcellus has done merits punishment according to military rules. And so, whereas Marcellus, who held the rank of centurion, first class, has confessed that he has disgraced himself by publicly renouncing his military oath, . . . I hereby sentence him to death by the sword.

Marcellus: Agricolanus, may God reward you.

Today the relics of Marcellus are preserved under the altar at the Basilica of the Sacred Heart at the University of Notre Dame in South Bend, Indiana.

5

The Cosmic Throne Room

Read Revelation 4:1–11

Around the throne, and on each side of the throne, are four living creatures, full of eyes in front and behind: the first living creature like a lion, the second living creature like an ox, the third living creature with a face like a human face, and the fourth living creature like a flying eagle. And the four living creatures, each of them with six wings, are full of eyes all around and inside. Day and night without ceasing they sing,

> "Holy, holy, holy,
> the Lord God the Almighty,
>   who was and is and is to come."

And whenever the living creatures give glory and honor and thanks to the one who is seated on the throne, who lives forever and ever, the twenty-four elders fall before the one who is seated on the throne and worship the one who lives forever and ever; they cast their crowns before the throne, singing,

> "You are worthy, our Lord and God,
>   to receive glory and honor and power,
> for you created all things,
>   and by your will they existed and were created." (4:6b–11)

Fig. 5.1. The reverse of this Domitian *denarius* from AD 81 depicts the emperor's throne, viewed from the front. A tasseled cloth is draped over the seat, and on top rests a winged thunderbolt reminiscent of what John saw emanating from the throne of God (Rev. 4:5). (Photo courtesy of Harlan J. Berk, Ltd.)

In the story of Tiridates bowing before Emperor Nero (see introduction), and in the correspondence between Pliny and Emperor Trajan (see chap. 4), we gather a sense of the power and influence of the Roman imperial throne. Much of the world known to John held the emperor in awe and bowed in devotion. In order to counter this global tide of idolatrous allegiance, John needed a transforming vision of alternative worship. In the throne vision (Rev. 4–5) he receives it: a dazzling panorama of worship in the presence of the living God.

John sees an open door in the heavens, and a voice like a trumpet invites him to ascend to the divine presence (4:1). The scene that greets him surpasses anything the emperors of Rome could have imagined (fig. 5.1). Symbols, most of which had established meaning in Jewish or pagan contexts, communicate the glory of God. A throne (symbol of sovereignty), surrounded by a rainbow (reminder of God's covenant with Noah), emits flashes of lightning and peals of thunder (echoes of Sinai). In front of the throne are seven flaming torches. Also in front of the throne is a sea of glass, just as the temple of Solomon once featured a massive "molten sea" water basin (1 Kings 7:23–26). The stilled waters reminded worshipers in the temple that God once had tamed a watery chaos at creation (Gen. 1:1–2).

With typical Jewish reverence for divine holiness, John uses simile rather than direct description to portray the one seated on the throne. God looks like jasper and carnelian. Around the throne are twenty-four elders, perhaps

Fig. 5.2. These terra-cotta images of mythical winged creatures were part of the Temple of Apollo built by Caesar Augustus on the Palatine Hill at Rome (36–28 BC).

Fig. 5.3. This *tetradrachm* from Asia Minor from about 27 BC features Caesar Augustus on the obverse and a sphinx on the reverse. (Photo courtesy of Harlan J. Berk, Ltd.)

signifying the twelve tribes of Israel (the Old Testament) and the twelve apostles (the New Testament).

Four winged creatures, perhaps representative of all living things, serve as worship leaders for the whole of creation. Such winged beasts commonly appear in portrayals of divine scenes in the ancient world—including in a temple built by Caesar Augustus (fig. 5.2) and on one of his coins (fig. 5.3). The beings in John's vision have the aspect of a lion (representing wild animals?), an ox (representing domesticated animals?), a man (representing humans?), and an eagle (representing birds?). It was standard practice in ancient pagan religion to worship heavenly bodies or forces of nature. Now, in contrast to such pantheism, John sees creation worshiping God. In ceaseless chorus the creatures proclaim,

> Holy, holy, holy,
> the Lord God the Almighty,
>   who was and is and is to come.

Then in words and gestures reminiscent of praise offered to Roman emperors, the twenty-four elders fall to the ground and sing,

> You are worthy, our Lord and God,
>   to receive glory and honor and power,
> for you created all things,
>   and by your will they existed and were created.

At a time when idolatrous pagan powers seemed to dominate the world, this vision of all creation worshiping the living God must have been exhilarating for John. Rulers of Rome craved glory, honor, and power, and John now sees that these appropriately belong to God.

Jews Are Sensitive to Political Symbols

The heavenly court abounds with symbols: throne, rainbow, white robes, golden crowns, thunder and lightning, torches, living creatures, and elders.

Fig. 5.4. In this second-century sculpture from Rome, the soldier on the right carries a standard (*signum*) that bears images or seals of the emperor.

Human experience of the divine usually involves symbol or icon, since that is the primary way mortals apprehend transcendent reality. When structured in liturgy or ritual, symbol and icon become doorways to a spiritual realm. Whether sacred or profane, symbols and icons can have a powerful impact on observers or participants, shaping allegiance and behavior.

Jews in the ancient world had keen sensitivity to the power of symbols, and these became points of conflict when pagan powers controlled Palestine. Pontius Pilate, procurator (and/or prefect) of Judea (AD 26–36), once tried to raise the profile of Roman presence in Jerusalem by publicly displaying icons of the emperor. These were on standards, which were hand-carried sacred poles ornamented with imperial symbols or small icons of the emperor and sometimes topped with an open hand that represented the oath of loyalty taken by soldiers (fig. 5.4).[1] Alarmed and outraged, a large number of Jews from Jerusalem and the surrounding countryside made their way to Pilate's residence at Caesarea on the Mediterranean seacoast. They pleaded with the procurator to respect their prohibition against images and remove the standards. When Pilate refused, the Jews stationed themselves around his house and protested for five days. Finally Pilate held court in the stadium at Caesarea Maritima, under the pretext of giving the protesters another hearing. Josephus reports that Pilate instead

> gave the arranged signal to his armed soldiers to surround the Jews. Finding themselves in a ring of troops, three deep, the Jews were struck dumb at this

1. For more on standards in the Roman army, see www.vroma.org/~bmcmanus/romanarmy .html.

unexpected sight. Pilate, after threatening to cut them down, if they refused to admit Caesar's images, signaled to the soldiers to draw their swords. Thereupon the Jews, as by concerted action, flung themselves in a body on the ground, extended their necks, and exclaimed that they were ready rather to die than to transgress the law.[2]

Astonished by the intensity of their religious fervor, Pilate ordered the immediate removal of the standards from Jerusalem.

Emperors Revel in Being Worshiped

John of Patmos was a radical Jew who resonated with this tradition of nonviolent resistance to political idolatry. The incident with the standards at Jerusalem occurred during the reign of Tiberius (AD 14–37), a relatively moderate emperor who generally did not promote himself as divine. But in the decades following his reign, Emperors Caligula and Nero brazenly presented themselves to the world as deities. Their blasphemies provide a background for John's vision of the beast and his urgent call for exclusive worship of the living God.

Caligula (AD 37–41; fig. 5.5), whose real name was Gaius, had a father who was a general in the Roman army. Soldiers nicknamed the future emperor Caligula, which means "Booties," when he appeared in public as a small boy wearing little army boots. Caligula became emperor at age twenty-four and claimed to believe in his own divinity. A contemporary, Philo of Alexandria, says Caligula liked to appear in public dressed as one of the gods:

> [Caligula] metamorphosed and transformed himself into Apollo, crowning his head with garlands, in the form of rays, and holding a bow and arrows in his left hand, and holding forth graces in his right, as if it became him to proffer blessings to all people from his ready store. . . . And immediately there were established choruses, who had been carefully trained, singing paeans to him, the same who . . . sang Bacchic hymns in his honor when he assumed the disguise of [the god] Bacchus.[3]

According to Suetonius, the vain emperor began to "lay claim to divine majesty." He ordered that statues of the gods that were "famous for their sanctity or artistic merit, including that of Jupiter of Olympia, should be brought from Greece, in order to remove their heads and put his own in their

2. Josephus, *Jewish War* 2.172–74; in Josephus, *The Jewish War*, vol. 2, trans. H. St. J. Thackeray, LCL 210 (1927–28; Cambridge, MA: Harvard University Press, 1967), 391.

3. Philo, *On the Embassy to Gaius* 95–96; in Charles Duke Yonge, trans., *The Works of Philo* (Peabody, MA: Hendrickson, 1993), 765.

Fig. 5.5. A modern reconstruction of Caligula's likeness, based on a cast of a first-century statue of the young emperor.

place." He "set up a special temple to his own godhead" that featured a life-sized statue of himself in gold.[4]

Caligula directed Governor Petronius of Syria to place a statue of the emperor in the Jewish temple at Jerusalem. Philo describes the reaction of one group of Jews when a messenger brought news of the impending sacrilege:

> [The man] with difficulty, sobbing aloud, and in a broken voice, spoke as follows: "Our temple is destroyed! Gaius [Caligula] has ordered a colossal statue of himself to be erected in the holy of holies, having his own name inscribed upon it with the title of Jupiter!" And while we were all struck dumb with astonishment and terror at what he had told us, and stood still deprived of all motion (for we stood there mute and in despair, ready to fall to the ground with fear and sorrow, the very muscles of our bodies being deprived of all strength by the news which we had heard), others arrived bearing the same sad tale.[5]

Tens of thousands of Jews in Palestine converged in Galilee in nonviolent protest to the governor, who was visiting the region. "Falling on their faces and baring their throats, they declared that they were ready to be slain" rather than see the offending icon introduced into their temple at Jerusalem.[6]

4. Suetonius, *Gaius* 22; in *Suetonius*, vol. 1, trans. and ed. J. C. Rolfe, LCL 31 (1913–14; Cambridge, MA: Harvard University Press, 1998), 437.

5. Philo, *Embassy* 188–89; in Yonge, *Works of Philo*, 774. Philo was part of a delegation from Egypt that had an audience with Caligula in Italy to request protection from harassment for Jews in Alexandria. Caligula scoffed at the delegation. While in Italy, Philo and the delegation received this report of the emperor's plans to place his statue in the temple at Jerusalem.

6. Josephus, *Jewish Antiquities* 18.271–72; in Josephus, *Jewish Antiquities*, vol. 7, trans. Louis H. Feldman, LCL 456 (Cambridge, MA: Harvard University Press, 1965), 159–61.

Given the volatility of the situation, Petronius delayed installation of the statue. When the governor dared to suggest that Rome rescind the statue order, Caligula ordered him to commit suicide. But the emperor himself soon died, the victim of assassination, and Petronius survived. The threat to Jewish worship that Caligula's statue represented, however, became part of a rising tide of resentment against Rome that eventually led to the Jewish War (AD 66–70).

Nero (AD 54–68), as we have seen, was an arrogant and violent ruler who erected a colossal statue of himself at Rome as the sun god Apollo. When he returned from a vanity tour of public singing and athletic competition in Greece, Nero received a triumphal reception at Rome. The contemporary Roman historian Dio Cassius reports that that city "was all decked with garlands, was ablaze with lights and reeking with incense, and the whole population, the senators themselves most of all, kept shouting" the following litany:

> Hail, Olympian Victor! . . . Augustus! Augustus!
> Hail to Nero, our Hercules! Hail to Nero, our Apollo!
> The only Victor of the Grand Tour,
> the only one from the beginning of time!
> Augustus! Augustus! O, Divine Voice!
> Blessed are they that hear thee.[7]

Some Jews Resist Roman Rule

Jesus carried out his public ministry during the reign of Emperor Tiberius (AD 14–37), before the excesses of Caligula or Nero. But emperor worship was well established already under Caesar Augustus (27 BC–AD 14). Jesus came face-to-face with Pontius Pilate, the governor who brought the Roman standards into Jerusalem. It is not clear whether the armed revolutionaries known as Zealots had yet emerged as an organized resistance movement. But Luke reports that among Jesus' twelve disciples was Simon the Zealot (Luke 6:15; Acts 1:13), which suggests that strains of political resistance appeared within Jesus' inner circle.

Jesus was alert to the rising tide of Jewish nationalism and gave instructions for how his followers should act when Jews revolted and Roman armies besieged Jerusalem:

> When you see Jerusalem surrounded by armies, then know that its desolation has come near. Then those in Judea must flee to the mountains, and those inside the city must leave it, and those out in the country must not enter it; for these are days of vengeance, as a fulfillment of all that is written. Woe to those who

---

7. Dio Cassius, *Roman History* 63.20.4–5; in *Dio's Roman History*, vol. 8, trans. Earnest Cary, LCL 176 (1914–27; Cambridge, MA: Harvard University Press, 1981), 169–71.

are pregnant and to those who are nursing infants in those days! For there will be great distress on the earth and wrath against this people; they will fall by the edge of the sword and be taken away as captives among all nations; and Jerusalem will be trampled on by the Gentiles, until the times of the Gentiles are fulfilled. (Luke 21:20–24)

What Jesus foresaw became awful reality in AD 66, when resentment boiled over into outright revolt. Violence irrupted first at Caesarea Maritima, when a Greek in that city deliberately violated Jewish worship sensitivities by offering a pagan sacrifice on a makeshift altar at the entrance to the synagogue.[8] Jewish appeals for the governor to intervene fell on deaf ears, and rebellion soon flared in Jerusalem, then spread to other parts of Judea and Galilee. By far the most successful insurgency against Rome anywhere in the first century, the Jewish War (AD 66–70) briefly ousted Roman armies from Palestine.

Rome Puts Down the Jewish Revolt

Wanting to eliminate all traces of emperor worship, the newly independent Jewish government melted down Roman coins bearing icons of so-called divine emperors and minted new money with no human images. But the insurgency was short lived. Nero directed General Vespasian (fig. 5.6) to retake Palestine, and within two years all territory except Jerusalem and the Masada fortress by the Dead Sea was back under Roman control (AD 66–68).

Josephus, commander of the Jewish rebels in Galilee, wrote a vivid account of the ghastly siege and fall of Jerusalem (AD 68–70). Residents of Jerusalem succumbed to starvation and civil war as Roman armies tightened the noose. Roman soldiers crucified Jewish captives outside the city walls to break the spirit of those inside, and so many died this way that "space could not be found for the crosses nor crosses for the bodies."[9] Panic and despair beset the trapped population, and visionaries claimed to see armies of heaven coming to the rescue. Josephus—who sided with Rome after being captured in Galilee—claims to have stood outside the walls of Jerusalem, exhorting the rebels to surrender: "Listen, that you may learn that you are warring not against the Romans only, but also against God."[10] Josephus declared to his fellow Jews that God had fled from the holy places of Jerusalem "and taken his stand on the side of those with whom you are now at war."[11]

Emperor Nero committed suicide at Rome (June 9, 68) while the Jewish War raged in Palestine. In the following eighteen months, three men briefly

8. Josephus, *War* 2.284–92.
9. Ibid. 5.451; in Thackeray, *Jewish War*, 3:341.
10. Ibid. 5.378; in Thackeray, *Jewish War*, 3:319.
11. Ibid. 5.412; in Thackeray, *Jewish War*, 3:331.

Fig. 5.6. General Vespasian (left) began the military campaign to retake Palestine. His son Titus (right) completed the reconquest and destroyed the temple at Jerusalem. Both went on to rule as emperors.

held the imperial throne, and all died violently before General Vespasian became emperor. Eventually Jerusalem fell to Vespasian's son Titus (fig. 5.6), who decimated the city and destroyed the temple in AD 70. Josephus says, no doubt with hyperbole, that 1.1 million Jews perished during the siege and fall of Jerusalem, and ninety-seven thousand were taken captive.[12] Titus took the "tallest and most handsome" Jewish youth to Rome for his triumphal procession. He sent "multitudes" of Jewish prisoners throughout the empire to be killed by wild beasts in the theaters, and condemned countless others to slavery in the mines of Egypt.[13]

Just as Jesus had directed (Luke 21:20–24), when the revolt began, Christians in Jerusalem fled across the Jordan valley to Pella.[14] The book of Revelation prominently features Jerusalem (Rev. 11) and the new Jerusalem (Rev. 21; 22), suggesting that John had emotional and spiritual ties to the holy city. It is possible that John was among the Christian refugees who fled Jerusalem as violence escalated. In any case, the flight of Jewish Christians from Jerusalem widened the gulf between Judaism and emerging Christianity.

12. Ibid. 6.420; in Thackeray, *Jewish War*, 3:497.
13. Ibid. 6.417–19; in Thackeray, *Jewish War*, 3:497.
14. Eusebius, *Ecclesiastical History* 3.5.

Radicals at Qumran Shed Light on Revelation

Christians who fled Jerusalem during the Jewish War were not alone in rejecting collaboration with both the Roman Empire and the Jewish priestly aristocracy at Jerusalem. In the parched badlands between the Dead Sea and the hills of the Judean Desert, a radical sect of Jews known as Essenes lived in a worshiping community at a place called Qumran.[15] The Essenes were not Christian; they followed their own apocalyptic leader, whom they called the Teacher of Righteousness.

Ruins from the Qumran community survive today (fig. 5.7), and starting in 1947 the renowned Dead Sea Scrolls were found in caves nearby. Members of the Qumran community apparently hid the scrolls in these caves for safekeeping when Roman armies approached during the Jewish War (AD 66–70).

We have no evidence that John of Patmos was an Essene. Yet the similarity between his writing and the practices of the Essenes suggests that their responses to empire at least were indexes of related religious impulses. Josephus says the Essenes generally did not marry, held all goods in common, and despised riches. They preferred white garments, wore white veils in worship, and took frequent ritual baths for spiritual purity.[16] From scrolls found at Qumran, we know that members of that community were alienated from the priestly hierarchy associated with the Jewish temple at Jerusalem.

These characteristics of the Essenes have parallels in Revelation, where saints whom John calls virgins follow the Lamb in heaven (14:4). Both the Essenes and John championed the ideal of a communal economy—the Essenes by having all possessions in common, John by envisioning a new Jerusalem in which all share the wealth. Both understood white clothing as a symbol of purity and as appropriate dress for worship (Rev. 3:4; 7:9). The Essenes took ritual baths, and Revelation says, "Blessed are those who wash their robes, so that they will have the right to the tree of life and may enter" the new Jerusalem (22:14). Also like the Essenes, John had a deep sense of being over against the dominant political and religious powers of the day.

A major difference between John and the Essenes, however, is that the latter prepared for actual physical warfare against the Romans. The Qumran *War Scroll* (or *War Rule*), about the struggle of the Sons of Light against the Sons of Darkness, sets out a battle plan for defeating the Romans. The document predicts that each side will win three battles over a period of forty years. In a seventh and final battle, the Sons of Light will triumph. The scroll gives instructions for the selection of soldiers, the use of trumpets in battle, and the

15. Not all scholars agree that the community at Qumran was Essene, but the majority opinion holds that it was. The Essene movement was larger than just Qumran, and some members did not live in monastic community.

16. Josephus, *War* 2.119–36.

Fig. 5.7. In the foreground is a *mikveh*, or ritual bath, used by members of the radical Jewish community at Qumran. Hills and caves in the background are where the group hid scrolls during the Jewish War.

deployment of troops. It also scripts a hymn of praise to be recited in worship after the final engagement. The following is an excerpt:

> Rise up, O Hero!
> Lead off Your captives, O Glorious One!
> Gather up Your spoils, O Author of mighty deeds!
> Lay Your hand on the neck of your enemies
>   and Your feet on the pile of the slain!
> Smite the nations, your adversaries,
>   and devour flesh with Your sword!
> Fill your land with glory
>   and Your inheritance with blessing. . . .
> O Zion, rejoice greatly!
>   Rejoice all you cities of Judah!
> Keep your gates ever open
>   that the hosts of the nations may be brought in!
> Their kings shall serve you
>   and all your oppressors shall bow down before you;
>   they shall lick the dust of your feet.[17]

17. *War Rule* (1QM, 4QM) 19; in *The Dead Sea Scrolls in English*, trans. G. Vermès, 3rd rev. ed. (1962; London: Penguin, 1994), 124, adapted.

Revelation Shifts to Grace and Redemption

We see intriguing parallels between Revelation and this sample of Qumran literature: defeat of the enemies of God, a focus on Zion, and the wealth of nations pouring into Jerusalem. But while the tenor of Revelation eventually shifts to grace and redemption, the Qumran War Scroll focuses relentlessly on the violent demise of all adversaries. Members of the Qumran community worshiped with the belief that in the end an exceedingly small group of mortals would be saved.

Josephus tells of the travail suffered by members of the Essene movement—which presumably included the Qumran community—when Roman armies moved in to quell the Jewish War:

> Racked and twisted, burnt and broken, and made to pass through every instrument of torture, in order to induce them to blaspheme their lawgiver [Moses] or to eat some forbidden thing, they refused to yield to either demand, nor even once did they cringe to their persecutors or shed a tear. Smiling in their agonies and mildly deriding their tormentors, they cheerfully resigned their souls, confident that they would receive them back again.[18]

Like John a generation later, the Essenes were willing to face martyrdom for their faith. The Qumran community—and the entire Essene movement—all but disappeared after the Jewish War, its members slain or scattered by the Roman army. It is possible that some members of the Qumran community retreated to the great desert escarpment called Masada, where the last Jewish rebels held out until their mass suicide in AD 73.

An Empire Humiliates Its Foes

All over the empire were reminders for Jews that insurrection had not served them well. Treasures from the plundered temple at Jerusalem flooded the regional market in such great quantity that the price of gold fell to half its previous value.[19] For a generation after the defeat of the Jews, Roman coins portray Judea as a woman in mourning (figs. 4.2; 5.8). The coin legends typically read *IVDAEA CAPTA* (Judea captive).

General Titus paraded in Rome as a hero, and the Romans placed a triumphal arch, reconstructed and standing today, in the forum at Rome to commemorate his victory. A frieze inside the arch depicts young men, likely Jewish captives, carrying sacred objects from the temple, including the seven-

18. Josephus, *War* 2.152–53; in Thackeray, *Jewish War*, 2:381.
19. Josephus, *War* 6.317.

Fig. 5.8. This Roman *as* coin from AD 77–78 portrays Judea as a defeated woman seated in mourning. The Romans issued such "Judea captive" coins for twenty-five years after the fall of Jerusalem. (Photo courtesy of Harlan J. Berk, Ltd.)

Fig. 5.9. Detail from the frieze inside the Arch of Titus shows the menorah and perhaps the table of showbread from the temple at Jerusalem being carried in triumphal procession along the Via Sacra in Rome.

branched golden menorah lamp (fig. 5.9). Both the arch and the coins gave an ominous message about the folly of resisting Roman rule.

The Power of Resurrection

In this chapter we have contrasted the awesome throne of God with the awful courts of Caligula and Nero; we also considered the fate of Jews in Palestine who rebelled against their Roman masters. While there is no indication that Christians joined in the revolt, from time to time they suffered harsh treatment similar to what the Roman government inflicted upon those it accused of insurrection. Jewish rebels had lethal weapons, and they actually succeeded for a while in ousting the enemy. Followers of the Lamb, in contrast, resisted the powers of death only with the Word of God, the power of the Spirit, and love of enemy.

"My kingdom is not from this world," Jesus told Pontius Pilate. "If my kingdom were from this world, my followers would be fighting to keep me from being handed over to the Jews [collaborating with Rome]" (John 18:36). The trial of Jesus looked like a mismatch, and Rome drove home the point on Thursday and Friday of that Passover week. No one observing those events foresaw the power of resurrection to reverse the tide of history.

An apparent mismatch of powers occurs today when followers of Jesus say no to a popular war, resist destruction of the environment by powerful corporations, or oppose Internet pornography. Christians who live simply and reject the consumerism of Western society are likely to be dismissed as cranks. People who champion global rather than national interests may come across as unpatriotic or ungrateful. Some Christians in totalitarian states or in countries where tension is high between religions face martyrdom for their loyalty to Jesus. The Lamb sometimes takes his followers to the margins of society, to places of vulnerability, to people who seem to lack power.

Worship of God and the Lamb is essential for Christians in such circumstances. Just as worship in the heavenly court galvanized John for sustained witness in the face of empire, worship of the creator God gives believers spiritual and emotional resources to resist the powers of death today. By joining the heavenly chorus, we align ourselves with God's future and find our strength renewed to follow the Lamb. We give our attention in the next chapter to this paradoxical Lamb, whose strength is made known in weakness.

For Reflection

1. What message do stamps and coins or other state-sponsored media in your country communicate? What stories of victory does your society retell to shape national identity and pride? Are there national holidays that Christians should refuse to celebrate or should mark with alternative celebrations?
2. If you were put on trial for being a believer, what evidence would prosecutors find to prove that you are a Christian?
3. In what circumstance can or should Christians speak to government, whether in protest or to provide counsel? In what circumstances can or should Christians take positions of leadership and responsibility in government? When would a Christian in government have to step down from office in order to be faithful to Jesus?

LIVING THE VISION
No Halfway House in Somalia

Ahmed Haile of Somalia became a Christian at age seventeen when he read the New Testament during a hospital stay. The change of allegiance could not have been greater. Somalia is 99 percent Muslim, and commitment to Jesus Christ meant alienation from family and clan. The Somali government, then officially atheist and aligned with the Soviet Union, had planned to send Ahmed to East Germany for a university education. But that opportunity was not open to Christians. "There was no 'halfway house' in Somalia during the years of Marxist rule," Ahmed says. "If you were a Christian, you had to be willing to die. We were sheep among wolves and had to depend on God." The church went underground, and Ahmed at age nineteen set out on foot for Kenya. Eventually he found his way to the United States for college and seminary.

Civil war raged in Somalia when local warlords tried to unseat the government, and Ahmed went back to his homeland to work for peace. He was recognized for his gifts in mediation and in 1992 served as the only Christian on a team of Muslims seeking to broker a settlement in the war at Mogadishu. "We were joined by a love for our people," he said, "believing that something stronger than guns could bring peace." The team conducted negotiations near the front line, but the house where they met was shelled by opponents of the peace process. Ahmed was grievously wounded and carried away semiconscious in a wheelbarrow. No hospital and no doctors were available. A friend who had no medical training did emergency surgery to amputate Ahmed's right leg. "I am going to die here," he thought. After the makeshift surgery, Ahmed asked his friend to retrieve three hundred fifteen dollars he had hidden in the shoe of his now-missing foot!

Warfare still plagues Somalia. "Somalis fight each other because each clan thinks theirs is the best," Ahmed says. "Clans traditionally resolved differences in meetings of the clan elders. Now they [try to] settle differences with an AK-47, and the cycle of violence grows." But Ahmed's wife Martha interjects, "Peace begins in the hearts of individuals, and people changed by Jesus can change the world."

Ahmed founded a peace studies program at Daystar University in Nairobi, Kenya, where he serves as a professor. Both he and his wife give encouragement and leadership to the Somali Christian community in Kenya.[20]

20. Ahmed and Martha Haile, interview by the author, May 22, 2008, Goshen, Indiana.

6

The Lamb Is Lord of History

Read Revelation 5:1–6:17

> Then one of the elders said to me, "Do not weep. See, the Lion of the tribe of Judah, the Root of David, has conquered, so that he can open the scroll and its seven seals." Then I saw between the throne and the four living creatures and among the elders a Lamb standing as if it had been slaughtered, having seven horns and seven eyes, which are the seven spirits of God sent out into all the earth. He went and took the scroll from the right hand of the one who was seated on the throne. When he had taken the scroll, the four living creatures and the twenty-four elders fell before the Lamb, each holding a harp and golden bowls full of incense, which are the prayers of the saints. (5:5–7)

With Jerusalem destroyed, fellow Christians slaughtered at Rome, and John himself apparently in trouble with imperial authorities, history must have seemed out of control. Is God truly sovereign in human affairs, or is history a meaningless cycle of injustice and suffering? As the throne vision unfolds, in the context of worship, John receives an answer to these questions.

Standing in the heavenly throne room, John sees a scroll in the hand of God (5:1). As was customary with confidential or official documents in ancient times, the scroll is sealed. Document seals in the ancient world were lumps of clay or wax, placed where strands of cord or papyrus around a rolled scroll were knotted. Into the clay or wax an authorized person made an imprint with a signet ring or stamp (fig. 6.1), so that any tampering with the scroll would be evident. Seven seals close this scroll, suggesting it contains the most sensitive or secret information. With seven being a biblical number of completion

Fig. 6.1. This signet ring from the Roman era makes an image of the god Mars when pressed into wax. (Photo courtesy of Ancient Caesar, LLC.)

all the way back to creation itself (Gen. 1), the seals also signal the fullness of time.

At the sight of the closed scroll in God's hand, John sinks into despair. It is only later, when the seals are broken, that we understand why. The scroll contains God's plan for—or perhaps God's foreknowledge of—the culmination of history. Events described in the scroll have already begun to take place but are not yet finished. Since no one is worthy to open the scroll, the destiny of the world remains a mystery to mortals, and the meaning of history remains hidden. John and his fellow believers have no way of being certain that the love and justice of God will prevail.

The Lion Is a Lamb

One of the elders tells John not to weep, because the "Lion of the tribe of Judah" has conquered and can open the scroll. What follows is a juxtaposition of symbols so profound that it is foundational to all of Christian theology. The weeping prophet, presumably standing with his head bowed in the heavenly court, raises his eyes to see the mighty Lion. This creature needs to be powerful enough to defeat the beast that casts a great shadow across the world (13:1–10).

Expecting to see a ferocious carnivore, John instead sees . . . a *Lamb*! The creature stands "as if it had been slaughtered" (5:6). The Greek word John uses for "slaughtered" carries more the meaning of murder than of sacrifice.[1] It is the same word John uses to describe both saints in heaven "who had been slaughtered for the word of God" (6:9) and all kinds of people "who have been slaughtered on earth" by Babylon/Rome (18:24). The Lamb that is worthy to reveal God's future for the world is himself a victim of violence.

From this moment onward, John is privy to the paradox of God's plan to redeem creation. God's fullest self-revelation has not come with brawn and bluster to match the muscle of Rome, but with the seeming weakness and vulnerability of a Lamb (fig. 6.2). Satan has deployed a devouring, seven-

---

1. Loren L. Johns, *The Lamb Christology of the Apocalypse of John: An Investigation into Its Origins and Rhetorical Force*, WUNT (Tübingen: Mohr Siebeck, 2003), 129.

Fig. 6.2. An early Christian representation of the Lamb from the catacombs at Rome.

headed monster upon the world. God chooses to meet Satan's ferocity with, of all things, a sheep.

The Lamb is worthy of praise, not just by the heavenly court, but also by all of creation. As the Lamb takes the scroll, the twenty-four elders fall down in worship. This index of devotion features harps for liturgical music (figs. 6.3; 6.4) and golden bowls of incense, "which are the prayers of the saints" (5:8). Emperor worship and other Roman religious ceremonies typically employed a shallow bowl called a *patera* for pouring libations (fig. 7.4). Now, in the heavenly court, John sees such bowls being used to hand deliver prayers of the church to the throne of God.

Fig. 6.4. Emperor Domitian featured the *cithara* harp on the reverse of this *denarius* minted at Rome in AD 95.

Fig. 6.3. A second-century sculpture of a *cithara* harp, played here by Apollo. This is the instrument John sees in the courts of heaven.

Followers of the Lamb Sing a New Song

In a burst of spontaneous praise, the four living creatures and the elders sing a new song:

> You are worthy to take the scroll and to open its seals,
>   for you were slaughtered and by your blood you ransomed for God
>   saints from every tribe and language and people and nation;
>   you have made them to be a kingdom and priests serving our God,
>   and they will reign on earth. (5:9–10)

In Jewish tradition, a new song is what the people of God offer in worship at a time of victory or deliverance. Most famously, Moses and the Israelites composed a hymn of praise at the Red Sea after their escape from the Egyptians:[2]

> Who is like you, O LORD, among the gods?
>   Who is like you, majestic in holiness,
>   awesome in splendor, doing wonders?
> You stretched out your right hand,
>   the earth swallowed them.
> In your steadfast love you led the people whom you redeemed;
>   you guided them by your strength to your holy abode. (Exod. 15:11–13)

The Lamb alone is worthy to open the scroll and reveal the meaning of history. His authority issues from the fact that he, like Moses, has ransomed a people. While Moses led a band of Hebrew slaves to freedom, the Lamb has redeemed individuals "from every tribe and language and people and nation" (Rev. 5:9). Out of this international and multiethnic group, the Lamb creates a kingdom and a priesthood serving God.

John and his seven churches functioned in an empire where few Christians could hope to enjoy the benefits of imperial citizenship. Followers of Jesus could not or would not belong to the *augustales*, the priests of emperor worship. Now the heavenly hymn proclaims that Jesus' death on the cross has created a new kingdom whose members belong to an alternative and eternal priesthood. The new song John hears reverberates with political, social, and economic implications.

Jesus' Death Is More Than Sacrifice

John keeps the cross itself at low profile in Revelation, which is typical of early Christian symbolism. In his Letters, Paul indeed frequently mentions the cross,

2. See also ibid., 168; Judg. 11:34; Ps. 40:3; 149:1–9.

and the crucifixion narrative is pivotal in all four Gospels. But Christians of the first centuries did not use the cross as a visual or liturgical symbol, and surely not as an ornament. Representing as it did a cruel death inflicted on those who threatened or offended the state, the cross was too gruesome and too subversive to be used as religious art. We find no crosses (fig. 6.5) in Christian art before Christianity became legal in the fourth century.[3]

Without mentioning the cross, John's vision nevertheless centers on the Lamb who died at Roman hands. What does John make of this great suffering? Many Christians today think of Jesus' death as a substitutionary sacrifice, in which Jesus laid down his life to atone for the sins of the world. Just as a ram or another animal bore the sins of the people of Israel in the Old Testament sacrificial system, Jesus paid the price for our sins by dying on the cross.

Fig. 6.5. Among ruins of ancient Laodicea is this undated image of a cross superimposed on a menorah. The cross was rare or nonexistent in Christian art before Constantine, so this image likely is from centuries after John wrote Revelation.

Such a substitutionary view of Jesus' death is valid and biblical, but it is not the main explanation the book of Revelation gives for the meaning of Jesus' death. In John's vision, Jesus confronts the powers of evil, absorbing the worst they can deliver (physical death) and triumphing over them through resurrection. This is a *Christus Victor* (Christ triumphant) view of salvation, in which followers of Jesus receive power through his victorious presence to live changed lives. Loren Johns says:

> The Lamb of Revelation is manifestly no cute, little nonviolent Lamb. It is a powerful and courageous Lamb who, through his consistent nonviolent and faithful witness, conquered evil. He did not deny the reality of evil or the reality of violence or "lie down with the lion" in some utopian idealism. . . . Rather, the Lamb overcame evil by refusing to adopt its methods and its rules and bearing its brunt. And he serves in the Apocalypse as a consistent and trustworthy model for believers facing the harsh realities of civic pressures to conform to the expectations of Graeco-Roman society.[4]

Jesus' victory over sin and death, through resurrection, makes him infinitely more worthy of praise than any mortal ruler. Emperors such as Nero or Domitian, who presumed to control history, are now upstaged by the Lamb.

3. Graydon F. Snyder, *Ante Pacem: Archaeological Evidence of Church Life before Constantine*, rev. ed. (Macon, GA: Mercer University Press, 2003), 58–64.

4. Johns, *Lamb Christology*, 198.

The beast killed the Lamb, and the Lamb came back! The Lamb has created a new political order by breaking the stranglehold of sin and death, giving believers power to live in redeemed community by standards of the kingdom of God. Such a momentous turn of events elicits exuberant worship.

John has already witnessed glorious worship in the heavenly court, but now something staggering happens. He catches a glimpse, perhaps a preview, of every creature in heaven and on earth and under the earth and in the sea singing: "To the one seated on the throne and to the Lamb / be blessing and honor and glory and might forever and ever!" (5:13).

It is more than a liturgical footnote when the four living creatures respond with "Amen!" In Hebrew the word means "truly, verily!" Saying amen is an index of heartfelt affirmation, imploring God to bring the petition to reality. Entering into prayer with all of their being, the elders again fall down in worship (5:14).

End-Time Events Unfold

Seal by seal the Lamb opens the scroll, revealing both the destructive character of the present age and the certainty that God will eventually intervene to end the chaos. The cosmos is in anguish as plague follows plague. The first four sufferings of this cycle seem, at least in part, to issue from human greed and violence. The following are possible meanings for the horsemen symbols that appear with the first four seals (6:1–8):

A *white horse*, whose rider carries a bow and sets out to conquer (6:2). The Romans were proud of the conquests that had brought them empire, and they highlighted military exploits in state propaganda. A coin issued by Domitian, for example, shows a soldier on a horseback charging in battle. The soldier has his sword raised for the kill, and the horse is running down a German tribesman (fig. 6.6). Such images underscore the brutality of Roman conquest.

A *red horse*, whose rider carries a great sword and takes peace from the earth so that people slaughter one another (6:4). Civil war ravaged parts of the Roman Empire in the year after Nero's death in AD 68, and unknown thousands of Jews died in and around Jerusalem during the Jewish War of AD 66–70.

A *black horse*, whose rider carries a pair of scales (6:5–6). A voice cries, "A quart of wheat for a day's pay, and three quarts of barley for a day's pay, but do not damage the olive oil and the wine!" Ancient sources indicate that staple foods sometimes became scarce in Asia Minor in the first century. Exporters catering to Rome had bought up agricultural lands and converted them to olive groves and vineyards. Even emperors in Rome understood that this change in land use in the provinces inflated the price of grains needed to feed the local population and their animals. Suetonius says that once,

Fig. 6.6. A *sestertius* coin from AD 85 features a portrait of Emperor Domitian, and on the reverse an image of a soldier (the emperor?) on horseback charging in battle. The horse tramples down a German tribesman, and the soldier has his weapon poised to kill. (Used by permission of Classical Numismatic Group, Inc., www.cngcoins.com.)

upon the occasion of a plentiful wine crop, attended by a scarcity of grain, thinking that the [grain] fields were neglected through too much attention to the vineyards, [Emperor Domitian] made an edict forbidding anyone to plant more vines in Italy and ordering that the vineyards in the provinces be cut down, or but half of them at most be left standing.[5]

The order was never carried out, and John's vision implies that grain had become so expensive that people had to pay a full day's wages for a mere quart of wheat (for human consumption) or for three quarts of barley (for animals).

A pale green horse, whose rider's name is Death (6:8). Hades (Greek god of death and the underworld) follows close behind. These two dark entities are "given authority over a fourth of the earth, to kill with sword, famine, pestilence, and by wild animals." For some Christians and other oppressed minorities, the empire brought death from the executioner's sword, from famine caused by Rome's enormous consumption, and from wild animals in the arena (fig. 6.7).

People in Anguish Pray for Justice

Because Jesus taught his followers to love their enemies, Christians sometimes imagine that we should not feel anger at evil. But Revelation seethes with anger, as do parts of the Old Testament. In worship, such anger appropriately filters up to the throne of God. When the Lamb opens the fifth seal, John sees the souls of Christian martyrs under the altar in heaven. As an index of their anguish they cry, "Sovereign Lord, holy and true, how long will it be before you judge and avenge our blood on the inhabitants of the earth?" (6:10)

The desire for revenge is a common human impulse, and we can find no better setting in which to acknowledge it than in worship. Martyrs in heaven are angry at the tyrants who have killed them, John is angry at Rome, and we should be angry at injustice in our day. But the point made in Revelation is that in God's own time and way, things will be made right. It is not our role as followers of the Lamb to answer violence with violence or to force matters with our own hands.

5. Suetonius, *Domitian* 7; in *Suetonius*, vol. 2, trans. and ed. J. C. Rolfe, LCL 38 (1913–14; Cambridge, MA: Harvard University Press, 1960), 353.

Fig. 6.7. This early Christian mosaic from North Africa depicts a believer facing lions in the arena.

The book of Psalms includes examples of rage channeled into prayer. One prayer, a song, registered anger and fear when a coalition of nations threatened to annihilate Israel:

> They say, "Come, let us wipe them out as a nation;
>   let the name of Israel be remembered no more.". . .
> O my God, make them like whirling dust,
>   like chaff before the wind.
> As fire consumes the forest,
>   as the flame sets the mountains ablaze,
> so pursue them with your tempest
>   and terrify them with your hurricane. (Ps. 83:4, 13–15)

John's vision shows heavenly courtiers carrying prayers of the saints to God like bowls of incense (Rev. 5:8). Some of these prayers must be petitions for retribution, for God to bring justice. In the meantime, martyrs already in heaven receive white robes, symbols of victory, and are told to wait a little longer. For God's people on earth, suffering will become worse before it becomes better.

The World Spins Out of Control

The first five seals, which likely represent identifiable events or circumstances in the Roman Empire, build to a crescendo of suffering. Then, like a spinning top that starts to wobble, the cosmos itself lurches out of control. The Lamb opens the sixth seal (6:12–14), and the earth quakes. The sun turns black, and the moon turns bloodred. Stars fall to earth, the sky rolls up like a scroll, and mountains slide out of place. The cataclysm envelops everyone, from kings in positions of power to freedmen and slaves at the bottom of the social pyramid (6:15–16).

These people still do not worship God, but at last they recognize the power of the Lamb. Terrified of coming face-to-face with the living God, they hide in caves and call for mountains and rocks to fall upon them. At one time, when they are rationalizing their collaboration with Rome, people of the earth ask rhetorically, "Who is like the beast, and who can fight against it?" (13:4). Now they fear the wrath of the Lamb and cry, "Who is able to stand?" (6:17).

God Hears When Saints Pray

The final verses of Revelation 6 depict such a high tide of catastrophe and judgment that John seems to be nearing the end of his vision. The great day of wrath has come, and we have reason to expect that the closing chapter of history is at hand. Instead, when the Lamb opens the seventh and last seal, there is silence in heaven "for about half an hour" (8:1).

In this liturgical pause, we once again see the integral part our prayers play in the heavenly court. While seven angels prepare to sound trumpets, another angel is given "a great quantity of incense to offer with the prayers of all the saints on the golden altar that is before the throne" (8:3; see 5:8). John does not reveal the content of these prayers carried into the presence of God—unless that is what John has heard in the fervent hymns of preceding events (5:9–13). In any case, John now knows that God hears when the saints on earth pray.

Jews had long believed that ceremonies in the temple at Jerusalem—now lying in ruins—mirrored what was happening in heaven (see Heb. 8:5; 9:23–24). John's reference to a half hour of silence in heaven (Rev. 8:1) in connection with incense offering (8:3–4) may reflect the approximate amount of time the incense ceremony had taken in the Jerusalem temple. We might infer that John and the early Christian community had a rhythm of morning and evening prayer, since that is how often incense offerings took place at the temple in Jerusalem (Exod. 30:7–9; Luke 1:9–10; Acts 3:1).[6]

But the silence at the seventh seal also is a reminder that worship is more about being in the presence of God than about giving the Lord of the universe a to-do list. During most of the time John is in heaven, he is observing, not speaking. The half hour of silence that prevails at the climax of history is far longer than most Western worshipers today will tolerate in corporate or personal prayer. But sometimes needs of the world, or events of our own lives, are so complex or so overwhelming that it is appropriate simply to be silent in the presence of God.

6. Richard Bauckham, "Prayer in the Book of Revelation," in *Into God's Presence: Prayer in the New Testament*, ed. Richard N. Longenecker, McMaster New Testament Studies (Grand Rapids: Eerdmans, 2001), 253.

The Kingdom Has Come!

What comes after the silence with the seventh seal is not the end of the world but another set of seven sufferings. As if John restarted a video of the end-time travail to show it from a different vantage point, the trumpets herald another sequence of plagues. When the seventh trumpet sounds, again there is a liturgical pause. This time loud voices in heaven cry that "the kingdom of the world has become the kingdom of our Lord" (Rev. 11:15), and the twenty-four elders fall down in worship (11:16–18).

Exuberant praise punctuates Revelation even in the midst of suffering and chaos. Celebration and jubilant worship would seem appropriate at the *end* of the vision, when the new Jerusalem has arrived and Babylon lies in ruins. Yet confident praise is woven throughout the fabric of Revelation. Those who experience the power of Jesus' resurrection know that it is only a matter of time until God defeats every abusive power and restores creation. For believers, heartfelt worship is vital in order to maintain hope amid adversity, and praise builds allegiance to the God who provides salvation.

For Reflection

1. What images of God do you have in mind as you pray and praise? Is your Jesus a Lion or a Lamb? How might your picture of God or Jesus affect your expectations of what God will do in the world, or of your part in God's mission in the world?
2. What is your explanation for the meaning of Jesus' death? Why do you or why do you not believe his death was a substitute for you, or a ransom? What difference does it make in your view of salvation if Jesus' death was the result of him courageously taking on the powers of sin, death, and empire?
3. How do tragedy, hardship, or poverty change the way people worship? What happens to worship when believers achieve security and status?

LIVING THE VISION

Liberating Worship in South Africa

For almost half a century after 1948, the government of South Africa enforced apartheid throughout society; it was a harsh system of racial separation. In 1986, black theologian Allan Boesak described the prayer of his people during this difficult time:

It is a cry black South Africans who find their help in Yahweh have been uttering for a long time. They have lived under racist colonial oppression for almost three and a half centuries, and under that particularly vicious form of racism called apartheid for nearly four decades. They have seen their land taken away and themselves stripped of human dignity. . . . From the earliest days of colonial rule, whole communities have been slaughtered to secure the continuation of white power. . . . During recent years there has hardly been a place where the police and the army have not wantonly murdered our children, piling atrocity upon atrocity for the sake of the preservation of apartheid and white privilege. And as they go from funeral to funeral, burying yet another victim of law and order or yet another killed by government-protected death squads, the cry continues to rise to heaven: "How long, Lord?" How long before this illegitimate power is removed? How long before the blood of our children is avenged?[7]

On one occasion, young black Christians danced and sang around a police vehicle just after a student was arrested at a church service. The worshipers sang, "Akanamandla, akanamandla, akanamandla, uSatani! Sim'swabisile, Alleluia! Sim'swabisile, uSatani! Akanamandla, uSatani!" (It is broken, the power of Satan is broken! We have disappointed Satan, his power is broken. Alleluia!) These indexes of praise disoriented the oppressors:

The police, somewhat confused, somewhat bewildered, somewhat scared, release our friend. Others join us as we march, singing and dancing, back into the church. This is a new song, a freedom song, and the power of it, the sheer joy of it, the amazing truth in it captivate and inspire thousands upon thousands throughout South Africa. . . . And we will sing this new song until "every creature in heaven and on earth and under the earth and in the sea, and all therein," will say: To him who sits upon the throne and to the Lamb be blessing and honor and glory and might for ever and ever![8]

7. Allan A. Boesak, *Comfort and Protest: The Apocalypse from a South African Perspective* (Philadelphia: Westminster, 1987), 69–70.
    8. Ibid., 61–62.

7

Seal of the Living God

Read Revelation 7:1–11:19

> After this I looked, and there was a great multitude that no one could count, from every nation, from all tribes and peoples and languages, standing before the throne and before the Lamb, robed in white, with palm branches in their hands. They cried out in a loud voice, saying,
>
> > "Salvation belongs to our God
> > who is seated on the throne,
> > and to the Lamb!"
>
> And all the angels stood around the throne and around the elders and the four living creatures, and they fell on their faces before the throne and worshiped God, singing,
>
> > "Amen! Blessing and glory and wisdom
> > and thanksgiving and honor
> > and power and might
> > be to our God forever and ever! Amen." (7:9–12)

In the last chapter we entered the cosmic throne room with John (Rev. 4–6) and saw that God remains in charge even when the world is in chaos. Worship opens the eyes of faith, giving John a long view of history from God's perspective. Believers who follow the Lamb know that in the end the Lamb's way of suffering love will prevail. Evil will implode, and God will finally eliminate the rebellion that does not self-destruct. But in the meantime it will be a rough passage for Christians and others as the beast of empire goes through its death throes. Revelation counsels readers to brace for persecution and to deepen their allegiance to the Lamb with indexes of devotion.

The beast will exploit every possible means of persuasion, especially the mark of the beast, to reinforce allegiance to itself (13:16–17). As we saw in Revelation 13, the mark likely was not a literal sign placed on hand and forehead. Rather, this mark was a metaphor for allegiance to Rome and participation in emperor worship. We also observed that actions and symbols related to the beast closely parallel or parody those used in the worship of God. Since the beast marks its followers, it comes as no surprise that followers of Jesus also carry a sign on their foreheads (7:3; 9:4; 14:1; 22:4).

Just as the four horsemen of empire have wreaked havoc across the world (6:1–8), four angels of God now stand at the corners of the earth to hold back the winds of destruction (7:1–3). Another angel, heralding a new day for humanity, comes from the rising of the sun to forestall further damage to the earth. The delay will last, the angel says, "until we have marked the servants of our God with a seal on their foreheads" (7:3).

A Seal Marks Ownership and Protection

The word *seal* literally refers to an official insignia printed on paper or parchment, or pressed into wax or clay (see fig. 6.1). It indicates that a powerful individual has authorized or validated a document. The angel in John's vision seals the foreheads of the saints, perhaps reenacting a scene from Ezekiel. In his vision of Solomon's temple in Jerusalem just before its destruction in the sixth century BC, Ezekiel witnesses rampant idolatry (Ezek. 9:1–11). Idolatry is so pervasive that God dispatches executioners to Jerusalem. Before swords flash, however, God sends a man dressed in linen through the city to "put a mark on the foreheads of those who sigh and groan over all the abominations that are committed" in the temple (9:4). The executioners spare those who carry God's mark on their forehead. Since Revelation has close parallels to Ezekiel, John may also have understood a seal on the forehead of Christians as a kind of protection.

Writings from the early church expand our understanding of what a seal meant among Christians in the Roman Empire. The apostle Paul says God has placed his seal on believers and put his Spirit in their hearts (2 Cor. 1:22). Twice in Ephesians (1:13–14; 4:30) *seal* refers to the gift of the Holy Spirit in the life of believers. A second-century Christian work, *The Shepherd of Hermas*, says that before an individual "bears the name of the Son of God," he or she is dead. But a person who receives the seal "puts away mortality and receives life." The author concludes, "The seal, then, is the water." Believers "descend into the water dead, and they arise alive."[1]

1. Hermas, *Similitudes* 9.16.3–4; in *ANF* 2:49; see Rom. 6:1–4.

Within the New Testament, baptism takes place in a variety of modes and with varying amounts of preparation. But the early church gradually standardized the form of this symbol, with an accent on allegiance and changed behavior. The *Apostolic Tradition*, commonly attributed to Hippolytus of Rome ca. AD 215, describes stages of preparation for baptism.[2]

Because the manual dates from more than a century after Revelation, we cannot flatly read its practices back into the time of John. But the *Apostolic Tradition* gives us the fullest description of the baptismal liturgy in the early church. It shows that baptism in the early centuries signaled a radical shift of allegiance, similar to what John portrays in Revelation. According to *Apostolic Tradition* 15–21, those wanting to join the Christian church at Rome would undergo scrutiny, instruction, and exorcism, and then baptism. Let's consider each in turn.

1. *Scrutiny.* The candidate, accompanied by a sponsor, met with teachers of the church. They asked questions about the candidate's lifestyle, to determine whether marital status, occupation, and values were consistent with the gospel. Unacceptable professions included, for example, gladiator and astrologer. Candidates who already were in the army would no longer be permitted to kill; those who joined the army after making a confession of faith were rejected for baptism.

2. *Instruction and exorcism.*[3] New believers would hear the word for up to three years, with attention to lifestyle. Teachers asked whether candidates had honored widows, visited the sick, and fulfilled all good works. Candidates received frequent exorcism for cleansing from patterns of greed, idolatry, and sin. Cyprian, a third-century church leader from North Africa, describes how his preparation for baptism involved giving up the banquets, fine clothes, and civic honors of his patrician past.[4]

3. *Baptism.* Candidates fasted on Friday of Holy Week, and on Saturday knelt for more exorcism to expel "every foreign spirit." The bishop

---

2. See Alan Kreider, *The Change of Conversion and the Origin of Christendom*, Christian Mission and Modern Culture (Harrisburg, PA: Trinity, 1999), 21–32; and Paul F. Bradshaw, Maxwell E. Johnson, and L. Edward Phillips, *The Apostolic Tradition: A Commentary*, Hermeneia (Minneapolis: Fortress, 2002), 82–135. The three-stage summary above is adapted from my article "What Madness Possessed You? Catechesis for New Allegiance," *Vision: A Journal for Church and Theology* 4, no. 2 (2003): 5–12.

3. The Greek verb for exorcism (*exorkizō*) means "adjure" or "charge under oath," frequently in reference to the expulsion of evil spirits. The New Testament does not use the term for Christian activity; Jesus and the disciples *cast out* (*ekballō*) demons. The third-century *Apostolic Tradition* is the earliest example of *exorkizō* being applied routinely in preparation for Christian baptism. Whether or not this use of the term was widespread, the early church understood that believers need cleansing and transformation from the warped values and allegiances of pagan society.

4. Cyprian, *Ad Donatum* 3; see Kreider, *Change of Conversion*, 7–9.

Fig. 7.1. Persons receiving baptism in this early Christian baptistery in Tunisia removed their clothes and walked down the steps. They went through the water and up the other side. The baptistery still is in situ among the ruins of an early Christian church at Sbeitla in Tunisia.

breathed on the candidates and sealed their foreheads, ears, and nostrils with the sign of the cross. The candidates kept vigil through Saturday night, listening to readings and instruction. Before dawn on Easter morning, they removed all clothing and received the anointing of exorcism. They said, "I renounce you, Satan, and all your service." Candidates then descended into the water to be baptized three times, with the confession "I believe, and submit myself to you and to all your service, O Father, Son, and Holy Spirit." They affirmed a version of the Apostles' Creed, then arose from the water to be clothed in white robes (see Rev. 7:9). They received milk mixed with honey to symbolize fulfillment of God's promise of a land flowing with milk and honey for the people of Israel. The new believers then received the Eucharist for the first time.

Most representations of baptism in the catacombs at Rome show the candidate (often Jesus, at his baptism) standing in water well below the waist. Another individual scoops water up over the head of the person being baptized. In typical baptisteries from the fourth and fifth centuries, several steps lead down into the water on one side and several more lead up the other side (fig. 7.1). Thus baptismal candidates literally went through the waters that symbolized death, the Jordan River, Noah's flood, and/or the Red Sea. Surviving baptisteries were usually in small rooms adjacent to the main meeting space of the congregation. Presumably this arrangement permitted privacy for the disrobed candidates, who may have been baptized in near darkness. It is possible that deaconesses presided at the baptism of women.[5]

5. We know of a woman, Phoebe, serving as deacon already during Paul's ministry (Rom. 16:1). The twelfth canon of the Fourth Council of Carthage (AD 398) refers to "widows and

Instructions for baptism in the *Apostolic Tradition* reveal that martyrdom was a distinct possibility for believers. "When a catechumen [a person receiving instruction for baptism] is arrested because of witness and killed before having been baptized, he is to be buried with all the martyrs, because he has been baptized in his own blood."[6]

The Roman State Sponsors Rituals of Life and Death

Early Christian worship gave prominence to symbols and rituals of life and death in baptism, Eucharist, hymnody, and other worship. Rituals of life and death also were prominent in ceremonies of the Roman Empire. Nowhere was this more evident than in the so-called games held in public arenas and amphitheaters throughout the Mediterranean world. Emperors, governors, and wealthy citizens sponsored shows in these venues, usually featuring gladiatorial battles and executions. At major celebrations, scores of humans and hundreds of animals would die as large crowds looked on. These exhibitions were more than mere entertainment. Romans sponsored ritual death with the belief that watching people die, especially if they died nobly, would build moral fiber in the spectators.

Roman orator and statesman Cicero (106–43 BC) said there was "no better schooling against pain and death" than watching criminals die in the arena.[7] Pliny the Younger praised Emperor Trajan (AD 98–117) for sponsoring gladiatorial games that were "nothing lax or dissolute to weaken and destroy the manly spirit of his subjects." Rather, the spectacles would "inspire them to face honorable wounds and look scorn on death, by exhibiting love of glory and desire for victory even in the person of criminals and slaves."[8] The Romans recognized that ritual activities, especially those with themes of life and death, could make a deep impact on spectators. Again, crowds would receive this supposed moral benefit if combatants died bravely.[9]

---

dedicated women (*sanctimoniales*) who are chosen to assist at the baptism of women" (Philip Schaff and Henry Wace, eds., *A Select Library of Nicene and Post-Nicene Fathers of the Christian Church*, 2nd series, vol. 14 [New York: Charles Schribner's Sons, 1905], 41). This late reference may reflect a longstanding assumed practice of women baptizing women.

    6. *Apostolic Tradition* 19.2; this text is from the Canons of Hippolytus, as cited in Bradshaw, Johnson, and Phillips, *Apostolic Tradition*, 103.

    7. Cicero, *Tusculan Disputations* 2.17; in Cicero, *Tusculan Disputations*, trans. J. E. King, LCL 141 (1927; Cambridge, MA: Harvard University Press, 1960), 193. See Thomas Wiedemann, *Emperors and Gladiators* (New York: Routledge, 1992), 38.

    8. Pliny the Younger, *Panegyricus* 33.1; in Pliny the Younger, *Letters and Panegyricus*, vol. 2, trans. Betty Radice, LCL 59 (Cambridge, MA: Harvard University Press, 1969), 393.

    9. See Joyce E. Salisbury, *Perpetua's Passion: The Death and Memory of a Young Roman Woman* (New York: Routledge, 1997), 119–48.

Christians Avoid Pagan Spectacles

Such public spectacles were always dedicated to the gods, and frequently to the emperor. Roman circuses (oblong racetracks) and arenas (amphitheaters) were laden with icons and symbols of pagan religion. Tertullian (ca. AD 155–230), a prominent early church leader from North Africa, said Christians should not attend spectacles in these settings because of commitments they made at baptism. "Every ornament of the circus is a temple by itself," he protested.

Tertullian condemned the idolatry he saw in these places "in the many images, the long line of statues, the chariots of all sorts, the thrones, the crowns, the dresses" featured in processions. He marveled that so many "sacrifices precede, come between, and follow" the games. Some of the sacrifices were to deities such as Mars (god of war) or Diana (goddess of the hunt); others were to emperors living or deceased. The circus racetrack at Rome had three altars to the gods Great, Mighty, and Victorious—attributes that figure prominently in the symbolic world of Revelation.[10]

Christian Worship as Alternative to Roman Imperial Ritual

Historian Joyce E. Salisbury, in her treatment of spectacles in the arena and circus,[11] says religious ritual in the Roman world usually followed a standard formula. Whether it was athletes preparing for competition in state-sponsored games, devotees of mystery religions holding a ceremony, or citizens of a town celebrating the emperor cult, the following sequence typically emerged:

1. Purification, which prepared the individual for the sacred and frequently included a ritual meal
2. Invocation, calling on the god
3. Vision, or the acknowledgment of the presence of the holy
4. Procession, by which the sacred was made public, and the space marked out as sacred
5. Fulfillment of the sacred ritual, which in many significant Roman rituals marked a victory over death

So gladiators, for example, joined a solemn and sacred meal on the night before they did battle in the arena. The games began with prayers and invocations, and all participants and spectators were treated to a vision of the emperor or an image of the emperor. The spectacle included a great procession (as described above by Tertullian), and finally the ritual acts of sacrifice, gladiatorial contests, and execution of criminals or captives. The entire event

---

10. Tertullian, *De spectaculis* 7–8; in *ANF* 3:82–83.
11. Salisbury, *Perpetua's Passion*, 123.

reinforced the notion that Rome had power over life and death and that the gods favored the empire.

Revelation resists the spiritual ideology of the Roman Empire by setting out alternative patterns of allegiance and worship. John's vision includes parallels to every step in the sequence of Roman public religious ritual:

1. *Purification and ritual meal.* "Blessed are those who wash their robes, so that they will have the right to the tree of life and may enter the city by the gates" (Rev. 22:14). "If you hear my voice and open the door, I will come in to you and eat with you" (3:20).
2. *Invocation.* "You are worthy, our Lord and God . . ." (4:11).
3. *Vision.* "There in heaven stood a throne, with one seated on the throne!" (4:2).
4. *Procession.* "There was a great multitude that no one could count, . . . standing before the throne and before the Lamb, robed in white, with palm branches in their hands" (7:9).
5. *Fulfillment.* "Let us rejoice and exult and give him glory, / for the marriage of the Lamb has come" (19:7).

Christian worship as presented in Revelation has close structural similarities to the imperial pagan ceremonies it displaces.

Innumerable Saints Unite in Worship

When John wrote Revelation, the human-made structure with the largest seating capacity in the Mediterranean world was the Circus Maximus, in a valley directly below Domitian's palace at Rome (fig. 7.2). Accommodating an audience of at least two hundred seventy thousand, one-quarter of the population of Rome, this circus was the grandest venue for state ceremonies and religious festivals. It was a racetrack, where chariot teams vied for glory. When a race was over, a presiding magistrate presented the victorious charioteer with a palm branch and a wreath, followed by monetary prizes.

In the courts of heaven, John of Patmos sees a celebration that is far bigger than any event in the Circus Maximus. The worshipers are standing (Rev. 7:9), the usual posture of prayer and praise in both Jewish and early Christian practice (fig. 7.3; see Matt. 6:5; Mark 11:25). In the inner circle of the mighty crowd are believers who have been sealed: one hundred forty-four thousand, "from every tribe of the people of Israel" (Rev. 7:4). Two millennia later, one hundred forty-four thousand may sound like a small number of Christians. But for John, writing to a few scattered house churches, it must have seemed an enormous tally. By saying that these saints are from the tribes of Israel, John implies that they are Jewish.

Fig. 7.2. This model of first-century Rome includes the Circus Maximus racetrack (bottom left) and the Coliseum amphitheater (upper right). The Circus Maximus could accommodate at least 270,000, and the Coliseum 50,000. The large complex of buildings (with the curved façade) just beyond the middle of the Circus is the palace of Emperor Domitian.

Fig. 7.3. Jews and Christians in the first century prayed standing, with hands raised to shoulder height. This sculpture is from the Christian catacombs at Rome.

John may be advancing the same argument that we find in Paul's Letters— that Jewish followers of Jesus have a kind of spiritual priority over Gentiles. When discussing the relationship between Jews and Gentiles in the Christian church, Paul tells Gentile readers, "It is not you that support the root, but the root that supports you" (Rom. 11:18). Now, in John's vision of heavenly worship, Jewish believers form the inner circle of saints gathered around the Lamb. But beyond the one hundred forty-four thousand is "a great multitude that no one could count, from every nation, from all tribes and peoples and languages, standing before the throne and before the Lamb, robed in white, with palm branches in their hands" (Rev. 7:9).

Like victorious chariot drivers in the Circus Maximus, believers from all nations wave palm branches of victory. But instead of having endured a grueling chariot contest with thundering steeds, saints in heaven have "come out of the great ordeal; they have washed their robes and made them white in the blood of the Lamb" (7:14). Presumably the great ordeal is the persecution or hour of trial that John sees "coming on the whole world" (3:10). A titanic spiritual contest is unfolding between the beast and the Lamb. Christians caught in this conflict signal their loyalties by receiving the seal or symbol of baptism.

The Emperor Claims Worship from All Nations

Revelation exposes worship of the beast and the emperor as a counterfeit of true praise to God. Archaeological discoveries at the ruins of ancient Aphrodisias, near Laodicea, show how closely the choreography of emperor worship could parallel the praise John describes in the heavenly court. A series of sculptural icons once adorned the grand entryway leading to a temple at Aphrodisias dedicated to Aphrodite (goddess of love) and the imperial family. The sculptures portray peoples and nations of the world subjected to Rome, each represented by a woman in ethnic attire. Just as John sees "all tribes and peoples and languages" worshiping God and the Lamb (7:9), these images depict the same for the emperor. Nations standing before the temple of the emperor include even obscure peoples such as the Andizeti, Callaeai, and the Iapodes.[12]

Historian Martin Goodman says this diverse representation "seems to have been intended to stress the extraordinary range and variety of peoples under Roman rule." The worship tableau conveys the notion that Rome and the emperor are benefactors to all these places and peoples.[13] In the *Res gestae divi Augusti* (*Deeds of the Divine Augustus*), a lengthy autobiographical funerary statement inscribed in stone throughout the empire after his death, Caesar Augustus catalogs peoples and nations supposedly blessed by his rule: "I restored peace to the Gallic and Spanish provinces and likewise to Germany. . . . I caused peace to be restored in the Alps, . . . without undeservedly making war against any people. . . . The Cimbrians, the Charydes, the Semnones, and other German peoples of the same region through their envoys sought my friendship and that of the Roman people." Caesar goes on to name Ethiopia,

12. R. R. R. Smith, "The Imperial Reliefs from the Sebasteion at Aphrodisias," *Journal of Roman Studies* 77 (1987): 89–98.

13. Martin Goodman, *Rome and Jerusalem: The Clash of Ancient Civilizations* (New York: Knopf, 2007), 118.

Fig. 7.4. Nero placed an icon of Salus (Salvation) on the reverse of this *denarius* issued in AD 67–68, the last year of his life. In her right hand Salus holds the *patera*—a shallow dish for pouring libations in religious ceremonies. Salus presumably represents the divine Nero bringing salvation to the world. Revelation counters such propaganda by declaring that salvation belongs to God (Rev. 7:10). (Photo courtesy of Harlan J. Berk, Ltd.)

Arabia, Egypt, Armenia, and Illyricum among the nations fortunate to come under his rule.[14]

The entire *Res gestae* inscription begins by saying, "Below is a copy of the accomplishments of the deified Augustus by which he brought the whole world under the empire of the Roman people." Roman emperors claimed to bring salvation (*salus*) to the world, as announced on a coin issued by Nero (fig. 7.4), and expected submission and praise from all peoples on earth. Over against such imperial hubris, John saw a multitude from all nations crying, "Salvation belongs to our God / who is seated on the throne, / and to the Lamb!" (7:10).

Struggle against the Beast Is Spiritual Combat

We must read Revelation 7 in tandem with Revelation 14, where the one hundred forty-four thousand appear again. In both chapters these saints worship ecstatically. They stand on Mount Zion (14:1), the most sacred spot on earth in Jewish cosmology, and sing a new song (14:3). No one can learn the song "except the one hundred forty-four thousand who have been redeemed from the earth." This privileged group are those "who have not defiled themselves with women, for they are virgins" (14:4).

It offends our social and political sensibilities today to read that these saints have not defiled themselves with women, as if sexual contact with women makes men unclean. We must interpret this unfortunate metaphor in light of Old Testament imagery and in the context of Roman imperial symbolism. Several Hebrew prophets describe the spiritual unfaithfulness of ancient Israel with the metaphor of sexual infidelity in marriage.[15] And in state propaganda, the goddess Roma routinely represents the capital city of the empire.

In Revelation, followers of the Lamb are virgins in the sense that they have not been whoring with Roma or embracing her ideology. So this imagery does not reflect a puritanical aversion to sex. As we will see later, what John calls fornication is compromise with the harlot Babylon (Rome) and participation

14. *Res gestae divi Augusti* 26–30; in Naphtali Lewis and Meyer Reinhold, eds., *Roman Civilization: Sourcebook 2, The Empire* (New York: Harper & Row, 1966), 9–19.
15. Ezek. 16:15–22; Hos. 1:2–3.

in the emperor cult (see, for example, 17:1–3). The word usually translated "virgin" (14:4) can also mean "chaste person." By ancient tradition, Jewish soldiers preparing for holy war abstained from sexual activity.[16] Struggle with the beast is spiritual combat, demanding a level of self-discipline once required for holy war. But this is most unusual warfare, because those engaged in battle follow the Lamb.

The fact that these saints have no lie in their mouths (14:5) is a clue to the nature of their victory. An issue the early church faced was what to do with believers who saved their lives by denying Christ when they were arrested and put on trial. After their release, such individuals sometimes repented and wanted to be reinstated as members of the church. According to John's vision, saints worshiping the Lamb on Mount Zion have not lied to avoid martyrdom.

All Nations Worship God and the Lamb

Although martyrs make up the inner circle on Mount Zion, there is room for many others to join the celebration. John sees a great multitude, from every nation and tribe and language, worshiping God and the Lamb. They are dressed in white, a traditional symbol of victory in Roman society. Here in Revelation (7:9), we catch our first glimpse of the global scale and ethnic diversity of the Christian church. Worship in the name of Jesus transcends every national and linguistic barrier.

"Salvation belongs to our God . . . and to the Lamb," the multitudes cry (7:10). This vision was good news for a vulnerable church caught in the cross-currents of imperial politics. No matter how hard they tried, believers could not save themselves or the world. God alone saves. Announcement of divine salvation elicits indexes of joyful worship that surpass any liturgy contrived for the Roman arena. Angels and elders around the throne fall to the ground and sing:

> Amen! Blessing and glory and wisdom
> and thanksgiving and honor and power and might
> be to our God forever and ever! Amen! (7:12)

These worshipers are survivors of the great ordeal, an intense period of persecution that John expects in the near future. They worship day and night, and God will shelter them. They will not hunger or thirst or suffer from heat. In a paradoxical role, the Lamb will become their shepherd (fig. 7.5) and guide them to springs of the water of life. God will wipe every tear from their eyes.

16. Deut. 23:9–14; 1 Sam. 21:5–6.

Hope Emerges in the Midst of Suffering

As the Lamb opened the sixth seal (6:12–17), the end-time trauma seemed to reach full force, and we got the sense that the end of history was at hand. Instead, there was an interlude for worship in Revelation 7. Now the Lamb opens the seventh seal, and (after the half-hour pause) seven angels step forward to blow trumpets that signal yet another series of disasters (8:1–11:19). When the last trumpet sounds, a third series of plagues follows, as seven bowls of God's wrath pour out on the earth (16:1–21).

We probably should not think of this triple series of plagues as sequential, as if they (seals, trumpets, bowls) follow one another chronologically. Rather, the three series portray the same events, each showing the end-time trauma with images that are increasingly more graphic and comprehensive. The plague cycles seem to spiral, with repeating views or vantage points that allow the reader to

Fig. 7.5. A fourth-century Christian statue of Jesus as the Good Shepherd.

gradually absorb the scale of devastation. The replay allows space for silence (8:1) and for John to insert visions that introduce the beast and other essential characters (esp. in Rev. 12–13).

At the end of the trumpet series, loud voices proclaim in heaven, "The kingdom of the world has become / the kingdom of our Lord / and of his Messiah, / and he will reign forever and ever" (11:15). The twenty-four elders fall prostrate to the ground and worship in song:

> We give you thanks, Lord God Almighty,
>   who are and who were,
> for you have taken your great power
>   and begun to reign.
> The nations raged,
>   but your wrath has come,
>   and the time for judging the dead,
> for rewarding your servants, the prophets
>   and saints and all who fear your name,
>   both small and great,
> and for destroying those who destroy the earth. (11:17–18)

In the midst of relentless end-time suffering, we unexpectedly receive a preview of how history will end: the kingdom of the world will become the kingdom of our Lord and his Messiah. God plans to redeem even fallen political structures, the kingdom(s) of the world.[17]

Heaven resounds with praise at this report, and mortals suffering on earth can take hope. "The nations raged," the choir sings, but God will reward his "servants, the prophets and saints" who remain true. Eventually the time will come "for destroying those who destroy the earth" (11:18). Mortals do not have the right to ravage the planet. Creation care is part of honoring the Creator, and this should inspire today's followers of Jesus to address issues of pollution, global warming, and conservation of resources.

Repentance Is the Purpose of the Plagues

Are the plagues of Revelation caused by human action or divine initiative? The first four seals (6:1–8) seem to portray war, famine, and casualties that follow in the wake of Roman conquest. But as the end-time traumas unfold, angels hurl destruction upon the earth at God's command (16:1). This scene raises questions about God's purpose in causing or allowing such suffering.

Just as plagues in the book of Exodus had redemptive rather than punitive purpose, so the sufferings in Revelation are designed to turn human hearts toward God. Moses called down a series of woes on Egypt, inviting Pharaoh after each plague to repent and save the people of Egypt from further suffering. While it is true that the Lord hardened Pharaoh's heart (Exod. 4:21; 10:1), Pharaoh himself was fully complicit in rebelling against God (Exod. 8:32; 9:34–35). The protracted plagues in Exodus and Revelation reveal that God repeatedly gives opportunity for mortals to repent but eventually lets disobedience run its course to destruction. The author of 2 Peter 3:9 similarly points to God's forbearance: "The Lord is not slow about his promise [of Christ's return], . . . but is patient with you, not wanting any to perish, but all to come to repentance."

There is no one-to-one correspondence between the plagues of Egypt and those in Revelation, but the parallels are unmistakable. The second trumpet of Revelation turns one-third of the sea to blood (8:8–9), just as Moses once turned the Nile River to blood (Exod. 7:20–21). Hail, fire, and blood of the seventh trumpet (Rev. 8:7) correlate to the thunder, hail, and fire of the sev-

17. The apostle Paul says that Christ, in the end, "hands over the kingdom to God the Father, after he has destroyed every ruler and every authority and power" (1 Cor. 15:24). Neither Paul nor John of Patmos envisions the destruction of all earthly things at the point where history fully transitions into the kingdom of God. Rather, at that time all pretenders to idolatrous power who usurp authority from God will have been defeated. Social, political, and economic systems—under the rule of Christ—will be redeemed as part of the kingdom. Even when 2 Peter says in the end "the elements will be dissolved with fire" (3:10), we must read this as purifying fire that saves what is good rather than as holocaust.

enth plague in Egypt (Exod. 9:22–26). In both Exodus and Revelation we find plagues of locusts, sores, and frogs.

These similarities suggest that we should interpret Revelation in light of the Exodus story, in which God uses plagues to liberate a people from slavery in Egypt. Yet freedom from bondage is not an end in itself. Again and again God tells Pharaoh, "Let my people go, so that they may worship me in the wilderness" (7:16; 8:1, 20; 9:13; 10:3). Empires—whether Egyptian, Roman, or modern—warp worship, and God wants his people to be free from their ideology.

Willful Humanity Ignores the Alarm

After witnessing a particularly ghastly plague, John seems amazed that people do not change their ways:

> The rest of humankind, who were not killed by these plagues, did not repent of the works of their hands or give up worshiping demons and idols of gold and silver and bronze and stone and wood, which cannot see or hear or walk. And they did not repent of their murders or their sorceries or their fornication or their thefts. (Rev. 9:20–21; see also 16:8–9)

Revelation sounds an alarm for all of humanity. Violence, greed, and blasphemy precipitate plagues of their own. In the first century the cycle of violence and destruction was evident for all to see. Nero's massacre of Christians at Rome and the crushing of Jerusalem by General Titus were catastrophic plagues. Emperor after emperor in that century met untimely death by suicide or assassination, demonstrating repeatedly that corrupt power often begins to self-destruct.

The spiral of sin and violence eventually gives way to chaos on a cosmic level, beyond what mortals can control. In John's vision, the very sun, moon, and stars turn against humanity by darkening or falling on the earth. These signs reveal a cosmos returning to primeval chaos, to the disorder that prevailed when God started creation (Gen. 1:1–2). Even so, each stage of the expanding turmoil also seems to be triggered by an action of the Lamb or of an angel at God's command. The trajectory of the universe remains firmly in God's hands.

Rejoicing Irrupts at Justice Meted Out

Revelation is consistent in signaling that followers of Jesus should not take up physical arms or otherwise participate in meting out punishment. Jesus' way of nonviolence is so much assumed in Revelation that it receives little direct comment. The Lamb is the governing image of John's vision, and his followers are to be lamblike. Just as Jesus was willing to lay down his life rather than take up the sword (Matt. 26:51–54; John 18:36), so saints in heaven have not clung to earthly life even in the face of (a martyr's) death (Rev. 12:11).

John of Patmos does not sanction the use of violence or coercion by followers of the Lamb, but he shows no qualms about rejoicing when evil meets its match. As the final round of plagues rains down on the earth, an angel proclaims:

> You are just, O Holy One, who are and were,
>   for you have judged these things;
> because they shed the blood of saints and prophets,
>   you have given them blood to drink.
> It is what they deserve! (16:5–6)

Another voice echoes, "Yes, O Lord God, the Almighty, / your judgments are true and just!" (16:7)

John is no armchair pacifist but a man fully engaged in spiritual battle with flesh-and-blood opponents. Fellow Christians have died at the hands of Rome, and he himself appears to be in trouble. John is angry, and we sense emotional release in the cry of victory when justice is visited upon oppressors.

Worship Sometimes Is Catharsis

Those who worship the beast and its image and who receive its mark on their forehead or hands will "drink the wine of God's wrath" (14:10). In the most unsettling passage of Revelation, an angel says they "will be tormented with fire and sulfur in the presence of the holy angels and in the presence of the Lamb." This torment will go on forever, since there is "no rest day or night for those who worship the beast" (14:9–11).

This awful scene does not reflect the kind of compassion we associate with Christ from accounts in the Gospels. However, the Lamb in this scene is the very one who loved his enemies and forgave the Roman soldiers who pounded nails into his hands and feet. Christ may yet offer forgiveness at a level John himself is unable to imagine or accept. The furthest John can go in his vision is to place the task of punishing people aligned with the beast into the wounded hands of Jesus.

The Lamb will not overlook evil or fail to call unrepentant sinners to account. Sin will be destroyed, and it is right for those who suffer to look forward to the time when creation will be free from bondage to death. Like those who composed the Psalms, suffering believers of every generation call on God to bring justice. Seething at their captors for having destroyed Jerusalem, Jewish exiles in Babylon once cried:

> O daughter Babylon, you devastator!
>> Happy shall they be who pay you back
>> what you have done to us!
> Happy shall they be who take your little ones
>> and dash them against the rock! (Ps. 137:8–9)

Jews in exile needed those words in their worship repertoire. John needed imagery of equal strength to register what he and other first-century Christians were experiencing under the Roman Empire. People today whose homes or lives are destroyed by war or injustice may need to cry out to God with vehement language. Worship sometimes must be catharsis, an opportunity to unload deep pain or anger on God, who can make all things new.

For Reflection

1. In your understanding, how does baptism mark a change of allegiance and identity today? What reflexes or influences need to be purged from persons receiving baptism in your culture?
2. What is the modern equivalent to the Roman games in the circuses and amphitheaters? What parallels to the Roman spectacles do you see in television, the cinema, or sports? When and how does your society ritualize death? Do these rituals have a political agenda?
3. Consider modern plagues such as environmental degradation, drug abuse, arms sales, and homelessness. What responsibility do humans have for these? What part does God play in such suffering? Should Christians be angry about these plagues? What should our response to these plagues be in worship and in action?

LIVING THE VISION
Beyond Blood Ties in Ancient Carthage

In AD 203, in the North African city of Carthage, a Roman aristocrat knelt before his twenty-two-year-old daughter, Perpetua. The mother of an infant son, Perpetua was in prison for being a Christian. Kissing her hand and weeping, her father said:

> Daughter, have pity on my grey head—have pity on your father.
> . . . Do not abandon me to be the reproach of others. Think of
> your brothers, think of your mother and your aunt, think of

your child, who will not be able to live once you are gone. Give
up your pride! You will destroy all of us!

At her trial the judge ordered Perpetua's father to be beaten in
order to play on her emotions. "Have pity on your infant son," the
judge said. "Offer sacrifice for the welfare of the emperors." Instead,
Perpetua was sentenced to die in the arena along with her Christian
slave Felicitas, who was pregnant. By Roman law Felicitas could not
be executed while pregnant. The two women prayed that childbirth
would come in time for them to die together.

On execution day, Perpetua and Felicitas marched joyfully from
the prison to the amphitheater. Perpetua "went along with shining
countenance and calm step, as the beloved of God, as the wife of
Christ, putting down everyone's stare by her own intense gaze."
At the arena the women were forced to put on robes of pagan
priestesses. As she came before the crowd, Perpetua sang a psalm.
The two women made gestures to the judge that communicated, "You
have condemned us, but God will condemn you."

Stripped naked, the two women faced a mad heifer. The crowd was
disconcerted to realize that Felicitas had just given birth. Dressed
again in a tunic, Perpetua was battered by the heifer. Her fellow
believer Saturus bled profusely from a leopard bite, whereupon
the crowd, ridiculing Christian baptism, roared, "Well washed! Well
washed!" When it was time for the games to end, the dazed women
were taken to a gladiator to have their throats cut. The two "went to
the spot of their own accord, . . . and kissing one another they sealed
their martyrdom with the ritual kiss of peace."[18]

---

18. "The Martyrdom of Perpetua and Felicitas," in *After the New Testament: A Reader in
Early Christianity*, ed. Bart D. Ehrman (New York: Oxford, 1999), 42–50.

8

A Harlot Drunk with Blood

Read Revelation 15:1–17:18

> Then one of the seven angels who had the seven bowls came and said to me, "Come, I will show you the judgment of the great whore who is seated on many waters, with whom the kings of the earth have committed fornication, and with the wine of whose fornication the inhabitants of the earth have become drunk." So he carried me away in the spirit into a wilderness, and I saw a woman sitting on a scarlet beast that was full of blasphemous names, and it had seven heads and ten horns. The woman was clothed in purple and scarlet, and adorned with gold and jewels and pearls, holding in her hand a golden cup full of abominations and the impurities of her fornication; and on her forehead was written a name, a mystery: "Babylon the great, mother of whores and of earth's abominations." And I saw that the woman was drunk with the blood of the saints and the blood of the witnesses to Jesus.
>
> When I saw her, I was greatly amazed. (17:1–6)

As we have seen, Revelation portrays an evil trinity: the dragon (Satan), a beast (Rome and the Roman Empire), and a second beast (the religious and political institutions that promote emperor worship). Revelation 17 introduces yet another figure of evil, a great whore named Babylon (17:5).

You Can Solve This Riddle

When the seventh angel has poured his bowl, "God remembered great Babylon and gave her the wine-cup of the fury of his wrath" (16:19). In case anyone hearing Revelation still has not figured out what the Babylon/harlot symbol represents, John offers precise giveaway clues. The harlot sits "on a scarlet beast that was full of blasphemous names, and it had seven heads and ten horns" (17:3). We recognize this figure as the beast of empire introduced in chapter 13. Now John once again gives a nudge to his first-century readers: "This calls for a mind that has wisdom" (17:9), by which he seems to mean, "You can solve this riddle." John says:

> The seven heads are seven mountains on which the woman is seated; also, they are seven kings, of whom five have fallen, one is living, and the other has not yet come; and when he comes, he must remain only a little while. As for the beast that was and is not, it is an eighth but it belongs to the seven, and it goes to destruction. And the ten horns that you saw are ten kings who have not yet received a kingdom, but they are to receive authority as kings for one hour, together with the beast. These are united in yielding their power and authority to the beast. (17:9–13)

Because the ancient world knew Rome as the City of Seven Hills,[1] most readers in Asia Minor would have understood the clue. John's explanation of the imagery, however, displays how symbolism in Revelation is multilayered and fluid. In Revelation 13, the beast seems to be the entire Roman Empire. Now in Revelation 17, we see that the heads of the beast are seven hills of the city of Rome, and they also are seven kings!

At the end of the harlot vision, an angel says bluntly, "The woman you saw is the great city that rules over the kings of the earth" (17:18). The first-century world knew there was no rival for that role: this vision is about Rome.

The Seven Kings Are Seven Emperors

The seven kings (17:9–10) probably are Roman emperors, but interpreters disagree on how we should count them. The most obvious solution is to begin counting kings with Caesar Augustus, the first ruler to take the title of emperor. Not counting the three emperors who each ruled for only a few months immediately after Nero's death, the following sequence emerges:

1. Augustus (27 BC–AD 14)
2. Tiberius (AD 14–37)
3. Caligula (AD 37–41)
4. Claudius (AD 41–54)
5. Nero (AD 54–68)

---

1. Virgil, *Aeneid* 6.782–83; *Georgica* 2.535; Martial, *Epigrams* 6.64; Cicero, *Epistulae ad Atticum* 6.5; *Sibylline Oracles* 2.18; 11.113–16; 13.45; 14.108.

6. Vespasian (AD 69–79)
7. Titus (AD 79–81)
8. Domitian (AD 81–96)

If five have fallen (17:10), John is writing sometime after the death of Nero. Some interpreters suggest that John begins counting emperors with Tiberius because the Christian church started during his reign. That would put Vespasian among the five fallen or deceased rulers. Or perhaps Caligula, the first emperor to promote worship of himself, should be the first beastly ruler in John's lineup. Thus when John says that five kings have fallen and the sixth one is living, he would have Domitian in mind.

Instead of taking John's enumeration of emperors too literally, however, we should understand the seven kings in more archetypal terms. The number "seven," in Revelation and in Hebrew tradition, symbolizes completion or fulfillment. It is likely that the five fallen kings represent all the deceased emperors, regardless of how we count them. The living emperor (17:10) may be Domitian, and the vision foresees yet another corrupt emperor to follow.

Empires Rule by Co-opting Indigenous Elites

Despite its considerable military power, Rome did not have enough soldiers to hold a far-flung empire in subjection by force alone. As is necessary for the success of any empire, key leaders among subject peoples had to side with the dominant power and help to keep their countrymen aligned with it.

Herod the Great (37–4 BC) is an example of a local ruler who collaborated with Rome. Born in southern Palestine of half-Jewish blood, Herod was from a politically powerful family that was savvy enough to side with Rome as the emerging empire began to assert itself in the Mediterranean world. Named governor of Galilee by his father, who had ruled Judea on Rome's behalf, Herod eventually received the title of king of the Jews from the Roman Senate. But few Jews wanted Herod to be their ruler, and it took the force of Roman arms to put him on the throne in Jerusalem.

Herod was a fox of a ruler[2] who could both ingratiate himself and bully. As king of the Jews, Herod courted local favor by building a magnificent temple to Yahweh in Jerusalem (fig. 8.1; see Mark 13:1). At the same time, he courted imperial favor by building temples for emperor worship at Caesarea Maritima (figs. 8.2; 9.5) on the Mediterranean coast, at Samaria-Sebaste, and at Caesarea Philippi (Banias), on the northern border of Israel. But at the slightest sign of a threat to his power, Herod wielded the sword. Matthew reports that

2. Jesus was referring to Herod Antipas, son of Herod the Great, when he said "Go and tell that fox" (Luke 13:31). The son displayed the same wiliness and cruelty as his father.

Fig. 8.1. A model reconstruction of the magnificent Jewish temple built at Jerusalem by Herod the Great. The structure with towers attached to the far right corner of the temple complex is the Antonia Fortress, which housed Roman soldiers prepared on short notice to stop any disturbance in or near the temple (see Acts 21:27–40).

Herod slaughtered male infants at Bethlehem in an attempt to kill a possible pretender to the throne (Matt. 2:16–18).

Such cruelty is in character for this provincial king, who governed on Rome's behalf. The beheading of John the Baptist by Herod Antipas (Mark 6:14–29),

Fig. 8.2. Even as Herod built the temple of Yahweh at Jerusalem, he also built a grand complex for emperor worship at the Mediterranean port of Caesarea. The structure was on a great stone platform (left of center in these ruins, where the crowd is gathered) overlooking the harbor. The temple featured a giant statue (colossus) of Caesar "not less than that of Jupiter Olympius, which it was made to resemble" (Josephus, *Jewish War* 1.414).

the son of Herod the Great, shows that the next generation in the Herod family continued the ruthless pattern. Herod Agrippa (AD 37–44), brother of Antipas, reflected the entire family's tendency to schmooze by issuing a coin bearing his own likeness and the legend "Great King Agrippa Lover-of-Caesar [ΦΙΛΟΚΑΙΣΑΡ]."[3]

Provincial rulers such as the Herods likely are what John refers to as the ten horns of the beast (17:3, 12–13). Daniel 8:21 already has used the horn of a beast to symbolize an individual ruler. In Revelation 17:12, the horns are ten kings who have not yet received a kingdom but "are to receive authority as kings for one hour." All provinces had ambitious local politicians who were ready to rule or help rule their own people on Rome's behalf. Such quislings were "united in yielding their power and authority to the beast" (17:13).

Many subject individuals and nations throughout the Mediterranean world voluntarily and gladly participated in the Roman Empire. The empire enjoyed enough spontaneous loyalty in Asia Minor that Rome did not have to base any of its twenty or more army legions in the region. The area of the seven churches of Revelation initially came under Roman control by the design of a native ruler, Attalus III. He governed the independent kingdom of Pergamum and came to believe that the security and well-being of his own people lay with the emerging power of Rome. Attalus directed in his will that the kingdom of Pergamum should become part of the Roman Empire—and it did so in 133 BC.

Such evidence of spontaneous and willing support appeared at many levels of society. Pressure to show allegiance to Rome came not so much from Italy as from friends, neighbors, or business associates in one's own province. Participation in emperor worship became an index of support for an empire that many people believed had brought peace and prosperity to the world.

Empires Unravel When Clients Turn against Them

John's vision indicts provincial rulers who side with Rome and "make war on the Lamb" (17:14). Kings of the earth, however, can quickly turn against Babylon/Rome. Anticipating such eventual insubordination, John sees that the ten horns (provincial rulers) and the beast (the Roman Empire) "will hate the whore [Rome]; they will make her desolate and naked; they will devour her flesh and burn her up with fire. For God has put it into their hearts to carry out his purpose by agreeing to give their kingdom to the beast, until the words of God will be fulfilled" (17:16–17).

3. Larry Joseph Kreitzer, *Striking New Images: Roman Imperial Coinage and the New Testament World*, JSNTSup 134 (Sheffield: Sheffield Academic Press, 1996), 21.

Fig. 8.3. The goddess Roma, personification of the city of Rome, in a second-century AD sculpture.

John's vision is a paradigm of how empires typically collapse. As long as it serves their own interests, proxy rulers in the provinces or satellite states pacify their own people and keep them aligned with the ideology of the empire. But when an empire weakens and can no longer deliver wealth or prestige to its henchmen, puppet rulers turn against the very power they once championed. Such an end to Rome's empire probably took longer than John imagined, but peoples that Rome once governed eventually sacked the city in AD 410.

In the language of Revelation, kings of the earth who ally themselves with Rome commit fornication with the harlot city (17:2). We have seen how Herod the Great built temples to honor Caesar Augustus, and how King Tiridates of Armenia bowed in worship to Emperor Nero. Drawing from a long biblical tradition, John condemns such acts of idolatrous allegiance as *fornication*. By kowtowing to the emperor and imperial interests, provincial power brokers and entrepreneurs gained political, social, or economic advantage.

The goddess Roma (fig. 8.3), symbol of the imperial city, appeared on coins and statues throughout the empire. John portrays her as a whore clothed in purple (17:4), the color reserved for imperial dress. Like a wealthy prostitute bedecked with gold and jewels and pearls, this mother of whores is drunk with the blood of the saints (17:6). The beast upon which she sits "was and is not and is to come" (17:8)—perhaps another allusion to Nero and the myth of his return to life after death.

Fig. 8.4. Emperor Domitian.

Domitian Was a Second Nero

Sometimes called a second Nero by contemporaries, Emperor Domitian (AD 81–96; fig. 8.4) killed many subjects whom he deemed a political threat or simply disliked, including senators and the governor of Asia. He cut off the hands of prisoners, was known to crucify a man with whom he had feasted the previous day, and executed his own cousin on a trivial pretext.[4] It is likely that some Christians were caught in the bloodbath that attended Domitian's reign.

Coins of the era call Domitian the father of the gods, and Roman contemporaries report that he wanted to be addressed as *Dominus et Deus noster* (our lord and god).[5] It is no accident that the heavenly court in Revelation 4:11 uses this exact phrase to worship God (see also John 20:28). John's vision presents a parallel reality, an alternative political allegiance, a counternarrative that stands over against the idolatrous expressions of emperor worship.

Celebrating a Tyrant's Demise

According to Suetonius, a Roman historian who survived the era, Domitian "became an object of terror and hatred to all."[6] When he was assassinated in AD 96, people across the Roman Empire celebrated the end of the emperor's brutal regime. Pliny describes the relief and jubilation that greeted news of his demise, as people spontaneously smashed icons—statues and images—of the emperor:

> Those innumerable golden images, as a sacrifice to public rejoicing, lie broken and destroyed. It was our delight to dash those proud faces to the ground, to smite them with the sword and to savage them with the axe, as if blood and agony could follow from every blow. Our transports of joy—so long deferred—were unrestrained; all sought a form of vengeance in beholding those bodies mutilated, limbs hacked to pieces, and finally that baleful, fearsome visage cast

4. Suetonius, *Domitian* 10–15.
5. Ibid. 13.2; Dio Cassius, *Roman History* 67.4.7; 67.13.4.
6. Suetonius, *Domitian* 14; in *Suetonius*, vol. 2, trans. and ed. J. C. Rolfe, LCL 38 (1913–14; Cambridge, MA: Harvard University Press, 1960), 369.

Fig. 8.5. A visitor at the ruins of ancient Ephesus points to the word *AUTOKRATOR* (autocrat, meaning emperor) on this inscription. To the left of the man's hand the name of a ruler has been erased—presumably a case of *damnatio memoriae*.

into the fire, to be melted down, so that from such menacing terror something for [human] use and enjoyment should arise from the flames.[7]

These comments from a pagan contemporary of John help us understand the vindictive celebrations over the end of the great whore in Revelation 16–19. We see Babylon/Rome being destroyed multiple times in Revelation. First, we learn that the city is split into three parts when "God remembered great Babylon and gave her the wine-cup of the fury of his wrath" (16:19). Then kings of the earth turn against the harlot Babylon/Rome and "devour her flesh and burn her up with fire" (17:16). Finally a mighty angel hurls a great millstone into the sea and says, "With such violence Babylon the great city / will be thrown down" (18:21).

Among ruins of the Roman Empire one still can find inscriptions in which the name of Domitian has been rubbed out (fig. 8.5). Just as they had done with Nero, the Roman Senate passed a *damnatio memoriae* (condemnation-of-memory) decree after Domitian's death, declaring that throughout the empire every trace of his existence should be removed. But senators who voted for such legislation, and most people who despised Domitian, wanted to see the end of a ruler, not the end of an empire.

7. Pliny the Younger, *Panegyricus* 52.4–5; in Pliny the Younger, *Letters and Panegyricus*, vol. 2, trans. Betty Radice, LCL 59 (Cambridge, MA: Harvard University Press, 1969), 441.

What Are We to Do with Violence in Revelation?

What are the spiritual and emotional effects on worshipers when they repeatedly dwell on the violent end of an adversary? John's obsessive focus on the fall of Babylon/Rome is unsettling, and some modern readers have condemned the book of Revelation as unethical. John Dominic Crossan, for example, claims that Revelation portrays Jesus as bloodthirsty. "To turn the nonviolent resistance of the slaughtered Jesus into the violent warfare of the slaughtering Jesus is . . . to libel the body of Jesus and to blaspheme the soul of Christ," he asserts. "It is Jesus, the dead-and-risen Lion-Lamb, who opens the scroll and unleashes its contents upon the earth."[8]

Crossan laments that we humans may actually end up destroying our own species; he adds: "But how do we dare say that God plans and wants it or that Jesus leads and effects it? For me as a Christian, that seems to be *the* crime against divinity, *the* sin against the Holy Spirit."[9]

These are strong words and most regrettable. It is unfortunate that interpreters such as Hal Lindsey (*The Late Great Planet Earth*) and Tim LaHaye (the Left Behind series) have given Revelation a sadistic and escapist interpretation. But we must not confuse such treatment of Revelation with what John intended. Unable or unwilling to wrestle with the juxtaposition of grace and judgment in Revelation, Crossan sets up a false dichotomy: the church, he says, must choose between the nonviolent Jesus of the Gospels and the violent Jesus of John's Apocalypse.[10] This approach effectively removes Revelation from the Bible, a solution that is simplistic and unacceptable.

Loren Johns agrees that Revelation is "arguably the most dangerous book in the history of Christendom" in terms of how it has been used. He cites various millenarian and apocalyptic movements, including the Branch Davidian cult in Waco, Texas, whose leaders quoted Revelation and steered their followers to catastrophe in 1993. Johns concludes, however, that "the more closely the symbolism of the book is read in light of actual first-century people and events, the more clearly does the book empower readers—ancient and modern alike—to adopt an ethic of nonviolent, faithful witness."[11]

It Matters How We Use Violent Imagery

Actual first-century people and events have featured prominently in our study of Revelation, giving a window to the hostile and potentially violent world

8. John Dominic Crossan, *God and Empire: Jesus against Rome, Then and Now* (San Francisco: HarperSanFrancisco, 2007), 224.

9. Ibid., 227.

10. Ibid., 217.

11. Loren L. Johns, *The Lamb Christology of the Apocalypse of John: An Investigation into Its Origin and Rhetorical Force*, WUNT (Tübingen: Mohr Siebeck, 2003), 187.

that some early believers faced. But even if John of Patmos and his community suffered persecution, should not they have been expected to live by Jesus' command "Love your enemies" (Matt. 5:44)?

How we interpret Revelation's violent images makes all the difference for whether this book of the Bible is a valid ethical resource for the church today. Those who use Revelation for insight into how Christians should conduct themselves might consider the following perspectives:

1. Revelation is set in *the context of worship*; it is not a strategic manifesto for bringing down a regime. To be sure, the book has all kinds of implications for political, social, and economic behavior. But the central focus is on worship of God and the Lamb, not on political activism.

2. A large amount of the *suffering* in Revelation is borne *by followers of the Lamb*, not only by followers of the beast. Looking under the altar in heaven, John sees the "souls of those who had been slaughtered for the word of God" (6:9) and learns that more will soon be killed (6:11). Later he sees "the souls of those who had been beheaded for their testimony to Jesus and for the word of God" (20:4).

3. The *prolonged suffering* brought by the plagues and the persistent witness of the martyrs *has the effect of bringing more people to salvation*. In heaven, John sees worshipers, likely martyrs, who "had conquered the beast and its image and the number of its name" (15:2). In 15:3–4, they sing:

> Great and amazing are your deeds,
>   Lord God the Almighty!
> Just and true are your ways,
>   King of the nations!
> Lord, who will not fear
>   and glorify your name?
> For you alone are holy.
>   All nations will come
>   and worship before you,
> For your judgments have been revealed.

John learns that all nations will come and worship God. This is a big vision of salvation, and the faithful testimony of martyrs is part of what draws others to faith. Tertullian famously said in his second-century letter to rulers of Rome, "The oftener we are mown down by you, the more in number we grow; the blood of Christians is seed."[12]

12. Tertullian, *Apology* 50; in *ANF* 3:55.

4. Because Revelation is a book of worship, we do well to stay for the entire service. While it is true that each individual vision in the book conveys a message, *a theological trajectory* shapes the entire work. The Apocalypse moves through long passages of suffering and violence but *ends with a vision of hope* (Rev. 21–22). The theological message is that a loving God is in control of history and ultimately will bring healing to a broken world.

5. While some imagery in Revelation is violent and vindictive, *the counsel for actual Christian behavior is nonviolence*. John repeatedly uses the word "endurance" (*hypomonē*), which connotes sustained nonviolent resistance. Immediately after contrasting worship of the Lamb and worship of the beast, John says, "Here is a call for the endurance of the saints, those who keep the commandments of God and hold fast to the faith of Jesus" (14:12). Loren Johns says the emphasis on endurance (which he translates "resistance") "is a clear 'No' to the possibility of humanity's bringing in the fullness of God's reign, and a joyful and confident 'Yes' to the way of Christ, demonstrated most poignantly in his faithful witness—a witness that led to his death on the cross."[13] Jesus said his witness on the cross would be powerful enough to "draw all people to myself" (John 12:32). God also works redemption through the nonviolent witness and suffering of Jesus' followers, who overcome evil by feeding the enemy (Rom. 12:17–21), win over patriarchal husbands by reverent conduct (1 Pet. 3:1–2), and even conquer Satan himself (Rev. 12:11).

6. It is imperative that we *read Revelation in the context of the entire Bible*—but especially in light of the whole New Testament. In the Gospels we see multiple examples of Jesus showing compassion or forgiveness, even to soldiers from the occupying forces of Rome.[14] In Acts 10 we see Peter proclaiming the good news of Jesus to Cornelius, a Roman centurion! Luke almost certainly wrote the Cornelius account after Peter, Paul, and other Christians had died under Roman persecution. We cannot let John's or other saints' *emotive* responses to evil in Revelation be the sole guide for our actions in confronting structures of sin today.

7. *The controlling metaphor* or governing symbol for the entire vision at Patmos *is the slain Lamb*.[15] Richard B. Hays writes, "A work that places the Lamb that was slaughtered at the center of its praise and worship can hardly

---

13. Johns, *Lamb Christology*, 187.

14. For example, Matt. 8:5–13; Luke 23:32–34.

15. See Ted Grimsrud, "Peace Theology and the Justice of God in the Book of Revelation," in *Essays on Peace Theology and Witness*, ed. Willard M. Swartley, Occasional Papers 12 (Elkhart, IN: Institute of Mennonite Studies, 1988), 154–78.

be used to validate violence and coercion."[16]
Symbols, especially when used repeatedly
in ritual, can have a profound effect on
participants. This reminds us of the importance of highlighting the right symbols from Revelation in our teaching and
worship today. The symbol of the beast
in preaching and teaching can open our
eyes to systemic and structural evil in our
world. Sometimes injustice or suffering
may make it appropriate for us to use
the rage passages of Revelation in prayer.
But always we must return, in worship
and obedience, to the central motif of
the Lamb. The example and teaching of
the Lamb must govern the lives of believers. Then the rage we bring to God and
leave at the throne of grace will find its
proper place.

Fig. 8.6. A sculpture at Aphrodisias depicts
Emperor Claudius preparing to slaughter
Britannia. (Photo courtesy of the New York
University / Institute of Fine Arts Excava-
tion at Aphrodisias.)

Fear and Anger in Worship

Everyone in John's day knew that the empire could be ruthless in gaining
or retaining power. Ruins of a grand temple at Aphrodisias, near Laodicea,
include a sculpture (fig. 8.6) portraying the conquest of Britannia by Emperor
Claudius (AD 41–54). The naked emperor stands triumphant, using his knee
to pin a partially naked Britannia to the ground, while the woman appears
to plead for mercy. Claudius pulls back her head by the hair, with his hand—
which once wielded a sword—held high for the deathblow.[17]

Regardless of whether John ever saw the sculpture of Claudius and Britannia
in nearby Aphrodisias, he was aware of imperial cruelty. Living under violent
and sometimes demented emperors, John had reason to be angry and afraid.
Worship in such circumstances can be catharsis, a cleansing of the bile that
accumulates in the souls of sufferers who cry out for justice. Modern readers
of Revelation who live comfortably in a stable democracy are presumptuous
to dismiss John's vision as sub-Christian.

16. Richard B. Hays, *The Moral Vision of the New Testament: Community, Cross, New
Creation; A Contemporary Introduction to New Testament Ethics* (San Francisco: HarperSan-
Francisco, 1996), 175; cited in Willard M. Swartley, *Covenant of Peace: The Missing Peace in
New Testament Theology and Ethics* (Grand Rapids: Eerdmans, 2006), 330.

17. R. R. R. Smith, "The Imperial Reliefs from the Sebasteion at Aphrodisias," *Journal of
Roman Studies* 77 (1987): 89–98.

Perhaps what the Christian church in the West today needs is more anger, not less. We may need Revelation to jolt us out of our slumber, to open our eyes to see the idolatry and injustice that pervade globalization and empire today. Something beastly is at work, for example, in a world where people starve to death or die of preventable disease while nations spend billions on weapons and leisure. Jesus reassured believers who pray for divine intervention: "Will not God grant justice to his chosen ones who cry out to him day and night? Will he delay long in helping them? I tell you, he will quickly grant justice to them" (Luke 18:7–8).

For Reflection

1. How does the international system of imperial power work in the modern world? What empires (political, military, or economic) can you name in the present or recent past? What ideology or professed values have been used to justify these empires?
2. Can you think of recent situations in which a people celebrated the end of an oppressive ruler? How did the ruler's fall from power happen? Did the means of bringing down the tyrant affect the long-term stability of the country?
3. What questions or concerns do you have about images of violence in Revelation? Under what circumstances, if ever, would you use violent imagery or language in worship? Would you ever use violence in conflict?

LIVING THE VISION

Art and Faith in Catacombs at Rome

Beginning in the second century, Christians at Rome buried their dead in underground tunnels outside the city. Believers sometimes put artwork on burial lids, sarcophagi, or fresco walls (figs. 8.7; 8.8). Artwork in the catacombs dates from two or more centuries after John was on Patmos, but it reflects faith and fears similar to what we find in Revelation. Themes of deliverance abound, including the (near) sacrifice of Isaac, three youths in the fiery furnace, and Christ healing the sick. The story of Jonah was popular as an example of divine deliverance—from a sea monster that looks more like a beast or dragon out of Revelation than the friendly beluga of modern children's books. Early Christians also used Jonah's escape from the big fish as a symbol of Jesus' resurrection after three days in the tomb (Matt. 12:40).

Fig. 8.7. This simple drawing etched into a burial lid in the Christian catacombs at Rome shows the sea monster hurling Jonah to dry land.

Fig. 8.8. A fourth-century Christian sarcophagus portrays scenes of deliverance: Abraham being told not to slaughter Isaac, Jesus healing a blind man, and Jesus telling a lame man to take up his bed and walk.

9

The Economics of Worship

Read Revelation 18:1–19:21

After this I heard what seemed to be the loud voice of a great multitude in heaven, saying,

> "Hallelujah!
> Salvation and glory and power to our God,
>   for his judgments are true and just;
> he has judged the great whore
>   who corrupted the earth with her fornication,
> and he has avenged on her the blood of his servants."

Once more they said,

> "Hallelujah!
> The smoke goes up from her forever and ever."

And the twenty-four elders and the four living creatures fell down and worshiped God who is seated on the throne, saying,

> "Amen. Hallelujah!"

And from the throne came a voice saying,

> "Praise our God,
>   all you his servants,
> and all who fear him,
>   small and great."

Then I heard what seemed to be the voice of a great multitude, like the sound
of many waters and like the sound of mighty thunderpeals, crying out,

> "Hallelujah!
> For the Lord our God
>   the Almighty reigns.
> Let us rejoice and exult
>   and give him the glory,
> for the marriage of the Lamb has come,
>   and his bride has made herself ready;
> to her it has been granted to be clothed
>   with fine linen, bright and pure"—

for the fine linen is the righteous deeds of the saints. (19:1–8)

At the site of ancient Ephesus, archaeologists found the following graffito
on the ruins of an elegant house: "Rome, queen over all, your power will never
end."[1] John of Patmos says the city has glorified herself and lived luxuriously. Rome chortled, "I rule as a queen; I am no widow, and I will never see
grief" (18:7).

John hated such smug complacency. Revelation 18 is a dirge over the demise
of "Babylon," John's contemptuous name for the imperial city he believes
soon will fall. To the mind of Jews, no epithet could have been more scathing; they remembered that Babylon destroyed Jerusalem and the temple of
Solomon in 586 BC.

Babylon/Rome Will Come to an End

"Fallen, fallen is Babylon the great!" cries the angel with a mighty voice (18:1–
2). Rome will perish for its arrogance and idolatry. Revelation warns Christians
not to participate in political, religious, or economic systems of an empire
about to collapse: "Come out of her, my people, / so that you do not take
part in her sins, / and so that you do not share in her plagues" (18:4). There
is vindictive energy in the celebration:

> Render to her as she herself has rendered,
>   and repay her double for her deeds;
>   mix a double draught for her in the cup she mixed.
> As she glorified herself and lived luxuriously,
>   so give her a like measure of torment and grief. (18:6–7)

---

1. Hermann Wankel et al., eds., *Die Inschriften von Ephesos*, vol. 2 (Bonn: Habelt, 1980),
no. 599.

The fate of Babylon triggers stupendous celebration in heaven. Full-volume "Hallelujahs" (Let us praise Yahweh) punctuate the cosmic liturgy as innumerable saints and heavenly beings rejoice. An oppressive empire has ended! For many people today, strains of Handel's "Hallelujah Chorus" resound in our ears when we read of this triumph over evil by the "King of kings and Lord of lords" (19:16).

Potsherd Mountain Reflects the Appetite of Rome

A visit to the landfill of ancient Rome confirms that the great city once "lived luxuriously." Still visible near the Tiber River is a huge heap of broken pottery called Monte Testaccio (Potsherd Mountain; fig. 9.1). The mound contains millions of smashed amphorae, heavy pottery containers that once carried wine, olive oil, fish sauce, and other foodstuffs by ship to Rome. The pile of unrecycled containers covers about two hundred eighteen thousand square feet (twenty thousand square meters) and probably was larger in ancient times.

Pottery near the surface of Monte Testaccio came from Spain or North Africa in the second and third centuries AD, but the core of the mound certainly is older. Each amphora carried about one hundred fifty pounds (seventy kilograms) of liquid. A modern observer says the heap "symbolizes the 'consumer city,' swallowing the produce of its mighty empire in a one-way trade, throwing away the 'empties' in a heap to one side."[2]

Even the philosopher Seneca, counselor to Emperor Nero, was appalled by the appetite of Rome. He wondered if nature gave Romans such insatiable bellies that they should "outdo the hugest and most voracious animals in greed."[3] Seneca cursed the "wretches whose luxury overleaps the bounds of an Empire that already stirs too much envy. . . . Why do you launch your ships?" he demanded. "Why do you pile riches on riches?"[4] He lamented that "an exhibition all too lavish is made of the spoils of conquered nations."[5]

Revelation Condemns the Greed of Rome

From his island vantage point at Patmos, along a shipping lane, John could watch raw materials, luxury items, and food supplies stream toward Italy.

2. Amanda Claridge, *Rome: An Oxford Archaeological Guide* (New York: Oxford University Press, 1998), 367.

3. Seneca, *Epistulae morales* 60.3; in Seneca, *Ad Lucilium epistulae morales*, vol. 1, trans. Richard M. Gummere, LCL 75 (1917–25; Cambridge, MA: Harvard University Press, 1961), 423.

4. Seneca, *De Consolatione ad Helviam* 10.2–7; in Seneca, *Moral Essays*, vol. 2, trans. John W. Basore, LCL 254 (1928–35; Cambridge, MA: Harvard University Press, 1958), 449–51.

5. Seneca, *Epistulae morales* 87.41; in Gummere, *Epistulae morales*, 2:347.

Fig. 9.1. Even the footpath to the top of Monte Testaccio in Rome is made of millions of pieces of broken amphorae from the Roman imperial era.

Someday, he declares, with the demise of Rome, markets there will dry up. Merchants of the earth will weep and mourn because "no one buys their cargo anymore" (18:11). With bitter precision, John lists luxury items first as he enumerates products that ships carry to Italy: "gold, silver, jewels and pearls, fine linen, purple, silk and scarlet, all kinds of scented wood, all articles of ivory, all articles of costly wood, bronze, iron, and marble, cinnamon, spice, incense, myrrh, frankincense, wine, olive oil, choice flour and wheat, cattle and sheep, horses and chariots, slaves—and human lives" (18:12–13).

This bill of lading reveals the perverse priorities of the empire: staple foods and human beings (slaves) appear at the end of the list, almost as an afterthought. When the oppressive economic system collapses, stunned merchants and shipmasters chant:

> Alas, alas, the great city,
>> clothed in fine linen, in purple and scarlet,
>> adorned with gold, with jewels, and with pearls!
> For in one hour all this wealth has been laid waste! . . .
> Alas, alas, the great city,
>> where all who had ships at sea grew rich by her wealth!
> For in one hour she has been laid waste. (18:16–19)

Saints and apostles and prophets of God are called to celebrate the demise of the greedy city (18:20). A mighty angel catalogs the arts, industry, and human society that will perish with Rome: the music of harp, flute, and trumpet; the creativity of artisans; the production of food by millstone; and celebration of marriage (18:21–23). In a sweeping indictment, the angel declares that in Rome "was found the blood of prophets and of saints, and of all who have been slaughtered on earth" (18:24). Here we see that Revelation's call for justice and judgment is not simply a response to the suffering of Christians. John stands in solidarity with all victims of imperial oppression—including, perhaps, the

Fig. 9.2. No structure represented Rome's excess and cruelty more than the Coliseum, an enormous amphitheater started by Emperor Vespasian in AD 70 and finished in AD 80. An ancient inscription at the main entrance reads, "Emperor Vespasian ordered this new amphitheater to be erected from his general's share of the booty . . ." This likely is a reference to the Jewish War and an indication that Jewish captives helped build this amphitheater where countless gladiators, prisoners, and animals died (AD 66–70; see Amanda Claridge, *Rome: An Oxford Archaeological Guide* [Oxford: Oxford University Press, 1998], 278).

Fig. 9.3. A *sester-tius* coin issued by Titus in AD 80–81 made the Coliseum an icon for people across the Roman world. (Photo courtesy of Harlan J. Berk, Ltd.)

thousands who died in the Coliseum (figs. 9.2; 9.3).

The dirge in Revelation 18 captures—for a fleeting moment—the tension that any thoughtful person feels in critiquing a great society. Evil does not usually come unadulterated; it is mixed in with the good. Even Hitler's regime promoted art and industry and creativity—along with horrific evil. The challenge for Christians who live at the heart of empire today is to recognize the good in society around us without being so enamored of it that we fail to see when our own country acts like a beast.

Merchants in Bed with a Whore

Kings of the earth have "committed fornication" with Rome, and "merchants of the earth have grown rich from the power of her luxury" (18:3). The prophets Ezekiel and Hosea used sexual infidelity as a symbol of illicit spiritual alliance (Ezek. 16:15–22; Hos. 1:2–3). Similarly, John describes the relationship between Rome and provincial merchants as fornication, an unholy collaboration between political powers and business leaders. Some kind of idolatry, probably emperor worship, had so penetrated the imperial economy that merely doing business with Rome contaminated those who engaged in it.

From various ancient sources, we know that people involved in international travel and trade were likely to venerate the emperor because they benefited from the security that Rome provided. "Caesar has obtained for us a profound peace," wrote the philosopher Epictetus during the reign of Domitian (AD 81–96). "There are neither wars nor battles, nor great robberies nor piracies, but we may travel at all hours, and sail from east to west."[6] Similarly, first-century Roman geographer Strabo expressed gratitude for the "present peace, because all piracy has been broken up, and hence the sailors feel wholly at ease."[7]

The ancient author Suetonius reported the following incident that took place at Puteoli, a port for Rome, in about AD 14:

> As [Caesar Augustus] sailed by the gulf of Puteoli, it happened that from an Alexandrian ship which had just arrived there, the passengers and crew, clad in

6. Epictetus, *Discourses* 3.13.9; in Epictetus, *The Discourses as Reported by Arrian, The Manual, and Fragments*, vol. 2, trans. W. A. Oldfather, LCL 218 (1926–28; Cambridge, MA: Harvard University Press, 1969), 91.

7. Strabo, *Geography* 3.2.5; in *The Geography of Strabo*, vol. 2, trans. Horace Leonard Jones, LCL 50 (1923; Cambridge, MA: Harvard University Press, 1988), 31. Also see Augustus's boast about ending piracy, in *Res gestae divi Augusti* 25; in Naphtali Lewis and Meyer Reinhold, eds., *Roman Civilization: Sourcebook 2, The Empire* (New York: Harper & Row, 1966), 17.

white, crowned with garlands, and burning incense, lavished upon him good wishes and the highest praise, saying that it was through him they lived, through him they sailed the seas, and through him that they enjoyed their liberty and their fortunes.[8]

Symbols of worship in this account—white garments, crowns, incense—also are prominent in Revelation. The recitation of benefits ascribed to Caesar—freedom to conduct maritime trade, wealth, and even life itself—is an index of praise similar to what Christians offer to God and the Lamb in worship (4:11; 5:9–10).

Patronage Held the Empire Together

A vast pyramid of power relationships, called the patronage system, linked every person in the Roman Empire from the emperor to the lowliest slave (fig. 9.4). John sees (emperor) worship—which has economic, social, and political dimensions—as the glue that holds the entire structure together.

Patrons in ancient society were people with political or economic power who provided *benefits* such as protection, loans, or employment to less powerful *clients*. Clients, in turn, variously gave service, allegiance, or public praise back to their patron. Unless they were at the very bottom of the pyramid of power, many clients in turn served as patrons to persons less powerful than themselves. When wealthy patrons gave money for public works projects, or when they gave public service by assuming a municipal office without pay, their offering was called a *liturgy (leitourgia).*[9]

Such liturgies had the dual effect of benefiting local communities and honoring the emperor. We see a parallel phenomenon in the early church, except that Christians performed liturgies (acts of generosity or service) to honor God. When Paul exhorts believers at Corinth to contribute generously to an offering for the impoverished church at Jerusalem, he says, "The rendering of this ministry [*leitourgia*] not only supplies the needs of the saints but also overflows with many thanksgivings to God" (2 Cor. 9:12). Paul's comment illustrates that it matters to which patronage system one belongs; Christians should be part of a system that generates praise to God.

The Romans relied on their vast patronage system, which generated praise to Caesar, to hold the empire together. Rome appeared to govern the ancient world so successfully because it provided tangible benefits to collaborators and was able to elicit gratitude from subject peoples. To client states, Rome

8. Suetonius, *Augustus* 98; in *Suetonius*, vol. 1, trans. and ed. J. C. Rolfe, LCL 31 (1913–14; Cambridge, MA: Harvard University Press, 1960), 277.

9. Peter Garnsey and Richard Saller, *The Roman Empire: Economy, Society, and Culture* (Berkeley: University of California Press, 1987), 33–34.

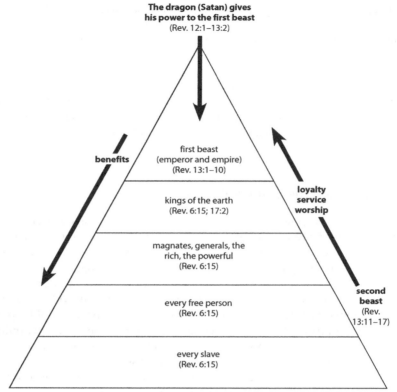

Fig. 9.4. This diagram shows how John of Patmos viewed the patronage system of the Roman Empire, an arrangement he lambasts as fornication. Patrons provided benefits downward to their clients, and clients responded upward with loyalty and service. Emperor worship, orchestrated by the second beast (the priesthood of emperor worship), was a primary index of participation in the entire system. Revelation condemns the benefits-for-worship exchange of Roman patronage as blasphemous, and offers an alternative patronage system of allegiance to God and the Lamb.

offered trade privileges, new roads, aqueducts, economic assistance in times of disaster, or other amenities. Many of these benefits were actually funded by local elites who aligned themselves with the imperial ideology.

Roman historian Suetonius says that Caesar Augustus on a personal level "united the kings with whom he was in alliance by mutual ties, and was very ready to propose or favor intermarriages or friendships among them. He never failed to treat them all with consideration as integral parts of the Empire, . . . and he brought up the children of many of them and educated them with his own."[10] Caesar Augustus served as patron to powerful clients (such as Herod the Great) in conquered nations, a pattern that later emperors continued.

10. Suetonius, *Augustus* 48; in Rolfe, *Suetonius*, 1:203.

Benefits from the System Come at a Price

The steady downward flow of benefits to clients in the patronage pyramid came with a price. Clients usually could not reciprocate on equal terms but were expected to offer indexes of loyalty, service, and praise to their patrons. In Roman cities it was not unusual for a group of clients to gather at their patron's home in the morning and offer greeting as the patron emerged for the day. They applauded when their patron gave a public speech.

Archaeologists have found thousands of stone inscriptions in which clients publicly expressed gratitude to patrons. The first-century Roman philosopher Seneca, tutor and adviser to Nero, wrote a book about the patronage system. Clients, he said, "must be willing to go into exile, or to pour forth your blood, or to undergo poverty" for their patrons.[11] Ironically, Seneca committed suicide when he fell under suspicion of having taken part in a plot to assassinate his patron Nero.[12]

Clients of Rome—especially government officials and priests who operated the far-flung institutions of emperor worship—constituted the second beast in John's vision (13:11–17). It is difficult to precisely identify this creature because it included a complex system of temples, altars, inscriptions, choirs, ceremonies, and other means of expressing loyalty to emperor and empire. The second beast "makes the earth and its inhabitants worship the first beast" (13:12) by promoting emperor worship at all levels of society. John is aware of the stratification of classes in the Roman world. He explicitly names classes of people who function in the bottom four tiers of a pyramid of power of which the beast—the emperor or the empire—is the apex. In descending order, the four subservient tiers are (1) kings of the earth; (2) magnates, generals, the rich, and the powerful; (3) every free person; and (4) every slave (6:15; fig. 9.4).

In one of the most caustic scenes of his vision, John sees that the first beast, representing the emperor or the empire, receives its power from Satan (13:2–4). Persuaded that Rome rules illegitimately by demonic mandate, John will have nothing to do with the imperial system—and especially not with any form of emperor worship.

Emperor Worship Pervades International Commerce

Avoiding emperor worship was difficult since religion pervaded all sectors of ancient society, including the economy. Ports and trade guilds in the first century were filled with temples to various gods, including the emperor. In the first century, Caesarea Maritima, principal Mediterranean port of Palestine, featured a temple of emperor worship built by Herod the Great as the

11. Seneca, *Epistulae morales* 81.27; in Gummere, *Epistulae morales*, 2:237.
12. Tacitus, *Annals* 15.60–64.

Fig. 9.5. This model reconstruction of the harbor built by Herod the Great at Caesarea Maritima shows how the temple to Caesar (bottom left) was the first building sea travelers encountered when they arrived at Judea. The entrance to the harbor is at top right.

first building that arriving sailors and visitors would encounter (figs. 9.5; 8.2). Among the ruins of Ostia, port for ancient Rome at the mouth of the Tiber River, a large building for priests of the emperor cult still stands. This structure illustrates the role emperor worship played in aligning international entrepreneurs with imperial ideology.

Rome needed thousands of collaborating merchants to maintain its standard of living. To mollify a restive population, the government regularly gave free grain to some two hundred thousand persons in the imperial capital.[13] Grain from beyond the Italian peninsula came on ships owned by private entrepreneurs because the Roman government did not have its own merchant fleet. We catch a glimpse of these privately owned merchant vessels in the New Testament. Paul was taken as prisoner toward Rome on a grain ship from Adramyttium, a port in Asia Minor just north of Pergamum (Acts 27:2, 38). He completed his journey on another ship from Alexandria that probably also carried grain (28:11).

There were many such vessels in the first century, and the Roman government provided economic incentives for shipowners to risk the dangerous sea journey to Italy. Shipwreck was common enough that Paul suffered it at least four times (Acts 27:39–44; 2 Cor. 11:25). Merchants who brought grain to Italy received insurance coverage from the emperor and enjoyed tax benefits. They were guaranteed minimum prices for their cargo and could perhaps obtain Roman citizenship for their service.[14]

13. At least this was the claim of Caesar Augustus. See *Res gestae* 15.
14. See further the discussion in my book *Imperial Cult and Commerce in John's Apocalypse*, JSNTSup 132 (Sheffield: Sheffield Academic Press, 1996), 117–21.

Thus a mutually beneficial relationship developed between Rome and entrepreneurs from the provinces. Although much of the freight going to Italy was grain, merchants also ferried a host of other products in ships that each carried up to four hundred tons of cargo, and a few up to a thousand tons.[15] Imports to Rome included silk and spices from the Orient, marble from Asia Minor, and ivory from Zanzibar.

Imperial Priests Have Power in Business

Familiar as he presumably was with the port city of Ephesus, and with international trade in general (Rev. 18), John understood how pagan rituals and emperor worship pervaded the imperial economy. A coin issued by Nero (fig. 9.6) shows one way common people such as John learned about the blend of commerce and worship in Italy. The coin depicts the new harbor of Rome at Ostia. At the top of scene, at the mouth of the harbor, stands a colossal statue either of the god Neptune or of the emperor posed as Neptune. Several merchant vessels with sails raised, and military ships with oars extended, move within the harbor. A personification of the river Tiber reclines at the bottom of the coin, with his hand on a ship's tiller. A temple, perhaps of emperor worship, appears at the upper left, at the end of warehouses built on the sea wall. Such coins showed to the world that ships going to Rome entered a port saturated with worship of the emperor and the gods.

At Ostia, archaeologists have found evidence of nearly forty trade guilds, and probably there were more. Guild sites typically had places for worship, as well as a hall for meetings and banquets. Inscriptions from Ostia indicate that men in guild leadership in the first century also usually had standing in the priesthood of the emperor cult. From ranks of the *augustales* came presidents of the shipbuilding guild and the wine-importing guild. Shippers sponsored a public inscription that honored a certain Faustus, a "priest of the divine Titus" and "patron of the Guild of Overseers of Seagoing Vessels."[16] The emperor cult so pervaded commerce in the Roman world that it was difficult to buy or sell without the mark of the beast (13:17).

Coins Carry the Mark of the Beast

Many first-century Roman coins bore legends such as "Emperor Caesar Domitian Augustus, Son of the Divine Vespasian, Pontifex Maximus [Chief

---

15. Fik Meijer and Onno van Nijf, *Trade, Transport, and Society in the Ancient World: A Sourcebook* (London: Routledge, 1992), 152.
   16. *CIL* 14.4142.

Fig. 9.6. The reverse of a *sestertius* coin issued during the reign of Nero gives a detailed image of the harbor of Rome at Ostia. At top center is a giant statue either of Neptune or of the emperor in divine guise. At bottom the river god Tiber reclines. (© The Trustees of the British Museum.)

Priest]." Coins of Nero and Domitian sometimes portrayed those emperors with the spiked crown associated with divinity. Jewish rebels, known as Zealots for their claim of radical obedience to God, refused to carry or even look at such money. When the Jewish War irrupted in AD 66, the newly independent Jewish government issued coins that bore no human likeness (fig. 9.7).

Ignatius of Antioch, an early second-century church leader martyred at Rome, recognized the power of symbol and used coins as a metaphor for spiritual allegiance: "Just as there are two coinages, the one of God, the other of the world, and each has its own stamp impressed on it, so the unbelievers bear the stamp of this world, and the believers the stamp of God in love through Jesus Christ, and unless we choose to die through him in his passion, his life is not in us."[17]

It is likely that both John and Ignatius were familiar with the response Jesus gives when asked about paying taxes to Rome (Matt. 22:17–21). As a radical Jew, Jesus carries no Roman money on his person. But when he asks for a coin, one of his critics compromises himself by producing a *denarius*.[18] Jesus asks whose image (*eikōn*) and whose title is on it, thus forcing his Jewish opponents to admit that they are carrying money inscribed with blasphemous claims. Then Jesus answers the question about paying taxes: "Give therefore to the emperor the things that are the emperor's, and to God the things that are God's" (Matt. 22:21). In other words, let the idolatrous emperor have the coins bearing his icon. Human beings, made in the image (*eikōn*) of their Creator, belong wholly to God.

Worship Issues in Action

Celebration over the fall of Babylon/Rome reverberates throughout Revelation 19, and "smoke goes up from her forever and ever" (Rev. 19:3). Indexes of worship include shouts of "Hallelujah" as the elders and living creatures fall prostrate before God in gratitude. Preparation is made for the marriage

17. Ignatius, *To the Magnesians* 5.2; in *The Apostolic Fathers*, vol. 1, trans. Kirsopp Lake, LCL 24 (1912–13; Cambridge, MA: Harvard University Press, 1985), 201.
18. Emperor Tiberius (AD 14–37) was the adopted son of Caesar Augustus, whom the Roman Senate declared divine upon his death in AD 14. Tiberius often included the legend *DIVI AUG F* ("son of the divine Augustus") on his coins (fig. 9.8).

Fig. 9.7. Rebels who ousted the Romans from Palestine in the Jewish War issued their own coins that bore no human likeness, such as this *shekel* from AD 67–68. (Photo courtesy of Zuzim Judaea.)

Fig. 9.8. The coin that featured in Jesus' exchange with the Pharisees about paying taxes (Matt. 22:15–22) most likely was this *denarius*. If so, the head to which Jesus referred was that of Emperor Tiberius, and the title on the coin was *DIVI AUG F* ("son of the divine Augustus"). (Photo courtesy of Harlan J. Berk, Ltd.)

supper of the Lamb, the union of Christ the bridegroom with the church as bride (see 2 Cor. 11:2; Eph. 5:25–33).

Amid the commotion, John makes the mistake of falling down to worship at the feet of an angel. Implying that God alone deserves worship, the angel rebukes John: "You must not do that! . . . Worship God!" (Rev. 19:10). John repeats the error near the end of his vision, and again receives a reprimand (22:8). In a world where most people reflexively bow before political rulers, even John needs to be reminded to worship only the triune God.

In Revelation, worship encompasses all of life, symbolized with the whole-body ritual of bowing low. The word John repeatedly uses for worship is *proskyneō*, which has the meaning of falling prostrate to the ground. Ten times John uses *proskyneō* as an index of worshiping God and/or the Lamb;[19] eleven times he uses it to refer to worship of the dragon, the beast, or an image of the beast.[20]

Worship in Revelation 19 takes place between the fall of Babylon/Rome (Rev. 17–18) and the appearance of the new Jerusalem (Rev. 21–22). Will John's readers bow toward Babylon or toward the new Jerusalem? More is involved than mere mental or spiritual disposition. The beast, in any case, is not satisfied to have people of the earth simply give intellectual assent to its supremacy; mortals must also offer indexes of fidelity. They follow the beast, make images of it, buy and sell with its symbol, and carry its mark on their bodies (13:11–17).

Likewise, those who reverence God and the Lamb show their own indexes of allegiance in new patterns of living, as reflected in the liturgy connected with the marriage celebration of the Lamb. The bride—the church—is "clothed with fine linen, bright and pure," and her wedding dress "is the righteous deeds of the saints" (19:8). This is not a "works righteousness," since it has been *granted* to the church by the gracious power of God to wear the garment

19. Rev. 4:10; 5:14; 7:11; 11:1, 16; 14:7; 15:4; 19:4, 10b; 22:9.
20. Rev. 9:20; 13:4 (twice), 8, 12, 15; 14:9, 11; 16:2; 19:20; 20:4. Three times John uses *proskyneō* to describe bowing before other entities (3:9; 19:10a; 22:8).

of holy living (see 6:11). Worship involves the whole self—mind, spirit, and actions. Those who die "in the Lord" are blessed, a voice from heaven says, "for their deeds follow them" (14:13).

On the day of final reckoning, all mortals will stand before God to be "judged according to their works, as recorded in the books" (20:12). Deeds do not save mortals, nor do beliefs or feelings; God and the Lamb save. But Revelation shows that deeds are indexes of what men and women actually worship. John of Patmos would have agreed with the Epistle of James: "So faith by itself, if it has no works, is dead" (James 2:17).

History Transitions to the Kingdom of God

Ritual, worship, and metaphor tumble over one another in rapid succession as history fully transitions from the kingdom of the beast to the kingdom of God. The heavens open, and a white horse of victory emerges (Rev. 19:11–16). We recognize the rider as Jesus because "from his mouth comes a sharp sword" (19:15; see 1:16). His name is The Word of God (see John 1:1), and his robe is splattered with blood—perhaps his own, poured out at Golgotha. The sharp sword with which he will strike down the nations is the Word of God (see Heb. 4:12). Just as God once spoke the word to bring creation out of chaos (Gen. 1:3), so Jesus speaks the word again to restore creation.

Good and evil have been mirror images throughout Revelation, so it is not surprising that there are two end-time banquets: the marriage supper of the Lamb (19:9), and a meal in which the menu is the flesh of kings, captains, horses, riders, and everyone who follows the beast (19:17–18). This foul feast makes a mockery of banquets held at imperial courts, guild halls, or political gatherings across the empire.

On the great day of God the Almighty, a climactic battle unfolds at a place John calls "Harmagedon," or "Armageddon" (16:16 RSV). In Hebrew, the name means Mount Megiddo and probably refers to an ancient mound at the edge of the Jezreel Valley, where the city of Megiddo once stood (fig. 9.9). Because of its strategic location on a plain at the intersection of major highways, Megiddo was the site of many pivotal battles in the ancient world.[21]

Megiddo is in the shadow of Mount Carmel, the mountain where Elijah once humiliated the prophets of Baal before leading them to execution (1 Kings 18). Now the forces of idolatry and violence from the whole world converge there for battle, this time apparently against God. The battle is a rout, with evil going down to defeat so swiftly that John simply reports:

21. For example, Megiddo was the place where Josiah, king of Judah, was mortally wounded in battle in 609 BC, when he intervened in the conflict between the empires of Assyria, Babylon, and Egypt (2 Kings 23:29–30; 2 Chron. 35:20–24).

Fig. 9.9. These ruins of ancient Megiddo are on a hilltop Revelation 16:16 calls Armageddon (mountain of Megiddo). In the distance is the broad Jezreel Valley where Revelation says an eschatological battle will take place.

> The beast was captured, and with it the false prophet who had performed in its presence the signs by which he deceived those who had received the mark of the beast and those who worshiped its image. These two were thrown alive into the lake of fire that burns with sulfur. And the rest were killed by the sword of the rider on the horse, the sword that came from his mouth; and all the birds were gorged with their flesh. (Rev. 19:20–21)

The false prophet is closely related to the second beast (13:11–17), the one who made people of the earth worship the beast of empire. The false prophet and the second beast personify rebellion against God; they are summarily hurled into the lake of fire. They are corrupt systems and structures, entities that need not arouse our sympathy. More sobering is the loss of human life in this passage: kings, captains, the mighty, free people, slaves, the small, and the great (19:18).

In a ghoulish parody of a banquet, birds gorge themselves on decaying human flesh (19:21). Note the symbolic nature of this passage: those who die are felled by a sword that issues from the rider's mouth. It is the sword of the Word of God, not a literal weapon. The rider *speaks* an end to those who, despite multiple warnings and plagues, insist on following the beast. Just as God repeatedly warned Pharaoh through ten plagues to change his heart, followers of the beast receive abundant warning through three cycles of seven woes. Those who perish have willfully and persistently chosen to worship the beast instead of God.

"Gonna Have to Serve Somebody"

The Apocalypse focuses on structural evil—in this case, vast networks of commerce and politics warped by greed, violence, and blasphemous ideology. John's purpose in highlighting systemic sin is to exhort individuals and congregations not to let themselves be caught up in a corrupt system.

Humans are not autonomous, and we are not gods. American troubadour Bob Dylan famously sang, "You're gonna have to serve somebody," whether that be the devil or the Lord.[22] Revelation unveils the spiritual realities of a first-century Roman world in which many people end up serving and worshiping an empire with depraved political and economic structures.

Thus Revelation reminds us that how we relate to money speaks volumes, and God is listening. As followers of Jesus, we cannot divide our lives neatly into spiritual, economic, and vocational compartments, because worship involves the whole of life. While Christians should engage political and economic institutions of our world, we must do so with kingdom values of justice and healing. We need to regularly worship God and the Lamb because other gods are ubiquitous and beguiling.

For Reflection

1. Where are the "potsherd mountains" in the modern economy? What evidence of wanton consumption will modern societies leave for future generations to uncover? To what extent are today's empires structured around economic objectives?
2. What does the patronage pyramid look like today? Who is at the top? Who is at the bottom? By what rituals or behaviors do we signal that we are part of the system? Does religion or some other comprehensive ideology play a part in holding the pyramid together?
3. What indexes of imperial allegiances do you see today—in trade agreements, in political alliances, or in places where elites around the world receive education? Which of these would John of Patmos call fornication? By what indexes or actions do you express allegiance to the kingdom of God?

LIVING THE VISION

Prescription for Healthy Community in Indiana

"The United States doesn't have a healthcare system," says James Nelson Gingerich, MD. "We have a medical industry that produces just

22. Bob Dylan, *Slow Train Coming*, LP record, Columbia Records/CBS Inc., 1979.

enough health care to maintain the illusion that its reason for being is health care rather than profits."

Not quite the outlook you expect from a graduate of a prestigious medical school! Gingerich recognizes that many doctors provide good care. But as one of his physician friends tells him, "Most of us just want our patients to be happy and to pay their bills on time." Gingerich's passion is for building healthy community with people that the medical system leaves out.

In 1988, Gingerich and other local visionaries set up Maple City Health Care Center in a racially mixed, economically struggling neighborhood in Goshen, Indiana. Volunteers helped to convert an empty fire station into a center offering accessible, affordable care. Gingerich learned Spanish, bought a house nearby, and works for a salary similar to that of a public schoolteacher.

The medical industry is a kind of pseudoreligion that gives allegiance to profit rather than the common good, Gingerich asserts. "Doctors in lab coats are priests with specialized knowledge, ministering behind closed doors to vulnerable patients. Advertising fosters faith in costly drugs promising youth, vigor, and a life free of pain." In contrast, the Maple City Health Care Center provides a setting in which neighbors—providers, patients, staff, and board— collaborate to improve the well-being of both individuals and the broader community.

The center provides a wide range of services, including comprehensive primary care, counseling, a drug assistance program, and support groups for persons with chronic conditions. Prenatal care includes culturally diverse gatherings of pregnant women, who bring their experience to the circle. The center's board converses in Spanish and English, across socioeconomic lines, to envision ways to foster the good of the neighborhood. Board members meet at table to share food and make decisions amid conversation about their families of origin and their experience as immigrants or long-term residents. They bring their knowledge of schools, businesses, law enforcement, or other local realities.

The vision that shapes the center is rooted in the example of Jesus, who spoke to the powerful and fraternized with the poor. It is about Jews and Gentiles, rich and poor, enjoying each other's hospitality, Gingerich says. Here the doors are open to people who are ready to bring their resources and needs and thereby help to create a healing community.[23]

23. James Gingerich, interview by the author, April 29, 2008, Goshen, Indiana.

10

Letters to Seven Churches

Read Revelation 2:1–3:22

And to the angel of the church in Pergamum write: These are the words of him who has the sharp two-edged sword: "I know where you are living, where Satan's throne is. Yet you are holding fast to my name, and you did not deny your faith in me even in the days of Antipas my witness, my faithful one, who was killed among you, where Satan lives. But I have a few things against you: you have some there who hold to the teaching of Balaam, who taught Balak to put a stumbling block before the people of Israel, so that they would eat food sacrificed to idols and practice fornication. So you also have some who hold to the teaching of the Nicolaitans. Repent then. If not, I will come to you soon and make war against them with the sword of my mouth. Let anyone who has an ear listen to what the Spirit is saying to the churches. To everyone who conquers I will give some of the hidden manna, and I will give a white stone, and on the white stone is written a new name that no one knows except the one who receives it." (2:12–17)

After exploring how John deals with large themes of empire and allegiance, we now have a broad context for understanding local issues facing the seven churches to which Christ speaks in Revelation 2 and 3. There is a specific message tailored for each congregation, but apparently all churches receive the entire set.

Each letter begins with the phrase "To the angel of the church in [city] write . . ." The word *angel* means messenger or envoy, and in Revelation only supernatural beings carry the title. Perhaps the one being addressed at the beginning of each letter is the guardian angel for the congregation in question. Just as the archangel Michael is guardian for the Jewish nation (Dan. 12:1), a divine deputy attends to each of these clusters of believers.

The vision leaves no doubt that it is Jesus who is speaking to the seven churches. John has just seen a vision of Christ standing among seven lampstands, symbols of the seven churches (Rev. 1:12–20). Now a different fragment of that vision appears at the beginning of each of the seven letters. The letter to Ephesus, for example, begins by saying, "These are the words of him who holds the seven stars in his right hand" (2:1). This statement lifts a detail from the earlier vision of Christ (1:16).

Christ Knows the Struggle of Every Church

The seven letters show that the exalted Christ is attentive to the distinct struggles, failures, and strengths of each congregation. Followers of Jesus at Ephesus have dealt with false prophets (2:2, 6), while those at Smyrna are living in tension with the Jewish community (2:9). A believer named Antipas has suffered martyrdom at Pergamum (2:13), and a woman named Jezebel is misleading the church at Thyatira (2:20). In contrast to the dead church at Sardis (3:1), Christians at Philadelphia have kept the word of Christ (3:8). Christians at Laodicea may be materially self-sufficient, but spiritually they are "wretched, pitiable, poor, blind, and naked" (3:17).

Christian churches likely had been in Asia Minor for half a century when John wrote his vision. Paul spent more than two years at Ephesus (Acts 19:1–10) but was not the first to bring the gospel there. As happened in other parts of the ancient world, Christianity emerged from within or in close proximity to long-established Jewish communities. This pattern set the stage for conflict as messianic and nonmessianic Jews became alienated from each other, and as Christian faith attracted a growing number of Gentiles. Since Asia Minor was precisely the region in which emperor worship first took root, believers there were quick to encounter political and social problems resulting from their exclusive worship of God and the Lamb.

In addition to the seven cities with Christian churches featured in Revelation, Paul's Letters mention congregations at Colossae and Hierapolis (Col. 1:2; 4:13). From letters to the seven churches of Revelation and from other ancient sources, we gather the following picture of believers' circumstances in Asia Minor, at the end of the first century:

1. *Christians in Asia Minor can stay out of trouble if they accommodate to society around them.* Most of the time in the early centuries, Christians were *not* persecuted. Provincial authorities engaged in occasional spates of persecution, but most believers suffered more from the stigma

Fig. 10.1. An inscription on this tomb of the late first-century merchant Flavius Zeuxis at Hierapolis says he "sailed on seventy-two voyages beyond Cape Maleus toward Italy." Cape Maleus (Malea) is a peninsula at the southern tip of the Peloponnesus in Greece.

of society than from government harassment. Revelation actually names only one person from seven churches who had been killed, Antipas at Pergamum (2:13). Issues other than government persecution are primary in most of the letters.

2. *Tension is high between some Christians and Jews.* Twice the letters refer to the synagogue of Satan (2:9; 3:9). This caustic phrase may indicate that John believes local Jewish congregations are collaborating with Rome and therefore are in league with Satan. At Smyrna there is "slander on the part of those who say that they are Jews and are not," which may be the reason Christ says to the believers, "The devil is about to throw some of you into prison" (2:9–10). Likewise, at Philadelphia there are "those of the synagogue of Satan who say that they are Jews and are not, but are lying" (3:9). Evidently there are bitter disputes about who are the true Jews: those who adhere to traditional Mosaic law, or those—including some Gentiles—who accept Jesus as the Messiah. Such disagreements within the Jewish community over messianic claims about Jesus have already caused trouble in Rome half a century earlier. Suetonius reports that Emperor Claudius in about AD 49 expelled the Jews from Rome for "making constant disturbances at the instigation of *Chrestus* [Christ?]."[1]

3. *Some Christians in Asia Minor are involved in trade with Rome.* We know from many sources that Asia Minor was a major trading partner with Rome. At Hierapolis (Col. 4:13), close to Laodicea, archaeolo-

---

1. Suetonius, *Claudius* 25; in *Suetonius*, vol. 2, trans. and ed. J. C. Rolfe, LCL 38 (1913–14; Cambridge, MA: Harvard University Press, 1960), 53. This probably is the same episode to which Acts 18:2 refers.

Fig. 10.2. While these ruins of ancient Sardis date from the second to fourth centuries, they illustrate the intersection of monotheism, commerce, and pagan culture that already was a concern for John of Patmos in the first century. In the foreground are stalls for shops along the street. In the background is a partially reconstructed Greek/Roman gymnasium that still bears inscriptions celebrating the emperor cult. Across the middle of the picture, just beyond the long wall, is the foundation of a synagogue. A large stone table in the synagogue, not visible in this picture, features Roman eagles on each end.

gists have reconstructed the tomb of the late first-century merchant Flavius Zeuxis (fig. 10.1). An inscription above the door indicates that he made seventy-two sea passages to Italy. We have no evidence that this entrepreneur was a Christian, but we know of other international businesspeople who were. According to Acts, the first believer on the continent of Europe was a merchant named Lydia, "from the city of Thyatira and a dealer in purple cloth" (Acts 16:14). Paul, Priscilla, and Aquila all moved internationally in commercial circles and had their own businesses. In the second century a Christian shipper from northern Asia Minor, Marcion, moved to Rome and arrived in his own vessel.[2] John of Patmos, in the middle of a dirge about politicians and merchants who have "fornicated" with Babylon/Rome, hears a voice cry, "Come out of her, my people, so that you do not take part in her sins" (Rev. 18:4).

4. *While some congregations are poor and powerless, others are rich and comfortable.* Only two congregations, Smyrna and Philadelphia, receive no rebuke from Christ. Smyrna suffers poverty (2:9), and Philadelphia has "but little power" (3:8). As we have seen, to compete economically and

2. Eusebius, *Ecclesiastical History* 5.13.3; Tertullian, *Prescription against Heretics* 30.1. This is the Marcion later rejected by the church for heresy.

Fig. 10.3. A sculpture of Nike, goddess of victory, among the ruins of ancient Ephesus. Her left hand holds a victory wreath.

politically in the first-century world, businesspeople may have felt they had to participate in emperor worship or other pagan rituals. Presumably, believers at Smyrna and Philadelphia have refused to compromise in this way and are suffering economically and politically as a result. In contrast, the church at Laodicea says, "I am rich, I have prospered, and I need nothing." Complacency has made Christians at Laodicea spiritually lukewarm—a familiar image in a region with water that sometimes was piped too far from local hot springs. Christ tells the congregation, "You do not realize that you are wretched, pitiable, poor, blind, and naked" (3:17).

5. *False teachers among the churches advocate syncretism and urge believers to participate in pagan society.* To Pergamum, Christ says, "You have some there who hold to the teaching of Balaam, who taught Balak to put a stumbling block before the people of Israel, so that they would eat food sacrificed to idols and practice fornication" (2:14). The prophet Balaam once incited Midianite women to lure Israelites into worship of Baal (Num. 31:16; 25:1–3).

At Thyatira, a prophetess whom Christ labels "Jezebel" is "teaching and beguiling my servants to practice fornication and to eat food sacrificed to idols" (Rev. 2:20). Jezebel of Phoenicia, wife of the wicked King Ahab, was instrumental in turning Israel to Baal worship (1 Kings 16:31–33). Both Balaam and Jezebel were spiritual two-timers, who blended pagan worship with worship of Yahweh. References to Balaam and Jezebel in Revelation are satirical, because no Christian or Jewish teacher would have accepted or assumed the name of these Old Testament villains. But Christ says those who advocate accommodation to pagan Roman values carry such identity. The Nicolaitans (Rev. 2:6, 15), teachers about whom we know almost nothing, may also have sought

Fig. 10.4. The reverse of this *denarius* of Nero from AD 64–65 portrays the goddess Roma holding the image of Victory (Nike) in her outstretched hand. (Used by permission of Classical Numismatic Group, Inc., www.cngcoins.com.)

to blend Christian faith with other religions. A setting such as that found by archaeologists at Sardis (fig. 10.2) may be the context in which some members of the seven churches advocated compromise with pagan society.

6. *Widespread persecution is imminent*, or at least John believes it is. "Do not fear what you are about to suffer," Christ says to the church at Ephesus. "Be faithful until death, and I will give you the crown of life" (2:10). To the church at Philadelphia, the Lord says, "I will keep you from the hour of trial that is coming on the whole world to test the inhabitants of the earth" (3:10). Each letter exhorts believers to conquer, which in Revelation means remaining faithful to Jesus despite persecution or martyrdom. Conquering was a common theme in Roman propaganda; symbols and icons of Nike, goddess of victory, were common (figs. 10.3–4). John's belief that Christians soon would need to overcome widespread persecution may have been a factor that prepared him for his vision.

Faith and Faithfulness Belong Together

The central strategy in Revelation for strengthening the church in Asia Minor is for believers to draw close to Christ in worship. In John's vision, Jesus tells believers at Ephesus, "You have abandoned the love you had at first" (2:4). It is not clear whether that comment refers to love for Christ or love between members of the church. Demonstrated love, in any case, is an index of faithfulness. Jesus says, "Listen! I am standing at the door, knocking; if you hear my voice and open the door, I will come in to you and eat with you, and you with me" (3:20). That is love-feast terminology, perhaps language of the Eucharist. Jesus is ready to host a meal among people who relate to one another in love.

Jesus is present among the churches to transform them with the love of God. Six times in the letters he uses the word *repent* (*metanoeō*), a Greek term with roots meaning to change one's mind. As we have observed, Hebrew linguistic and thought patterns lie behind Revelation's Greek text, and the Hebrew word for *repent* (*shuv*) literally means "turn around." What mortals believe matters, but the accent in John's vision falls on behavior. Believers at Ephesus are told to "do the works you did at first" (2:5). Christ tells the church at Sardis to remember "what you received and heard; obey it, and repent" (3:3). Later in the visions, as plagues fall upon the earth, John expresses amazement that sufferers "did not repent of the works of their hands or give up worshiping demons and idols" (9:20; see 16:11).

Revelation resonates with the rest of the Scriptures by insisting that faith (what we believe) is inseparable from faithfulness (actions consistent with what we profess).[3] The first words Jesus speaks to the church at Thyatira are "I know your works—your love, faith, service, and patient endurance" (2:19). Since Jesus in John's vision notices behavior first, perhaps we also should put orthopraxis ("right practice") on the same level as orthodoxy ("right belief").

Early Christians Disagree on How to Act in the World

Revelation is spiritually polarized, with a strong tendency to place all persons and entities into categories of light and darkness, good and evil, truth and lie. In the midst of this polarized universe, God remains sovereign. But great swaths of the created order have fallen into rebellion; Roman ideology and the structures of empire are so corrupt that followers of Jesus must abandon all relationship with them.

We have few clues about what "Jezebel" promoted at Thyatira, but her doctrine involved "teaching and beguiling my servants to practice fornication and to eat food sacrificed to idols" (2:20). Since fornication in John's vocabulary means illicit engagement with pagan society, we can guess that Jezebel was teaching some strategy for Christians to survive economically or politically by accommodating to pagan practices.

It is unlikely that Christians disposed to eat food sacrificed to idols simply were spiritually careless. Rather, participating in meals that included worship of the gods or the emperor may have been required for membership in trade guilds or political associations. Abundant archaeological and literary evidence shows that trade guilds were present in the commercial city of Thyatira and elsewhere in cities of the New Testament. The guilds typically held ceremonial meals where relationships developed that enhanced business.

Instead of being a willful idolater, Jezebel may simply have been a pragmatist. She may have insisted that, in order to survive economically and socially, followers of Christ had to participate in guilds or other associations where pagan ceremonies were part of doing business. John viewed such pragmatic participation as an index of loyalty to the beast.

---

3. Both the Old Testament Hebrew word for faith (ĕmûnâ) and the New Testament Greek word for faith (pistis) convey notions of faith *and* faithfulness.

Paul Counsels Cautious Engagement with Pagan Society

Other parts of the New Testament show that believers had diverse opinions about the appropriate way for Christians to participate in pagan society. In his letters to the church in Corinth, Paul recognizes that some believers there claim special knowledge that allows them to eat food offered to idols. When discussing of this issue, Paul inserts quotes from such persons:

> As to the eating of food offered to idols, we know that "no idol in the world really exists," and that "there is no God but one." Indeed, even though there may be so-called gods in heaven or on earth—as in fact there are many gods and many lords—yet for us there is one God, the Father, from whom are all things and for whom we exist, and one Lord, Jesus Christ, through whom are all things and through whom we exist. (1 Cor. 8:4–6)

Paul at first almost seems to say that Christians can interact with pagan society without scruples because they know that other gods do not even exist. But he immediately goes on to say that the liberty this insight affords can become an obstacle to faith for the weak—probably a reference to Gentile believers who have only recently abandoned a pagan worldview to accept Christ:

> It is not everyone, however, who has this knowledge. Since some have become so accustomed to idols until now, they still think of the food they eat as food offered to an idol; and their conscience, being weak, is defiled. "Food will not bring us close to God." We are no worse off if we do not eat, and no better off if we do. But take care that this liberty of yours does not somehow become a stumbling block to the weak. For if others see you, who possess knowledge, eating in the temple of an idol, might they not, since their conscience is weak, be encouraged to the point of eating food sacrificed to idols? (1 Cor. 8:7–10; see also Rom. 14)

Paul does not reject all Christian participation in settings of society where there may be *indirect* connection with pagan rites. He advocates a "don't ask" policy, for example, when believers have food set before them that possibly once was part of a pagan offering (1 Cor. 10:27–30). But he is categorical in condemning outright Christian participation in pagan rituals and ceremonies, telling the Corinthian Christians to "flee from the worship of idols. . . . I do not want you to be partners with demons. You cannot drink the cup of the Lord and the cup of demons" (10:14, 20–21). The Apostle thus gives nuanced guidelines for Christians to cautiously engage the Roman world and even goes so far as to express qualified support for the Roman government:

> Let every person be subject to the governing authorities; for there is no authority except from God, and those authorities that exist have been instituted by God. Therefore whoever resists authority resists what God has appointed, and those

who resist will incur judgment. For rulers are not a terror to good conduct, but to bad. Do you wish to have no fear of the authority? Then do what is good, and you will receive its approval; for it is God's servant for your good. But if you do what is wrong, you should be afraid, for the authority does not bear the sword in vain! It is the servant of God to execute wrath on the wrongdoer. Therefore one must be subject, not only because of wrath but also because of conscience. For the same reason you also pay taxes, for the authorities are God's servants, busy with this very thing. (Rom. 13:1–6)

Both Paul's treatment of the issue of idol worship and his attitude toward the Roman government would have seemed inadequate to John of Patmos. Revelation is categorical in condemning the Roman Empire and any association with its pagan rites.

Paul and John Lived in Different Contexts

We can understand the contrast between Paul's Letters and John's vision when we place the two authors chronologically in first-century politics. Paul conducted much of his ministry before Emperor Nero developed terminal megalomania, before he turned against the church in AD 64. Paul died before Roman armies destroyed Jerusalem in AD 70.

John, writing in about AD 96, knew that the Roman government was responsible for the deaths of Paul, Peter, and other believers at Rome. John knew about the horrendous destruction of Jerusalem in AD 70, and perhaps was himself a refugee from that conflagration. The moral outrages of emperors Nero (AD 54–68) and Domitian (AD 81–96) were common knowledge in the Roman world. Such abuses probably played into John's bleak view of Rome and imperial society.

Reading both Paul's Letters and John's Apocalypse in their respective historical settings might help us discover how to apply these Scriptures today. Do governments we know today act more like "God's servant" (Rom. 13:4) or like the beast "uttering haughty and blasphemous words" (Rev. 13:5)? Is it possible that part of a given government or society might be doing God's will, while another part is acting beastly? If so, should followers of Jesus Christ accept the authority of government in one area of society while rejecting it in another?

In any case, Christians seeking to be faithful today must draw insight from the whole of Scripture. In determining how to engage government and society, we cannot simply find one proof text from Romans, or from Revelation, or from any other part of the Bible, and give that excerpt universal application. We need to view issues of Christian faithfulness from diverse biblical vantage points; together as the people of God, we need to listen for what the Spirit is saying to the churches today.

A Day of Reckoning Is Coming

At the end of each of the seven letters in Revelation 2 and 3, Christ speaks words of invitation and warning that point to a future day of reckoning: "To everyone who conquers, I will give permission to eat from the tree of life" (2:7); "I will give authority over the nations" (2:26); or "I will make you a pillar in the temple of my God" (3:12).

In John's vision, "to conquer" means to consistently resist the threats and allurements of empire and remain loyal to the Lamb, even in the face of death. Judgment scenes in Revelation 20 show the ultimate vindication of those who triumph with the Lamb. The chapter begins with an angel binding Satan for a thousand years, a symbolic number that probably just means a long time. At last the prime perpetrator of evil no longer is able to deceive the nations (20:3), and a great reversal takes place: martyrs in heaven who once received death sentences at Roman tribunals now take thrones and themselves have authority to judge. A qualification for this role is that the saints "had not worshiped the beast or its image and had not received its mark on their foreheads or their hands" (20:4).

This passage is heavy with symbolism, and we should not read it literally. Based on a misunderstanding of 1 Thessalonians 4:13–18, premillennial interpreters claim that Christ will return to take saints to heaven before his thousand-year reign. This might be harmless speculation, except that premillennialism sometimes includes the notion that biblical teaching about the kingdom of God, such as that found in the Sermon on the Mount, applies only to some indeterminate future and not to the present. If that assertion were true, followers of Lamb today would not need to love enemies or otherwise live out the hard teachings of Jesus. We would not need to work for healing and hope in a fractured world if we believe God soon will whisk us away from a planet headed for sure destruction.

The point of Revelation 20 is simply that evil someday will suffer utter defeat, and followers of the Lamb will receive honor. For a thousand years Satan will be powerless, locked and sealed in a pit. Then, at the time of God's choosing, Satan will briefly be out on parole. He will make one last desperate attempt at global mischief, rallying armies from many nations to intimidate the people of God (20:9). Then in one definitive stroke of divine justice, fire will come down from heaven to destroy armies aligned with evil. Into the lake of fire and sulfur will go Satan and the beast and the false prophet (the second beast)—all symbols of systemic and structural evil.

At last the moment arrives in John's vision for individuals to stand before the throne of God and give account for their lives. Before a great white throne, all of humanity, living and dead, receive judgment "according to their works, as recorded in the books" (20:11–15). Behavior, not belief, is the standard for how God views mortals on judgment day. This portrayal is similar to Jesus' teaching about final judgment hinging on whether an individual has fed the hungry, welcomed the stranger, and clothed the naked (Matt. 25:31–46).

With conduct factoring so large in the final judgment, it is not surprising that messages to the seven churches in Revelation 2 and 3 put an accent on action. Be faithful, Christ says, by showing with your lives that you follow the Lamb.

For Reflection

1. Imagine the letter (on the model of Rev. 2:1–3:22) that Christ might write to your congregation. What would Jesus bless? What challenge might he give you for faithful living?
2. What do you observe about the effect of poverty or wealth on the spiritual vitality of the church? What false doctrines or false teachers circulate today, and how do they get their message to churches?
3. What is the modern equivalent of eating food offered to idols? In what ways are you more like John of Patmos or the apostle Paul in your attitude toward Christian involvement in wider society?

LIVING THE VISION

Is the Pledge of Allegiance Religious?

In the United States, religion and patriotism often blend. Millions of schoolchildren and countless adults in civic settings stand daily to offer the loyalty index of placing hand over heart and saying: "I pledge allegiance to the flag of the United States of America, and to the republic for which it stands, one nation under God, indivisible, with liberty and justice for all."

A Christian minister wrote the pledge to the flag in 1892, but the words "under God" were not added until 1954. With the rise of atheistic communism elsewhere in the world, politicians in the 1950s felt that reference to God would strengthen American patriotism and moral fiber. In 2004, the United States Supreme Court issued a ruling that the words "under God" in the pledge do not violate the constitutional principle of separation of church and state. Supreme Court Chief Justice William Rehnquist declared that the pledge is in no sense a prayer, nor an endorsement of any religion. "Reciting the Pledge," he said, "is a patriotic exercise, not a religious one; participants promise fidelity to our flag and our Nation, not to any particular God, faith, or church." Justice Sandra Day O'Connor added that the pledge has nothing to do with "individual submission to divine authority."[4]

But discipleship to Jesus Christ has everything to do with individual submission to God. John of Patmos, with his global view of the people of God, would be wary of any rite suggesting that God is particularly favoring one nation. The following lines, written for twenty-first-century Christians in America, provide an alternative for followers of Jesus to say in our worship or when others are pledging allegiance to flag and country: "I pledge allegiance to Jesus Christ, and to God's kingdom for which he died, one Spirit-led people the world over, indivisible, with love and justice for all."[5]

4. Chief Justice Rehnquist, concurring in judgment, Supreme Court of the United States, No. 02-1624, On Writ of Certiorari to the United States Court of Appeals for the Ninth Circuit, June 14, 2004.

5. A Christian Pledge of Allegiance, © 2003, June Alliman Yoder and J. Nelson Kraybill.

11

All Things New

Read Revelation 11:1–19; 20:1–22:21

Then I saw a new heaven and a new earth; for the first heaven and the first earth had passed away, and the sea was no more. And I saw the holy city, the new Jerusalem, coming down out of heaven from God, prepared as a bride adorned for her husband. And I heard a loud voice from the throne saying,

> "See, the home of God is among mortals.
> He will dwell with them as their God;
> they will be his peoples,
> and God himself will be with them;
> he will wipe every tear from their eyes.
> Death will be no more;
> mourning and crying and pain will be no more,
> for the first things have passed away."

And the one who was seated on the throne said, "See, I am making all things new." Also he said, "Write this, for these words are trustworthy and true." Then he said to me, "It is done! I am the Alpha and the Omega, the beginning and the end. To the thirsty I will give water as a gift from the spring of the water of life." (21:1–6)

The water of life! Like an oasis after a journey through the desert, the new Jerusalem comes into view at the end of Revelation. Chaos and suffering are

Fig. 11.1. A Jewish worshiper weeps against the Western Wall, part of the massive foundation that once supported the great temple of Yahweh at Jerusalem.

relentless in John's vision, and it must have seemed too good to be true when John "saw the holy city, the new Jerusalem, coming down out of heaven" (Rev. 21:2). Death will be no more!

We generally think worship means coming into the presence of God. In this last vision of Revelation, the reverse happens: the presence of God comes to humans. For Jewish Christians who grieved the loss of Jerusalem, and for others who suffered persecution, the "loud voice from the throne" (21:3) brought wonderful news: God soon will dwell among mortals. God will wipe every tear from their eyes, and mourning and crying and pain will be no more (21:4).

Heaven Comes to Earth in the Form of a City

Jerusalem, so recently ruined by warfare, appears gloriously restored. With his use of the present active participle (coming down), John implies that arrival of the new Jerusalem—at least in some preliminary way—is a *present* reality. Believers are not wafted to heaven while the earth suffers final destruction; instead, heaven comes to earth in the form of a city.

Devout Jews today still weep for the temple lost at Jerusalem (fig. 11.1), echoing grief that followed the disaster in AD 70. For a thousand years before Roman armies destroyed the city, Jews had understood Jerusalem and/or the temple to be God's footstool, the place on earth where Yahweh was most present.[1] Destruction of the holy city was profoundly disorienting to people of faith. Did not the Scriptures say, "God is in the midst of the city; it shall not be moved" (Ps. 46:5)?

1. 1 Chron. 28:2; Ps. 99:5; 132:7; Lam. 2:1; 2 Esd. 6:4.

John of Patmos believed in Jesus and possibly was among those who had fled Jerusalem when revolt irrupted in AD 66. He was also Jewish, and it is not surprising that Jerusalem figures prominently in his vision. In Revelation 11, one of the more obscure passages of the book, John receives a measuring rod and instructions to measure the temple of God. Presumably the setting of this vision is before Rome's destruction of the temple in AD 70, which might indicate that John received his revelation over a period of decades.

The Two Witnesses Die at Jerusalem

The vision in Revelation 11 anticipates imminent occupation of Jerusalem by pagan armies: the court outside the temple will be "given over to the nations, and they will trample over the holy city for forty-two months" (11:2).[2] John expects two sackcloth-clad witnesses to prophesy and suffer martyrdom (11:3). We cannot be certain about the identity of these individuals, but we know they are victims of the beast. Apparently they are followers of Jesus who die in Jerusalem, "the great city that is prophetically called Sodom and Egypt, where also their Lord was crucified" (11:8). By preventing the heavens from raining, they stand in the tradition of Elijah (1 Kings 17:1). In turning the waters to blood and striking the earth with plagues, they recall Moses. It is not clear what these allusions meant to John.

Since John bitterly calls Jerusalem "Sodom and Egypt," we infer that it had become a difficult place for Christians. Sodom was the quintessential city of evil in Jewish memory, and Egypt was a place of slavery and oppression. Perhaps the two witnesses were followers of Jesus who had remained in Jerusalem as the Jewish revolt gathered momentum. Brutal martial law prevailed as rebel leaders—called robbers by Josephus—vied with one another for control of the insurrection. If Christians or others had wanted to negotiate peace with the Romans when Jerusalem was under siege (AD 68–70), they would have been in trouble. Josephus says leaders of the insurrection, who were "divided on all else, put to death as their common enemies any in favor of peace with the Romans or suspected of any intention to desert."[3]

Whoever the two witnesses are, their corpses lie unburied for three days, and people celebrate their demise (Rev. 11:9–10). This picture fits what we know about horrendous conditions in Jerusalem during the siege of AD 68–70. So many who were trapped in the city died from famine or internal strife that

2. Forty-two months is three and one-half years. In the book of Daniel, three and one-half indicates a brief, intense period of suffering or persecution (7:25; 9:27; 12:7).

3. Josephus, *Jewish War* 5.30; in Josephus, *The Jewish War*, vol. 3, trans. H. St. J. Thackeray, LCL 487 (1927–28; Cambridge, MA: Harvard University Press, 1967), 209.

Josephus says the piles of corpses presented a horrible spectacle, emitted a pestilential stench, and were an "impediment to the combatants in their sallies."[4] Famine became so bad in Jerusalem that some desperate occupants resorted to cannibalism.[5]

Worship Transports Us Forward

John finally sees Jerusalem decimated by a great earthquake that kills thousands (11:13), an apt metaphor for the cataclysm that ensued when Roman armies finally overran the city in AD 70. The seventh angel blows his trumpet, and loud voices in heaven cry,

> The kingdom of the world
>   has become the kingdom of our Lord
>   and of his Messiah,
> and he will reign forever and ever. (11:15)

In this liturgical fragment from the heavenly courts, we see an important function of worship: to transport participants forward in time to God's final victory—or to bring the future into the present. "The kingdom of the world / has become the kingdom of our Lord!" Through the Messiah, God is asserting sovereignty over the earth now, even when history looks bleak. The glories of all human achievement will someday come under the lordship of Christ.

To be sure, this anticipatory victory celebration unfolds in heaven, not on earth. John and his fellow Christians can hardly have rejoiced when Jerusalem was reduced to rubble. But John's vision of worship in heaven is meant to elicit a parallel response within the church on earth. Throughout history, Christians in the midst of suffering have offered heartfelt praise to God. From ancient Rome to modern China, the church has grown when persecution bears down. Worship is always at the heart of spiritual renewal in the midst of suffering.

People who have no hope of saving themselves, who risk everything of this world because of allegiance to Christ, place their hope in God without reservation. Loren Johns writes, "Hope—if it derives from a clear empowering vision of God's reality—is itself *an effective action* insofar as persons in community act on the basis of a new understanding or interpretation of reality."[6]

---

4. Ibid. 6.1; in Thackeray, *Jewish War*, 3:379.
5. Ibid. 6.201–13.
6. Loren L. Johns, *The Lamb Christology of the Apocalypse of John: An Investigation into Its Origins and Rhetorical Force*, WUNT (Tübingen: Mohr Siebeck, 2003), 203.

Jews Need an Alternative Future after AD 70

With the holy city of Jerusalem in ruins after AD 70 (fig. 11.2), Jewish leaders regrouped elsewhere in Palestine to forge a new future. The priestly class of Judaism was gone, and rabbis (teachers) became the primary guides for a people finding their way after catastrophe. Even before the fall of Jerusalem, a prominent rabbi named Yochanan (Yokhanan/ Yoḥanan) ben Zakkai (fig. 11.3) escaped the city and secured permission from the Romans to teach Jewish law at a town west of Jerusalem called Yavneh (Jabneh/Jamnia), near the Mediterranean seacoast. Citing the words of God in Hosea 6:6, "I desire mercy, not sacrifice" (NIV), Rabbi ben Zakkai taught his people to replace animal sacrifice with deeds of loving-kindness and prayer.[7]

Fig. 11.2. Gigantic stones, once part of the magnificent temple built by Herod the Great, still lie where they fell from the Temple Mount when Roman armies destroyed Jerusalem in AD 70.

After AD 70 the core of Jewish identity shifted from temple to Scripture. Worship of Yahweh now took place in homes and synagogues rather than in the Jerusalem temple. The Torah—the first five books of the Old Testament—provided a steady anchor for a people cast away from their homeland. Rabbis put into writing the vast code of oral tradition— the Mishnah, eventually incorporated in the Talmud—that taught the faith community how to apply the Scriptures to daily life.

In this way, Diaspora (dispersed/scattered) Judaism could survive without a base in Jerusalem, and Jewish communities remained strong in cities across the Mediterranean world. Because Christianity emerged from within Judaism, Christian congregations often formed in close proximity to Jewish synagogues. But while Judaism was largely an ethnic phenomenon, with actual blood ties among its adherents, Christianity quickly jumped the fence to become a faith for all peoples. At Caesarea Maritima on the Mediterranean coast (fig. 11.4), Peter brought the gospel to a Roman centurion named Cornelius (Acts 10:1–48), a representative of the very army that had crucified Jesus and would eventually destroy Jerusalem. Paul became an apostle to the Gentiles (Rom. 11:13) and wanted to carry the gospel of Jesus Christ as far as Spain (15:28).

The missionary impulse of Christianity was unsettling to some pagans. The Romans generally found Jewish monotheism unappealing and the practice of circumcision barbaric. But for strategic purposes, Jews and Romans

7. *'Aboth d' Rabbi Nathan* 4.

Fig. 11.3. At Tiberias on the Sea of Galilee, the tomb of Yoḥanan ben Zakkai (front left) stands before a modern steel memorial marking the tomb of medieval Jewish scholar Maimonedes.

had established diplomatic ties already in the second century BC.[8] Rome had made peace with the Jews, at least until the revolt of AD 66–70, and treated Judaism as a tolerated religion. There were Romans and Greeks who were attracted to aspects of Judaism, and some even affiliated with the religion as proselytes or "God-fearers" (e.g., Acts 2:9–11; 6:5; 13:43; 16:14). But Judaism largely confined itself to descendants of Abraham and Sarah, and there was little chance that the religion would significantly penetrate pagan society.

Christianity Reaches to the Ends of the Earth

In contrast to the self-defined ethnic boundaries of Judaism, Christianity was set to communicate its message "in Jerusalem, in all Judea and Samaria, and to the ends of the earth" (Acts 1:8). Not only did Christians have global objectives; they also used the politically loaded language of the kingdom of God. Yet this was no conventional kingdom with palaces and armies and conquests. Jesus had told Pilate, "My kingdom is not from this world. If my kingdom were from this world, my followers would be fighting to keep me from being handed over to the Jews [who collaborated with Rome]" (John 18:36).

Nevertheless, the gospel had real political implications. The charge against Christians at Thessalonica was that they were "turning the world upside down" and "acting contrary to the decrees of the emperor, saying that there is another king named Jesus" (Acts 17:6–7). Christians not only believed their crucified Lord had risen from the dead; they also believed Jesus had ascended to heaven and would come again to reign on earth with the saints. Romans rightly feared that Christians would give their allegiance to this Jesus rather than to Rome and its empire.

8. Josephus, *Jewish Antiquities* 12.413–19; 1 Macc. 8:17–30.

Fig. 11.4. Herod this Great built this aqueduct to provide water for his magnificent port city of Caesarea Maritima—where Peter shared the gospel with a centurion (Acts 10) and Paul appeared in trial before the Roman procurator Festus and the Jewish ruler Herod Agrippa II (Acts 25, 26).

Believers Escort Christ to Earth

John's description of a new heaven and new earth (Rev. 21:1) brings to mind a popular teaching among modern Christians that believers will be "raptured"[9] or snatched up to heaven when Christ returns. This notion developed only in recent centuries; it stems from a misunderstanding of Paul's teaching in a letter to the church at Thessalonica. At the coming (*parousia*) of Christ, Paul reports, "the dead in Christ [believers who have died] will rise first" to meet him. "Then we who are alive, who are left, will be caught up in the clouds together with them to meet the Lord in the air; and so we will be with the Lord forever" (1 Thess. 4:16–17).

"Parousia," a familiar word in the ancient world, could mean "arrival" in an ordinary sense—such as the arrival of fellow believers Stephanas, Fortunatus, and Achaicus to be with Paul at Ephesus (1 Cor. 16:17). The New Testament never uses the phrase "second coming" in reference to Jesus; it simply speaks of his imminent "coming" (parousia).

"Parousia" also had a more technical political meaning, referring to the arrival of a king or other ruler for a state visit. Josephus, for example, tells about the parousia of Alexander the Great at Jerusalem in 332 BC. Alexander had already conquered Damascus, Sidon, and Tyre, and intended to pass through

9. The English term *rapture* comes from the Latin word *rapio*, "to carry off." In 1 Thess. 4:17 the ancient Latin Vulgate translation of the Bible uses this word in the form *rapiemur* (we will be caught up), first-person plural, future passive indicative.

Judea on his way to Egypt. Jaddus, the Jewish high priest in Jerusalem, had previously refused a request from Alexander for tax payments and supplies for his troops. Now Jaddus awaited the arrival of the conqueror and his entourage with foreboding.[10]

But according to Josephus, Jaddus had a dream indicating that he should "adorn the city with wreaths and open the gates and go out to meet them, and that the people should be in white garments." Jaddus acted accordingly as he prepared for the "coming [*parousia*]" of the king. When he learned that Alexander was not far from Jersualem, Jaddus processed out with priests and a body of citizens to meet him. The delegation greeted Alexander and escorted him into the city, where Alexander invited the Jews to "ask for any gifts which they might desire."[11]

This political meaning is how we should understand the parousia of Christ in the New Testament. Rather than imagining that Christians will be whisked away from a planet going up in flames, we should anticipate a day when we will go out to meet Christ "in the air" and welcome him to earth again. This hope has broad implications for how we care for the environment and otherwise share in God's long-term plan to restore creation.

New Jerusalem Is the Church in Mission

Jesus taught his followers to pray, "Your kingdom come. Your will be done, on earth as it is in heaven" (Matt. 6:10). This reflects longing for a new political and social order, for heavenly values of justice and love to find tangible expression on earth. John witnessed a fulfilment of this radical petition, telling us, "I saw the holy city, the new Jerusalem, coming down out of heaven from God, prepared as a bride adorned for her husband" (Rev. 21:2). Just as God once inhabited Zion, God now will inhabit the new Jerusalem.

Modern interpreters sometimes complain that John of Patmos was escapist, seeming to advocate withdrawal from society (see 18:4) in hopes that a new world would come into being by divine intervention. When assessing John's understanding of mission, we do well to remember that he likely was the target of persecution, confined to Patmos against his will. Direct action to transform the Roman world was simply not an option for him, and he expected that the same would soon be true for his readers. Even Christians from the seven churches who remained free were not living in a participatory democracy, in which it is possible to lobby legislators or otherwise influence the political process.

10. Josephus, *Jewish Antiquities* 11.317–26.

11. Ibid. 11.327–39. For discussion of the parousia, see John Dominic Crossan and Jonathan L. Reed, *In Search of Paul: How Jesus's Apostle Opposed Rome's Empire with God's Kingdom* (San Francisco: HarperSanFrancisco, 2004), 167–71.

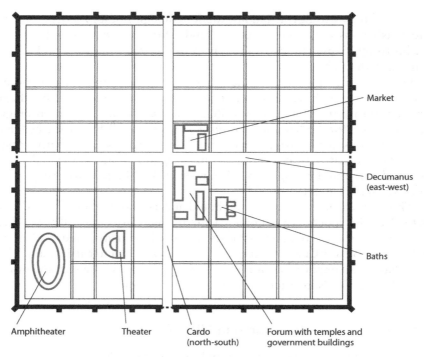

Fig. 11.5. If site conditions allowed, the Romans would lay out a new city in a square or rectangle. The main street running north-south was the *cardo*, and the east-west counterpart was the *decumanus*. These two main streets passed through the city walls at triple-door gateways on the north, south, east, and west. At the center of the city was the *forum* with temples and government buildings. A source of water supplied baths, and there was a theater and amphitheater for large groups to take part in ceremonies or entertainment. The new Jerusalem has parallels to all these features but is a cube. It has a footprint large enough to encompass all the territory from Jerusalem to Rome and is approximately equal in size to the total land mass of the Roman Empire (see map on p. 212).

If the new Jerusalem is entirely in the future—even in John's future—then perhaps he was escapist. But if we understand the arrival of the new Jerusalem to have started already in John's day, and to continue in our own, then the holy city is a symbol of God restoring the world in the present. Someday, when Christ returns, the restoration will be complete.

The new Jerusalem, as an image for the kingdom of God, should inspire tangible acts of discipleship for followers of the Lamb. Although the kingdom of God is more than the church, the church is a primary means by which God has chosen to embody the good news. The *global* church, encompassing all who truly know and follow Jesus, is the Christian's most important place of belonging.[12] The new Jerusalem image in Revelation suggests the following for the church's theology of salvation and mission:

12. Paul perhaps goes so far as to equate the (new) Jerusalem with the church in Gal. 4:26.

1. *Salvation is corporate*, not just individual; a *city* is the vehicle of redemption. Although it matters what individuals believe and do, saved individuals are brought into a worshiping, healing *community* when they give allegiance to Jesus.

2. *The scope of salvation is enormous*: the new Jerusalem is twelve thousand stadia (one thousand five hundred miles) in length, width, and height (21:16). The city has a footprint approximately equal in size to the entire land mass of the Roman Empire (see p. 212)! The cube shape of the city harks back to the same configuration of the holy of holies in the temple of Solomon (1 Kings 6:20). But whereas one room in Solomon's temple offered access to God for a privileged few, the divine presence now is accessible to all who seek God throughout the world.

3. *The old and the new covenants are both integral to the structure of the redeemed community.* The wall of the city has twelve foundations, each bearing the name of one of the twelve apostles (Rev. 21:14). Gates of the city feature the names of the twelve tribes of Israel (21:12). This blend of symbols from both Testaments suggests that Christians cannot abandon their ties to Judaism. The canon—the collection of authoritative Scripture—includes both the Old and the New Testaments.

4. *People of the Lamb enjoy astonishing wealth in an egalitarian society.* Suetonius reports that Augustus so beautified the city of Rome that he could "justly boast that he had found it built of brick and left it in marble."[13] Now, in John's vision, the new Jerusalem is *pure gold*, built on a foundation of precious stones, with gates made of pearls (21:18–21)! In contrast to the elitist Roman economy, wealth here is shared by all. The new Jerusalem has no hoarding, no exclusive neighborhoods, and no poverty.

5. *All followers of the Lamb have fellowship with God*, without intermediary. All followers of the Lamb are priests (1:6; 5:10). The city has no temple, for God and the Lamb are themselves the temple (21:22). Christians need not await the rebuilding of the physical temple at historic Jerusalem because God can be worshiped any place on earth.

6. *Improbable people are part of the redeemed community.* "The nations will walk by its light, and the kings of the earth will bring their glory into it" (21:24). Kings of the earth! They were the ones so recently fornicating with the beast (17:2), and now they are coming into the presence of the Lamb! The prophet Isaiah once had a vision of foreign kings coming into Jerusalem, evidently as prisoners of war (Isa. 60:11–12). John foresees a time when kings of the earth apparently will choose to enter the new Jerusalem.

13. Suetonius, *Augustus* 28; in *Suetonius*, vol. 1, trans. and ed. J. C. Rolfe, LCL 31 (1913–14; Cambridge, MA: Harvard University Press, 1960), 167.

Fig. 11.6. From these ruins at Hierapolis near Laodicea we get an idea of what John meant by three gates on each side of the city. Emperor Domitian built this triple gate in AD 83.

7. *There is free access to the new Jerusalem.* The city has three gates on the east, three on the north, three on the south, and three on the west. Its gates will never be shut by day, and there will be no night there (Rev. 21:13, 25; fig. 11.6). This community is more concerned with having God and the Lamb at the center than with gatekeeping.

8. *Healing of the nations is the mission* of the holy city. John sees the river of the water of life flowing from the throne of God and the Lamb. The river issuing from Jerusalem is an ancient symbol from the Garden of Eden (Gen. 2:10) and from visions of the Hebrew prophets (Ezek. 47:1–12; Zech. 14:8). The water nurtures the tree of life, and "the leaves of the tree are for the healing of the nations" (Rev. 22:1–2).

9. *Those who willfully reject God and the Lamb remain outside* the new Jerusalem. These include "the cowardly, the faithless, the polluted," as well as murderers, fornicators, sorcerers, idolaters, and liars (21:8). No one "who loves and practices falsehood" (22:15) will enter. This last category provides a critical clue for understanding why some are excluded: there are people who love something else more than obedience to God, so they do not want to enter.

10. *Worship is the central activity* of the new Jerusalem. The throne of God and the Lamb are in it, "and his servants will worship him; they will see his face, and his name will be on their foreheads" (22:3–4). The beast is gone, along with the mark it put on the forehead of its followers.

A Divine Christ Gives Meaning to History

From start to finish in Revelation, Jesus is the key to understanding both God and history. "I am the Alpha and the Omega," Jesus says, "the first and the last, the beginning and the end" (22:13). Revelation reflects a high Christology, making lofty claims about the divinity of Jesus. At the beginning of Revelation, John sees Jesus: "His head and his hair were white as white wool, white as snow; his eyes were like a flame of fire, his feet were like burnished bronze, refined as in a furnace, and his voice was like the sound of many waters" (1:14–15). This imagery parallels Old Testament descriptions of God (Ezek. 1:26–27; Dan. 7:9).

Now, at the close of his vision, John refers to the throne (singular) of God and the Lamb (Rev. 22:1, 3). Although the church had not yet articulated a doctrine of the Trinity when Revelation appeared, John uses imagery in which God and Jesus seem to coalesce into one entity. After Christ addresses each of the seven churches in chapters 2 and 3, he enjoins each to "listen to what the Spirit is saying to the churches" (as in 2:7). In this case Christ seems to coalesce into one entity with the Spirit. An incipient doctrine of the Trinity is evident in Revelation.

Worship Is a Staging Area for Spiritual Resistance

With sin and death still present, the new Jerusalem was not yet a full reality in John's day. Nor does any part of the church today embody all of the holy city. But in this time between the times, worship becomes the central means by which God orients individuals and congregations toward God's future. Among the seven churches of Revelation, worship is more than just a setting in which Revelation will be heard. Worship, says Jean-Pierre Ruiz, is "the staging area from which and on the basis of which John mounted a minority counter-attack against the powerfully convincing claims" of the Roman Empire.[14] A titanic spiritual struggle is underway to win the hearts and minds of peoples and nations.

A faith community in the midst of this epic contest needs worship with robust rituals, and we find marks of such worship at the end of Revelation. John hears this benediction:

> Blessed are those who wash their robes,
> so that they will have the right to the tree of life
> and may enter the city by the gates. (22:14)

Washing robes in the blood of the Lamb may be an allusion to baptism (see 7:14). The blood of Jesus, as a parallel to Old Testament sacrifice, takes away sin (see 1 John 1:7). Paul says those receiving baptism in the name of

---

14. Jean-Pierre Ruiz, "Praise and Politics in Revelation 19:1–10," in *Studies in the Book of Revelation*, ed. Steve Moyise (Edinburgh: T&T Clark, 2001), 74.

Jesus are "baptized into his death" (Rom. 6:3), which for many early believers meant martyrdom.

Through worship that embodies a lively eschatology—an understanding of where God is taking history—the church finds power to live faithfully in the present. Christian eschatology is more about the end (purpose) of history than about the terminus (finishing point) of history. Because Christians believe God intends to restore creation through Christ, we pray daily for his coming in our lives and in our world.

After a lengthy discussion of Christian conduct in 1 Corinthians, Paul concludes his letter with the Aramaic words *Marana tha* ("Our Lord, come!" 1 Cor. 16:22). John ends Revelation similarly:

> The Spirit and the bride say, "Come."
> And let everyone who hears say, "Come."
> And let everyone who is thirsty come.
> Let anyone who wishes take the water of life as a gift. (Rev. 22:17)

Jesus, "the bright morning star" (2:28; 22:16), is the sure sign of a new day dawning. The planet Venus, brightest object in the heavens after the sun and moon, is the morning star. It orbits so close to the sun that it is only visible in the sky shortly before or after sunrise and sunset. Anyone awaiting dawn knows the hour is close when Venus rises in the east. The appearance of Jesus—both in his earthly ministry and in the vision of John—is a signal that the time when God will restore all things is near.

Revelation begins and ends with an invitation to eating (3:20) and drinking (22:17). These invitations may be related to the Lord's Supper, the central act of worship in the Christian community. The apostle Paul understands communion in eschatological terms: "For as often as you eat this bread and drink the cup, you proclaim the Lord's death until he comes" (1 Cor. 11:26). The last words of Revelation reflect the same hope and offer a closing benediction:

The one who testifies to these things says,

> "Surely I am coming soon."
> Amen. Come Lord Jesus!

The grace of the Lord Jesus be with all the saints. Amen. (Rev. 22:20–21)

For Reflection

1. Are you satisfied to let the specifics of Christ's return remain a mystery? What are the dangers of becoming too certain about when and how

the parousia will take place? Why might it matter if we pay too little attention to Christ's return?

2. What would the new Jerusalem look like if it were coming to the place where you live? Do you see signs of its presence? What does an emerging new Jerusalem mean for relationships between nations or ethnic groups?

3. Have you experienced worship transporting you forward to something for which you long? What role did Scripture, song, or body posture have in that experience?

LIVING THE VISION

The New Jerusalem in Nebraska

For more than thirty years, Nadine and Al Peters have been bringing something of heaven to a place of brokenness in Nebraska. Once a week, these gentle-spirited farmers drive fifteen miles to visit prisoners at the Nebraska Correctional Center for Women. "We are just trying to do what Jesus would have done," they say. "He reached out to the downtrodden. He did not come for those who have it together."

Nadine and Al dispense business cards describing their specialty: "Building relationships—horizontal & vertical," and "Peace work." They felt called to become involved in prison ministry in 1974 when they led a young adult Bible study group that was captivated by James 2:17: "Faith by itself, if it has no works, is dead."

"Once you are in prison," the Peters say, "you literally have been stripped, deloused, and humiliated. By the time we get to see the prisoners, they are in a lot of pain." Many have had shattering life experiences. One prisoner confided that her father had raped her for sixteen years. "Now at last I can talk about it," she said. Over the years Al and Nadine have been in pastoral relationship with more than a thousand prisoners.

"We are allowed to hug the women," Nadine says, "and for some that's the only physical contact they have all week." Community emerges among prisoners who commit their lives to Christ. "You are my family," a woman exclaimed to a group of Christian inmates when she came to faith. Al and Nadine make phone contact with former prisoners and sometimes drive hundreds of miles to visit a woman after her release.[15]

15. Nadine and Al Peters, interview by the author, April 15, 2007, Henderson, Nebraska.

12

Long-Term Hope

The one who testifies to these things says,
"Surely, I am coming soon."
Amen. Come, Lord Jesus! (Rev. 22:20)

We began this book with a letter from Trevor, for whom a worship experience soon after September 11, 2001, marked a change in his ethics and worldview. The patriotic and military symbol of the American flag, incorporated into Christian worship, became the focal point of his allegiance to empire. "If my identity as an American makes me a target," he wrote, "I have an obligation to defend myself, my family, and my neighbors." Deciding factors in his shift of loyalty were pride in nation and desire for security, which eclipsed a lifelong commitment to the way of the Lamb.

In both the Roman world and the modern era, symbols and rituals have been means of promoting political, national, and class loyalties. Incorporated into ceremony or worship, symbols and rituals reinforce belief systems and shape values. Revelation unmasks the manipulation of ritual and worship by malevolent forces, and it shows the life-giving power of worshiping God and the Lamb.

Hammers and Crocuses Focus Anger and Hope

Soon after September 11, 2001, the seminary where I worked chose to grieve the loss of so many human lives by pounding thousands of wooden stakes into the lawn of our campus. The stakes—one for each victim—formed a

Fig. 12.1. Students and faculty at Associated Mennonite Biblical Seminary in Indiana form a cross on the lawn with wooden stakes representing victims of the 2001 terrorist attacks. (J. Tyler Klassen/*The Elkhart Truth*)

one-hundred-twenty-foot cross next to the seminary chapel (fig. 12.1). Students, faculty, and visitors gathered to lament and pray, then silently picked up hammers and went to work. While pounding out our grief and fear onto the cross, we remembered the words of Jesus at Golgotha: "Father, forgive" (Luke 23:34). The sound of our hammers reminded us of the brutality of our Lord's death and the cost of loving the enemy.

As winter approached in 2001, students and faculty pulled up the thousands of wooden stakes and slipped a crocus bulb into each wound in the ground. Every spring for several years, a colossal cross appeared on the lawn as the crocuses sprang up and bloomed. The seminary community gathered on the lawn to celebrate Jesus' victory of life over death. The stakes and crocuses did not change the world or stop the war, but the symbolic action changed us. We affirmed our conviction that someday "death will be no more; mourning and crying and pain will be no more" (Rev. 21:4), and wars will cease. Hope enables us to take risks for healing and reconciliation in a broken world.

It is difficult to argue that, in the short run, following the Lamb in circumstances of violence will "work." Jesus died on a Roman cross. Peter, Paul, and countless other followers of Jesus suffered violent deaths. There were millions of Christian martyrs in the twentieth century alone. Jesus was blunt about the cost of being a disciple: "If any want to be my followers, let them deny themselves and take up their cross and follow me" (Mark 8:34).

Discipleship Requires a Theology of the Future

Living out the way of the Lamb makes little sense without a God-centered eschatology or theology of the future. Important as it is to work for an end to violence and injustice, humans are not going to gradually improve until we ourselves usher in a golden age. A restored humanity and a new creation will come by divine initiative, when God at last chooses to "reconcile to himself all things" in Christ (Col. 1:20).

In the meantime, we worship daily with the prayer of Jesus, "Your kingdom come. Your will be done, on earth as it is in heaven" (Matt. 6:9). That is the most radical of prayers because it calls for the justice and healing of heaven to become reality on earth. By praying these words, we signal our citizenship in the new Jerusalem.

The author of Hebrews understands the importance of worship as the way to endure suffering and claim citizenship in the heavenly city:

> Jesus also suffered outside the city gate in order to sanctify the people by his own blood. Let us then go to him outside the camp and bear the abuse he endured. For here we have no lasting city, but we are looking for the city that is to come. Through him, then, let us continually offer a sacrifice of praise to God, that is, the fruit of lips that confess his name. (Heb. 13:12–15)

The book of Hebrews, like Revelation, points to a city—presumably with economic, political, and social dimensions—that God is about to bring into being. Hope is the hallmark of those who live into this future, and worship is their defining agenda.

Sometimes Worship Is Play

Revelation conveys an earnest message about suffering and faithfulness, but its imagery sometimes seems playful. This especially is true when John describes worship. Around the throne of God are fantastic creatures with heads like a lion, an ox, an eagle, and a human (4:6–7). These are not lovable beasties from Maurice Sendak's *Where the Wild Things Are*, but they tease the imagination. Jesus, the one we worship, is a Lamb! Rome, whom we must not worship, is an outlandish streetwalker. Evil is lampooned as a trio of beasts. Saints in heaven participate in massive victory celebrations—wearing party clothes (white robes), or waving branches (fig. 12.2), or falling to the ground, or casting crowns before the throne.

Scientific study of play is still in a fledgling state, but it may be able to shed

Fig. 12.2. This coin from about 15 BC portrays Emperor Augustus seated on a platform before worshipers waving branches. (Photo courtesy of Harlan J. Berk, Ltd.)

light on the nature and function of worship. Psychiatrist Stuart Brown, founder of the National Institute for Play, says that play

> reduces the social distance between individuals and assists in the development of more intricate intimate bonds. . . . Play and games seem necessary for the development of community, which requires mutual trust, cooperation and common goal setting. They are necessary to develop a sense of future optimism and perseverance. Handicapping, the play induced behavior where the strong voluntarily withholds domination in a situation of unequal power, is learned in the crucibles of solitary and social play by all social creatures. . . . For humans, play is also surprisingly active in the shaping of one's own inner private narratives (actual sense of self), and thus is directly related to mental health and elasticity. It is also the means by which we shape a model world.[1]

Brown's description of play has parallels to worship in Revelation. Worship in John's vision reduces social distance as the seer finds himself in the very presence of God, as he joins a mighty chorus of great and small united in praise. Worship builds community as John shows Christians that they are part of a cross-section of the universe that honors God. Optimism emerges as worshipers see the victory of the Lamb and are motivated to persevere. There is voluntary handicapping, as the Lion of Judah chooses to operate as a Lamb. Imaginative worship shapes the private inner narratives of believers, and they come to see themselves as having "washed their robes and made them white in the blood of the Lamb" (7:14). Believers in Asia Minor have their eyes opened to a model society in the form of the new Jerusalem, a vision of reconciled mortals living communally in the presence of God.

Worship Turns Chaos to Order

Walter Brueggemann speaks of Christians organizing our lives around "counterimagined worlds"[2] that stand over against empire and evil. The world around us may be full of violence and greed. But in the act of worship, we imagine the world as God created it and as God will re-create it. By the power of the Spirit, we receive an actual foretaste of the new creation. God's design for the future begins to take tangible form, at least in part, through healing and hope in the restored community called the church. Because followers of Jesus counterimagine a world different from what we see, we live differently.

1. Stuart Brown, in the Public Broadcasting Service series "The Promise of Play." This quote is from the "Touch the Future" website, http://ttfuture.org/authors/stuart_brown (accessed July 16, 2009). See Stuart Brown and Christopher Vaughan, *Play: How It Shapes the Brain, Opens the Imagination, and Invigorates the Soul* (New York: Avery, 2009).

2. Walter Brueggemann, *Texts under Negotiation: The Bible and Postmodern Imagination* (Minneapolis: Fortress, 1993), 12–18.

Worship in Revelation has roots in Jewish tradition, especially in the Torah, the first five books of the Old Testament. Samuel Balentine underscores that worship in the Torah functions to bring order out of chaos. Just as Revelation emerged while the Roman Empire dominated the world, the Torah began to take final shape when the Jewish people were under the yoke of the Persian Empire (539–333 BC).

As the era of Persian dominance began, the Jews—defeated and disoriented—were allowed to return from Babylon to Jerusalem. The restoration was bittersweet since the throne of David was gone, and the temple of Solomon lay in ruins. Once free and self-confident, Jews now were subject people in a pagan empire. The Persians used every means at their disposal to bring order to the realms they dominated. But from a Jewish religious and political perspective, the world was in chaos.

The Torah, Balentine writes, provided raw material for worship in a chaotic world. Through an assortment of narratives, songs, and liturgical texts, Jewish worship (or cult, as Balentine prefers to call it) "was the occasion for returning symbolically to primordial time, to the primal assertions of Genesis 1: God created the world, brought order to disorder, established a divine purpose for the cosmos that is secure and sustainable, and created humankind in the divine image with the responsibility and the capacity to fulfill God's creational design for the cosmos."[3]

Jews worshiped with stories and symbols that pointed to a reality larger than the Persian Empire. Worship reminded them that God still had the power to end darkness and to bring order to the bleakest circumstances. By liturgically affirming this hope, God's people strengthened their conviction that the Persian Empire was not the culmination of history.

John Howard Yoder points to a similar function of worship in the book of Revelation. To sing, "The Lamb is worthy to receive power," as did the early Christian communities in their hymnody, "is not mere poetry. It is performative proclamation. It redefines the cosmos in a way prerequisite to the moral independence that it takes to speak truth to power and to persevere in living against the stream when no reward is in sight."[4]

Revelation Illuminates the Landscape of Worship

Revelation is the longest continuous worship text in the Bible. The vision illuminates the landscape of both emperor worship and Christian worship, teaching us the following:

3. Samuel E. Balentine, *The Torah's Vision of Worship* (Minneapolis: Fortress, 1999), 13–14.

4. John Howard Yoder, *The Royal Priesthood: Essays Ecclesiological and Ecumenical*, ed. Michael G. Cartwright (Grand Rapids: Eerdmans, 1994), 8.

1. *True worship of God transcends time, culture, language, and nation.* When we worship God and the Lamb, we join a vast multitude of saints from all peoples and all eras of history (Rev. 7:9–17). Seeing ourselves as part of this multitude makes us less likely to be co-opted by idolatrous allegiance to tribe or nation. We are less likely to let issues and perspectives of our own generation eclipse the shared wisdom of saints through the ages. We will respect and learn from the theological reflection, spiritual disciplines, creeds, and ethical convictions of believers around the world and across the centuries. We will not abandon parts of sacred Scripture that happen to grate against our political or cultural preferences.

2. *Jesus is central to Christian worship.* Revelation's steady focus on the Lamb reminds us of the centrality of Jesus for worship and discipleship. By opening the heavens, the incarnate Christ makes possible a new creation and a new humanity. Jesus is the new Adam (1 Cor. 15:45), the bright morning star (Rev. 22:16) that heralds the dawn of a new era. Revelation's high Christology, symbolized by the coalescing of God and the Lamb, signals that Jesus is more than just a good role model. Jesus is God-with-us, Emmanuel. When we worship Jesus, we worship God (see John 20:28). Worshiping Jesus shapes our loyalty to the kingdom of God just as emperor worship consolidated allegiance to Rome. Emperor worship frequently happened over meals in the guild halls and political associations of the Roman world. In Christian worship, especially in the eucharistic meal, we open the door to the risen Christ so he will enter and dine with us (Rev. 3:20).

3. *Christian worship is steeped in Scripture.* There are some four hundred allusions to the Old Testament in John's vision, evidence that he knew the Bible well. Believers need to replenish our spiritual wells with words and images from the Psalms, the Prophets, the teachings of Jesus, and all of Scripture. The Bible gives us prayer vocabulary. It offers models for structuring worship and living holy lives that honor God and the Lamb.

4. *Other gods use symbols, icons, and indexes to attract our worship.* What is the meaning of symbols such as patriotic lapel pins or commercial brand names? Do we crave status symbols such as fine cars, club memberships, or academic degrees? What is the appropriate Christian attitude toward icons of nationalism, such as war heroes or political party candidates? How should we view men and women who become icons of fashion, business, sports, or cinema? When we are exposed daily to a tsunami of advertising messages, how do we avoid the index of craving things we do not need and most of the world cannot afford?

Young people in the Western world, who see tens of thousands of television or Internet commercials a year, are particular targets of consumer seduction. Nathan Dungan, a financial services professional, speaks of youth being targeted by a "three-headed monster—a high-powered triumvirate of consumer-products companies, media conglomerates, and advertising agencies."[5] Dungan describes the sophisticated marketing and enormous amounts of advertising that induce young people to buy clothing, soft drinks, cell phones, or health and beauty products—many of which become status symbols in youth culture. The monster systematically uses television, Internet, text messaging, and social networks to influence the values of youth, millions of whom bow in submission through the index of making a purchase. Dungan does not connect his imagery to Revelation, but his beast language has parallels to John's vision and may help us see the importance of following the Lamb in all areas of life.

5. *The patronage system of Babylon will try to enlist us.* Today we generally do not speak of patrons and clients with the meanings those words had in John's era. But institutions, businesses, and professional organizations still operate today as pyramids of power. John's vision should make us circumspect about what we must do to be employed or to advance in the corporate or professional culture. Must we sell our souls to achieve success, violating the values and teaching of the Lamb? Revelation might inspire us to ask whether companies for which we work, or in which we invest our money, behave ethically. Do they care for creation, treat workers at home or around the world with dignity, and deliver goods or services that benefit humanity?

6. *We can name and confront the powers during Christian worship.* Not all human ills, personal or social, can be reduced to psychological or scientific explanations. Evil has an agent behind it, a predatory spirit of greed and death. Symbols in Revelation—such as the beast, the harlot, or Babylon—can help Western Christians recover an awareness of structural evil and the malevolent source of sin. We must take care, however, not to employ such symbols in self-serving ways simply to beat up on national or tribal foes. There is a tragic history of Christians using beast language, for example, to stoke nationalism in war or to discredit believers of other denominations or world religions. Let us look first for beastly forces within our own power structures; let us consider the possibility that we in the industrialized West might be living in Babylon.

During the American war in Vietnam, several Christians broke into military draft board offices and destroyed files at Catonsville, Maryland. William Stringfellow said this was a "sacramental protest against the

5. Nathan Dungan, *Prodigal Sons and Material Girls: How Not to Be Your Child's ATM* (Hoboken, NJ: John Wiley & Sons, 2003), 70.

Vietnam war—a liturgy of exorcism" that "exposed the death idolatry of a nation that napalmed children."[6] Revelation provides worship language and symbols for believers to take up such resistance to the powers.

7. *Christian worship has allegiance-shaping power.* Hymns, creeds, communion, baptism, weddings, funerals, and other rituals and symbols have the capacity to define and shape loyalty. Architecture, dance, procession, body posture, and other ways of using space or movement can penetrate deep into our souls and change us. Revelation majors in such aspects of worship, and we should pay attention to these in our homes and churches. We might want to draw on biblical symbolism to create worship spaces in our homes and in our daily schedules.

When my daughter was a child, I often walked her six blocks across north London to school. On the first day I accompanied her, we had just moved to England, and she was afraid to meet classmates in a new culture. She asked me to pray for her as we walked through a long narrow alley. That spot forever became prayer alley, where we remembered to pray aloud each day as we walked together to school. I have sought prayer alleys in my life ever since, because a rhythm of prayer woven into the daily routine is life-giving. More recently I have benefited from the discipline of practicing the daily office, using a book of Scripture, song, and prayer structured for personal or corporate worship.[7]

8. *Worship requires a contemporary idiom.* Rituals of allegiance and worship in John's vision would have felt contemporary to his first readers, since they reflected commonly recognized political and religious realities of the ancient world. Symbols such as thrones, crowns, and white clothes must have made sense immediately to members of the seven churches. The same is true for the indexes of bowing, singing praises, and burning incense. In a similar way, our forms of worship need to be in an idiom that connects with the lived experience of today's believers. We can make judicious use of contemporary technology, music, and art. To stay grounded in the historical foundations of Christian faith, we also will need to use symbols, icons, and indexes from the Bible and Christian tradition. Some expressions—such as footwashing, or the sign of the cross, or the word "amen"—might require interpretation.

9. *Deeds are a vital aspect of worship.* Ethics and manner of life, not just belief, matter in the eyes of God. Deeds are evidence of faith, a necessary

---

6. William Stringfellow, in *A Keeper of the Word: Selected Writings of William Stringfellow*, ed. Bill Wylie Kellermann (Grand Rapids: Eerdmans, 1994), 307.

7. Catholic, Anglican, Orthodox, and other Christian groups have a long and rich tradition of daily office prayers. For a recent version of the daily office that emphasizes discipleship and peacemaking, see Arthur Paul Boers et al., *Take Our Moments and Our Days: An Anabaptist Prayer Book*, rev. ed. (Scottdale, PA: Herald, 2007).

manifestation of the allegiance we express in prayer, song, and creed. The messages to the seven churches in Revelation 2 and 3 end with practical instruction about behavior, upon which salvation depends. Christ says, "Repent, and do the works you did at first. If not, I will come to you and remove your lampstand from its place" (Rev. 2:5). It is Christ, not fellow Christians, who finally removes unfaithful congregations. When mortals stand before God on the day of reckoning, they receive judgment "according to their works, as recorded in the books" (20:12).

The world watched in 2006 when an Amish community in Pennsylvania reached out to love and forgive the family of a man who shot and killed five of their schoolchildren before turning a gun on himself. Despite deep anguish, the Amish impulse to forgive was spontaneous and universal in their faith community. When asked about the origins of this shared response, the Amish consistently pointed to the Lord's Prayer, with its petition that God forgive our sins as we forgive others. "The Lord's Prayer is said in *every* church service," an Amish minister reported. "We don't have a church service, a wedding, a funeral, or an ordination without the Lord's Prayer." Amish toddlers learn the Lord's Prayer, and schoolchildren recite it every morning.[8] The Lord's Prayer is at the heart of Amish worship, shaping allegiance to Jesus and inspiring reflexive behavior patterned on his words and actions.

Worship Empowers the Marginalized

Because many Christians in North America live at relative ease in the heart of empire, it may be difficult for us to identify with the countercultural nature of worship in Revelation. We are tempted to the diversion of using Revelation as a horoscope for predicting the future rather than as a handbook for radical Christian living in the present. Believers in the two-thirds world who deal daily with poverty or violence, however, may help us grasp the function of worship among suffering people.

Sociologist David Martin reports that evangelicalism in Latin America, especially the fast-growing Pentecostal variety, is deeply grounded in worship. Evangelicalism flourishes among economically and politically marginalized people, among self-governing worshiping communities in slums and impoverished villages. In these places there are islands of Christian hope in which believers

are able to devise their own social world for themselves. And as these worlds expand numerically they gain a sense of latent power, which above all becomes

8. Donald B. Kraybill, Steven M. Nolt, and David L. Weaver-Zercher, *Amish Grace: How Forgiveness Transcended Tragedy* (San Francisco: Jossey-Bass, 2007), 91.

manifest as they come together in vast public gatherings [for worship]. The growing network of chapels represents a walkout from society as presently constituted. The evangelical believer is one who has symbolically repudiated what previously held him in place, vertically and horizontally.[9]

Martin does not call these communities the new Jerusalem. But in language reminiscent of Revelation, he says that their "adoption of a new life means drinking pure and 'living water.'" Worshipers have their identities set free from a hierarchy of military and economic patronage that reaches to the top of society, and often to an empire beyond. The result of worship in these communities is tangible social and economic change in the lives of participants. Destructive machismo diminishes, and people whom Jesus delivers from substance abuse lead stable lives that allow for greater financial security. The church offers opportunity to develop leadership skills that open vocational doors elsewhere.[10]

Martin's analysis of Pentecostalism in Latin America illustrates that healthy worship is not escapism. In the act of worshiping God, believers receive a new identity not defined by the hierarchies of Babylon. In their walkout from society as presently constituted, followers of the Lamb experience an alternative society in which they find meaning and hope.

With Long-Term Hope, Christians Live Differently

Encounter with the living God changes individuals, communities, and eventually the world. It is the *eventually* part of change that tempts us to abandon the way of the Lamb and take ethical shortcuts. We know that Jesus called his followers to put away the sword, to lay up treasure in heaven, and to love the enemy. But when terrorists strike, or when we fear for our security, the dominant culture socializes us to be "realistic." We want short-term, surefire ways to alleviate fear and insecurity.

But Christian eschatology takes a long-term view of change. To be sure, many early Christians anticipated that the end of earthly empire was imminent. "I am coming soon," Jesus tells John (Rev. 22:12, 20). And Jesus reminds his followers, "You must also be ready, for the Son of Man is coming at an unexpected hour" (Matt. 24:44).

For two thousand years Christians have waited in divine suspense, looking for the final revelation of Jesus even as we move on with our lives. While some believers get caught up in speculations about the temporal proximity of Christ's appearance, it is more important to live in spiritual proximity to

9. David Martin, *Tongues of Fire: The Explosion of Protestantism in Latin America* (Cambridge, MA: Blackwell, 1993), 285.
   10. Ibid., 108, 231.

our Lord. That happens in worship, when the presence of Jesus truly is near and soon.

Hope Energizes Mission

When Jesus appears to his disciples soon after the resurrection, their minds immediately turn to political forecasting. "Lord, is this the time when you will restore the kingdom to Israel?" they ask (Acts 1:6). Jesus steers them away from such speculation: "It is not for you to know the times or periods that the Father has set by his own authority. But you will receive power when the Holy Spirit has come upon you; and you will be my witnesses in Jerusalem, in all Judea and Samaria, and to the ends of the earth" (Acts 1:7–8). In other words, forget about predicting the future and get on with the task of mission!

We must read Revelation in the spirit in which John wrote it, learning how worship of God can shape allegiance to Jesus and empower us to invite others to the new Jerusalem that is our true home.

Amen. Come, Lord Jesus!

For Reflection

1. Have you witnessed or experienced cases when worship seemed to re-order a chaotic world for an individual or community? What exactly did worship do to transform the situation? Do you ever find worship playful?
2. Now that you have traversed the whole of Revelation, how has your view of the book changed? In what ways has this experience affected your view of symbols, rituals, and other signs in church and society?
3. What questions or unresolved issues about Revelation remain for you?

LIVING THE VISION
Seeds of the Kingdom in Rural Japan

Aki and Ray Epp manage a twelve-acre farm called Menno Village near Aki's birthplace on the Japanese island of Hokkaido. There they model sustainable agricultural practices, build Christian community, and ask questions about modern farming techniques. International seed companies, Ray says, threaten the global environment by aggressively promoting a few genetically engineered varieties of seed. This practice reduces the gene pool and makes agriculture too vulnerable to disease.

Members of seventy-five local Japanese households help on the Epp farm, sharing in the bounty and risk. Ray observes that the average food item in the United States travels one thousand three hundred miles to the consumer, wasting energy and polluting the environment. As a result, consumers lose touch with the natural world, and rural communities are destroyed as agribusiness displaces traditional farms.

The Epps practice traditional Japanese *polyculture* farming, with up to ten different crops in one field. "Japanese young people are beginning to awaken to the economic and ecological maladies of the modern world," Ray says. "Menno Village provides a way for Japanese people to discover their traditional community life and agriculture. We work with government officials and nongovernment organizations to give shape to agricultural policy and local food systems." Menno Village produces rice, potatoes, wheat, soybeans, and thirty varieties of vegetables. Instead of buying chemical fertilizer, Epps produce their own fertilizer from tofu production waste, rice husk charcoal, and chicken manure.

A rhythm of worship "reminds us that God made the world right, and we need to *faith* that into action," states Ray. "We will not save the world ourselves, but our actions bear witness to what God has done and will do: unite all things—including principalities and powers—in Christ."[11]

11. Aki and Ray Epp, interview by the author, November 26, 2007, Sapporo, Japan.

Time Line of Events, People, and Empires That Figure in Revelation

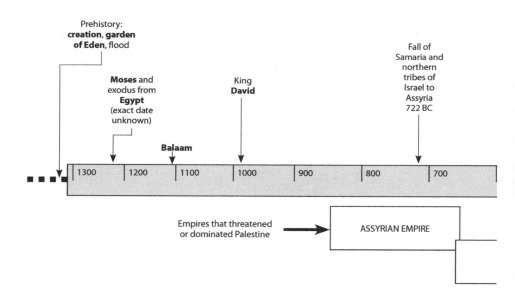

Prehistory: **creation, garden of Eden**, flood

Moses and exodus from **Egypt** (exact date unknown)

Balaam

King **David**

Fall of Samaria and northern tribes of Israel to Assyria 722 BC

| 1300 | 1200 | 1100 | 1000 | 900 | 800 | 700 |

Empires that threatened or dominated Palestine

ASSYRIAN EMPIRE

Items in **bold** receive particular attention or allusion in John's vision

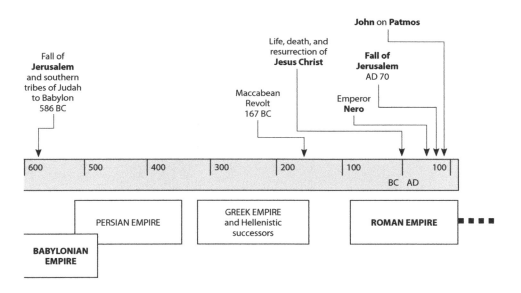

Fall of
Jerusalem
and southern
tribes of Judah
to Babylon
586 BC

Life, death, and
resurrection of
Jesus Christ

John on **Patmos**

**Fall of
Jerusalem**
AD 70

Maccabean
Revolt
167 BC

Emperor
Nero

| 600 | 500 | 400 | 300 | 200 | 100 | 100 |

BC   AD

PERSIAN EMPIRE

GREEK EMPIRE
and Hellenistic
successors

ROMAN EMPIRE

**BABYLONIAN
EMPIRE**

Glossary

Africa: A Roman imperial province located in the north-central coastal region of what is known today as the continent of Africa.

Ahab: The ninth-century BC king of the northern nation of Israel whom the prophet Elijah confronted for tolerating Baal worship promoted by Ahab's Phoenician wife, Jezebel (1 Kings 16:29–22:40).

Alexander the Great (356–323 BC): The king and general from Macedonia, north of Greece, who conquered the eastern Mediterranean (including Judea), Mesopotamia, and part of India in the last twelve years of his life. His conquests consolidated the Greek cultural dominance that still shaped the ancient world in the New Testament era.

amillennialism: The belief that the thousand-year reign described in Revelation 20 is largely symbolic and that to the extent it is literal it began at Pentecost and will end at the **parousia**. *See* **eschatology**.

amphora: A tall two-handled ceramic vase carrying about one hundred fifty pounds (seventy kilograms) of liquid and used in the ancient world to transport olive oil, wine, fish sauce, and other commodities. Amphorae usually were not recycled, and a huge pile of smashed amphorae called Monte Testaccio remains in Rome today from goods imported in the imperial epoch.

Ancient of Days: The divine judge—presumably God—in the final judgment scene of Daniel 7:9 RSV.

Antiochus IV Epiphanes (reigned 175–164 BC): The Hellenistic (Greek-culture) tyrant king of Syria who conquered Cyprus and much of Egypt and adopted the surname "Epiphanes" ("[god] manifest"). He brutally suppressed Jewish religion and ritually violated the temple in Jerusalem, triggering a revolt led by Judas Maccabaeus and a cleansing of the temple that Jews commemorate today as Hanukkah (1 Macc. 1–6; 2 Macc. 1–9).

Antipas: An otherwise unknown Christian martyr at Pergamum (Rev. 2:13). The only believer named in Revelation as having been put to death.

Aphrodisias: A small city near Laodicea named for Aphrodite, goddess of love, where archaeologists have found a fine first-century marble Sebasteion, or temple of the imperial cult.

apocalypse: A Greek word meaning "unveiling" or "uncovering," and the first word of the book of Revelation. The term often refers to a type of prophetic writing produced by postexilic Jews and later by early Christians. It commonly features dreams, visions, heavenly journeys, and extensive symbolism. Most apocalypses (but not Revelation) are pseudepigraphical: they purport to have been written by some ancient notable person who accurately "predicts" events of world history up to and just after the time of the actual writing.

Apollo: Greek god of sun, light, poetry, and music; the son of Zeus; and twin of Artemis, whose temple was prominent at Ephesus (Acts 19:23–41). Nero liked to impersonate Apollo and erected an enormous statue of himself in the likeness of the god at Rome.

apostle: A title meaning "one who is sent" by Jesus in mission to the world. Sometimes a technical term referring just to the specially authorized Twelve, though Paul insists that he too has apostolic authority.

Apostolic Tradition: An early manual of church discipline and worship (ca. AD 215), commonly attributed to Hippolytus, a third-century theologian at Rome.

Aramaic: A Semitic language closely related to Hebrew that probably was the primary language of Jesus, his disciples, and early Christians of Jewish background.

Armenia: A kingdom in the mountainous region between the Caspian Sea and the Black Sea whose empire extended to the Mediterranean Sea early in the first century BC. Contested territory between the Roman and **Parthian** Empires in the first century AD, Armenia definitively became a client state of the Roman Empire when King **Tiridates** presented himself to Nero at Rome in AD 66.

Asia/Asia Minor: Asia was a province of the Roman Empire located in the western third of the region called Anatolia or Asia Minor (most of modern Turkey). The province Asia was governed by a proconsul sent from Rome and included the cities of the seven churches of Revelation.

augustales: An order of priests established by Emperor Tiberius to preside at ceremonies of Roman emperor worship. In the provinces these priests usually were wealthy freedmen.

Baal: The Canaanite storm and fertility god whom Queen Jezebel promoted in ninth-century BC Israel, whose prophets Elijah humiliated on Mount Carmel and killed at the nearby Wadi Kishon (1 Kings 18).

Babylon: An ancient city located in what today is Iraq. It became capital of the Babylonian Empire, which defeated the Assyrian Empire in 612 BC to dominate Mesopotamia. Babylonians conquered Jerusalem in 586 BC, destroyed the Jewish temple, and took thousands of captives to Babylon—making Babylon an enduring symbol of idolatry, injustice, and hubris in some Jewish circles.

benefits: A technical term for goods, services, employment, or other advantages provided by patrons to their **clients** in the **patronage system** of the ancient world.

Bithynia: A Roman province in northwest Asia Minor. When **Pliny the Younger** was governor of Bithynia in (ca.) AD 111–112, he wrote a letter to Trajan about prosecuting Christians in the province. This marks the earliest extant reference to followers of Jesus in Roman imperial records.

Caesarea Maritima: A port city on the Mediterranean coast that was the capital of Roman government in Palestine and the site where Herod the Great built a magnificent harbor with a temple of emperor worship. Disturbances between Jews and pagans that led to the Jewish War irrupted first at Caesarea in AD 66.

Caiaphas: Jewish high priest at Jerusalem at the time of the trial and execution of Jesus (Matt. 26:3; John 18:13).

Christology: Theology about the person and work of Christ. High Christology emphasizes the divinity of Christ.

client: A participant in the **patronage system** of the Roman world who was beholden to and often dependent upon a patron to whom the client looked for **benefits** and to whom the client offered allegiance, praise, and service.

Dead Sea Scrolls: Scrolls of the Hebrew Bible and other documents from about 150 BC to AD 70 that were found in caves near the Dead Sea in 1947 and following years. The scrolls probably belonged to the radical Jewish sect of the **Essenes**, who had a monastery nearby.

Dio Cassius: A Roman historian who wrote a fourteen-hundred-year history of Rome in eighty volumes, many fragments of which survive. Born in Nicaea in **Asia Minor** around AD 165, Dio was a friend of several emperors. He served as a senator and consul in Rome and as a governor in Smyrna.

eschatology: "Last" things, from (Greek) *eschatos*, meaning "last"; the theology of where history is headed and how the world will end or be transformed in the future. Christian eschatology includes the return of Christ and a full realization of the kingdom of God.

Essenes: A diverse Jewish religious movement that flourished in the New Testament era and had similarities with the early Christian movement, including a vibrant eschatology and messianic expectations. It is almost certain that the monastic Qumran community that produced the **Dead Sea Scrolls** was Essene.

Gaul: A region of the Roman Empire comprising what today is France, Belgium, Luxembourg, and Western Germany.

gematria: The modern term for an ancient system of assigning numerical value to letters of the alphabet, thereby determining a specific sum for any word.

Hades: The Greek god of death; also the underworld or place of the dead in Greek mythology.

Herod the Great (ruled 37–4 BC): The half-Jewish, half-Nabatean collaborator with Rome who was made king of Judea by the Romans. He splendidly rebuilt the Jewish temple at Jerusalem even as he also built temples of emperor worship at **Caesarea Maritima,** Caesarea Philippi, and Samaria-Sebaste.

index: A sign that communicates because it is affected by or changed by the phenomenon it registers.

Josephus (AD 37–ca. 100): Jewish historian who served as commander in Galilee for the Jewish War against Rome. He narrowly escaped execution when captured by General Vespasian, then became a Roman citizen. His primary works, which provide valuable though sometimes inaccurate information on the late New Testament era, are *Jewish Antiquities* and *Jewish War.*

Jupiter: Chief deity in Roman mythology, equivalent to Zeus in Greek religion, whose temple was the largest at Rome.

Maccabean Revolt: A successful Jewish revolt begun in 167 BC against the Seleucid Empire when its pagan king, **Antiochus IV Epiphanes,** sought to destroy Jewish religion by desecrating the temple at Jerusalem and banning practice of the Torah. The book of Daniel, the earliest full-blown Jewish apocalypse, likely took its current form during early years of the revolt (see also 1 and 2 Maccabees).

monotheism: The belief that there is only one God.

Mount Zion: An ancient name for Jerusalem, especially the raised area called the Temple Mount.

Nebuchadnezzar (ruled 605–562 BC): King of the Babylonian Empire (*see* **Babylon**) and army general who besieged Jerusalem in 597 BC and eventually destroyed the temple and the city in 586 BC, carrying thousands of Jews into captivity. Jewish narratives preserved in the book of Daniel tell of heroic Jewish resistance to Nebuchadnezzar's idolatrous actions and decrees.

Neptune: God of sea and water in Roman mythology.

Olympia: The city in southwestern Greece where the Olympic games began; not to be confused with Mount Olympus, highest mountain in (northeastern) Greece and home of the gods in Greek mythology.

pagan: An adherent of a polytheistic religion; from (Latin) *paganus,* "country dweller, rustic."

parousia: A Greek word (loanword in English) that in the ancient world meant "coming," either in the ordinary sense of a common person's arrival, or of the state visit of an emperor or other powerful person. Early Christians adopted the word to refer to the anticipated (second) coming of Christ. *See* **eschatology.**

Parthia: An area of northeastern Iran, from which the Parthian Empire reigned between 238 BC and AD 226. At its greatest extent the Parthian Empire reached into **Armenia** and eastern Turkey and was a longtime political threat to the Romans.

patronage system: The pyramid of power relationships that linked every person in the Roman Empire, from the emperor to the lowliest slave, through a chain of patron-client pairings. Patrons gave **benefits** to **clients**, who returned allegiance, praise, and service.

Pax Romana: Latin propaganda term meaning "Roman peace"; the order, prosperity, and end to war ostensibly brought about by Roman rule in the ancient world.

Persia: An area in the southeastern region of modern Iran that ruled the vast Persian Empire. The empire was founded by Cyrus the Great, who defeated the Babylonians in 539 BC and permitted captive Jews to return to their homeland (Ezra 1).

Philo of Alexandria (20 BC–AD 50): Jewish philosopher and prolific author in Alexandria, who famously joined a Jewish delegation that personally appealed to Emperor Caligula for help in AD 40, when tensions ran high between Jews and pagans in Egypt.

Pliny the Younger: A Roman lawyer, senator, and bureaucrat whom Emperor Trajan sent to serve as governor of **Bithynia**, a province north of the seven churches of Revelation, in (ca.) AD 111–112. Pliny served as judge for the earliest trials of Christians for which we have record in Roman imperial sources.

Pontius Pilate: Procurator/prefect of Judea (AD 26–36), who presided at the trial of Jesus and provoked protest from Jews of Jerusalem by publicly displaying icons of the Roman emperor.

postmillennialism: The doctrine that Christ will return after the thousand-year reign anticipated in Revelation 20. *See* **eschatology**.

premillennialism: The doctrine that Christ will return before the thousand-year reign anticipated in Revelation 20. *See* **eschatology**.

Res gestae divi Augusti: A lengthy inscription cataloging accomplishments of Caesar Augustus during his reign, commissioned by the emperor before his death for his mausoleum, and titled "Deeds of the Divine Augustus." The original at Rome is lost, but stone inscriptions of it were made throughout the Roman world. The best surviving today is at Ankara (ancient Ancyra) in Turkey.

Seneca (ca. 4 BC–AD 65): Stoic philosopher and rhetorician who became tutor to the lad Nero and later served as his adviser. Seneca was the author of plays, dialogues, and satires—the most famous of which is *Apocolocyntosis divi Claudii* (Pumpkinification of the Divine Claudius), a satire on Emperor Claudius becoming divine at his death. Seneca's proconsul brother, Gallio, presided over a court proceeding for the apostle Paul (Acts 18:12–17). Nero eventually suspected Seneca of joining a plot against him and induced him to commit suicide.

sestertius (Latin pl.: *sestercii*; French pl.: *sesterces*): A common large brass (with the reform of Augustus) coin of the Roman Empire, worth one-fourth *denarius*. Its size made it an ideal medium for state propaganda, especially for detailed images of reigning or deceased emperors and the gods or conquests with which they were associated. See chart at end of glossary.

Son of Man: Early Christian title for Jesus, especially in the Gospels, implying that he was the fulfillment of a prophecy in Daniel 7:13–14 about a messianic ruler who would usher in the eternal kingdom of God.

standard: A pole topped with an eagle or small bust of the emperor(s) that heralded a Roman army camp or official procession.

Suetonius (ca. AD 69–ca. 130): Historian who famously wrote biographies of twelve successive Roman rulers from Julius Caesar to Domitian, in a volume called *The Twelve Caesars* (*De vita Caesarum*). Suetonius also served on the staff of **Pliny the Younger** when the latter was governor of **Bithynia**.

syncretism: The combining or blending of religions, common in the ancient world but unacceptable in the **monotheism** of Jews and Christians.

Tacitus (ca. AD 56–117): Roman senator and historian who wrote accounts—only parts of which survive—of the Roman Empire from *Caesar Augustus* to near the end of the first century AD. His primary works are the *Histories* and the *Annals*. The latter includes discussion of Nero's persecution of Christians, the earliest known reference to Jesus and Christians in secular Roman sources.

Tertullian (ca. AD 155–230): Church leader from Carthage in **Africa**, who was raised in a **pagan** family and became a prolific author of Christian apologetic and polemical works. His essays give insight into how early Christians related to Roman society, and his *Apology*, addressed to the Roman rulers, is a classic defense of Christian faith.

tetradrachm: The most common ancient Greek coin in centuries leading up to the emergence of the Roman Empire. Made of silver, it was equivalent to four drachmas. The drachma was approximately one day's wage for a skilled worker.

Tiridates: King of **Armenia**, from the border and disputed territory between the Roman Empire and the Parthian Empire (*see* **Parthia**), who famously journeyed to Rome in AD 66 to appear before Nero in the forum and publicly align himself and his people with Rome.

Yahweh: Hebrew name (יהוה) for the God of Israel, never vocalized by devout Jews; commonly capitalized in English versions of the Scriptures as LORD.

Zealots: Jewish revolutionaries who took inspiration from the violent zeal of Phinehas in Numbers 25 and 31 and fostered resistance to Roman rule in Palestine. Scholars differ on the degree to which Zealots were an organized or coherent movement. They perhaps should be seen as a diverse grouping of insurgents, bandits, and religious idealists who helped generate ferment leading to the Jewish War of AD 66–70.

Zion: *See* **Mount Zion.**

Relative Value of Roman Coins in the First Century AD

Name of coin	Metal	Value
as	copper	base unit
dupondius	brass	2 asses
sestertius	brass	4 asses
denarius	silver	16 asses
aureus	gold	400 asses

Bibliography

Achtemeier, Paul J. "Revelation 5:1–14." *Interpretation* 40 (1986): 283–88.

Aune, David E. *Revelation*. WBC 52A, 52B, 52C. Dallas: Word Books, 1997–98.

Balentine, Samuel E. *The Torah's Vision of Worship*. Minneapolis: Fortress, 1999.

Barr, David L., ed. *Reading the Book of Revelation: A Resource for Students*. Atlanta: Society of Biblical Literature, 2003.

———. *Tales of the End: A Narrative Commentary on the Book of Revelation*. Santa Rosa, CA: Polebridge, 1998.

Bauckham, Richard. *The Theology of the Book of Revelation*. Cambridge: Cambridge University Press, 1993.

Beale, G. K. *The Book of Revelation: A Commentary on the Greek Text*. New International Greek Testament Commentary. Grand Rapids: Eerdmans, 1998.

Blount, Brian K. *Can I Get a Witness? Reading Revelation through African American Culture*. 2005.

———. *Revelation: A Commentary*. New Testament Library. Louisville: Westminster John Knox, 2009.

Boesak, Allan A. *Comfort and Protest: The Apocalypse from a South African Perspective*. Philadelphia: Westminster, 1987.

Boring, M. Eugene. *Revelation*. Louisville: Westminster John Knox, 1989.

Bradshaw, Paul F. *Early Christian Worship: A Basic Introduction to Ideas and Practice*. Collegeville, MN: Liturgical Press, 1998.

Bradshaw, Paul F., Maxwell E. Johnson, and L. Edward Phillips. *The Apostolic Tradition: A Commentary*. Hermeneia. Minneapolis: Fortress, 2002.

Brueggemann, Walter. *Texts under Negotiation: The Bible and Postmodern Imagination*. Minneapolis: Fortress, 1993.

Caird, George B. *The Revelation of St. John the Divine*. New York: Harper & Row, 1966.

Charlesworth, James H., ed. *The Old Testament Pseudepigrapha*. 2 vols. Garden City, NY: Doubleday, 1983–85.

Claridge, Amanda. *Rome: An Oxford Archaeological Guide*. New York: Oxford University Press, 1998.

Collins, Adela Yarbro. *Crisis and Catharsis: The Power of the Apocalypse*. Philadelphia: Westminster, 1984.

Crossan, John Dominic. *God and Empire: Jesus against Rome, Then and Now*. San Francisco: HarperSanFrancisco, 2007.

Crossan, John Dominic, and Jonathan L. Reed. *In Search of Paul: How Jesus's Apostle Opposed Rome's Empire with God's Kingdom*. San Francisco: HarperSanFrancisco, 2004.

Dungan, Nathan. *Prodigal Sons and Material Girls: How Not to Be Your Child's ATM*. Hoboken, NJ: John Wiley & Sons, 2003.

Ehrman, Bart D., ed. *After the New Testament: A Reader in Early Christianity*. New York: Oxford University Press, 1999.

Eller, Vernard. *The Most Revealing Book of the Bible: Making Sense out of Revelation*. Grand Rapids: Eerdmans, 1974.

Fant, Clyde E. *A Guide to Biblical Sites in Greece and Turkey*. Oxford: Oxford University Press, 2003.

Fiorenza, Elisabeth Schüssler. *The Power of the Word: Scripture and the Rhetoric of Empire*. Minneapolis: Fortress, 2007.

———. *Revelation: Vision of a Just World*. 2nd ed. Proclamation Commentaries. Minneapolis: Augsburg Fortress, 1998.

Friesen, Steven J. *Imperial Cults and the Apocalypse of John: Reading Revelation in the Ruins*. Oxford and New York: Oxford University Press, 2001, 2006.

Garnsey, Peter, and Richard Saller. *The Roman Empire: Economy, Society, and Culture*. Berkeley: University of California Press, 1987.

Gonzalez, Justo L. *Faith and Wealth: A History of Early Christian Ideas on the Origin, Significance, and Use of Money*. San Francisco: Harper & Row, 1990.

Goodman, Martin. *Rome and Jerusalem: The Clash of Ancient Civilizations*. New York: Knopf, 2007.

Gradel, Ittai. *Emperor Worship and Roman Religion*. New York: Oxford University Press, 2004.

Grimsrud, Ted. *Triumph of the Lamb*. Scottdale, PA: Herald Press, 1987.

Hays, Richard B. *The Moral Vision of the New Testament: Community, Cross, New Creation; A Contemporary Introduction to New Testament Ethics.* San Francisco: HarperSanFrancisco, 1996.

Horsley, Richard A. *Jesus and Empire: The Kingdom of God and the New World Disorder.* Minneapolis: Augsburg Fortress, 2002.

―――. *Paul and Empire.* Harrisburg, PA: Trinity, 1997.

Howard-Brook, Wes, and Anthony Gwyther. *Unveiling Empire: Reading Revelation Then and Now.* Maryknoll, MD: Orbis Books, 1999.

Hurtado, Larry W. *At the Origins of Christian Worship: The Context and Character of Earliest Christian Devotion.* Grand Rapids: Eerdmans, 2000.

Jensen, Robin Magaret. *Understanding Early Christian Art.* New York: Routledge, 2000.

Johns, Loren L. *The Lamb Christology of the Apocalypse of John: An Investigation into Its Origins and Rhetorical Force.* WUNT. Tübingen: Mohr Siebeck, 2003.

Kovacs, Judith, and Christopher Rowland. *Revelation: The Apocalypse of Jesus Christ.* Oxford: Blackwell, 2004.

Kraybill, Donald B., Steven M. Nolt, and David L. Weaver-Zercher. *Amish Grace: How Forgiveness Transcended Tragedy.* San Francisco: Jossey-Bass, 2007.

Kraybill, J. Nelson. "Apocalypse Now." *Christianity Today*, October 25, 1999, 30–40.

―――. *Imperial Cult and Commerce in John's Apocalypse.* JSNTSup 132. Sheffield: Sheffield Academic Press, 1996. Translated into Portugese by Barbara Theoto Lambert as *Culto e Comércio Imperiais no Apocalipse de João.* São Paulo: Paulinas, 2004.

―――. "The New Jerusalem as Paradigm for Mission." *Mission Focus: Annual Review* 2 (1994): 123–32.

Kreider, Alan. *The Change of Conversion and the Origin of Christendom.* Christian Mission and Modern Culture. Harrisburg, PA: Trinity, 1999.

Kreitzer, Larry Joseph. *Striking New Images: Roman Imperial Coinage and the New Testament World.* JSNTSup 134. Sheffield: Sheffield Academic Press, 1996.

Lewis, Naphtali, and Meyer Reinhold, eds. *Roman Civilization: Sourcebook 2, The Empire.* New York: Harper & Row, 1966.

Longenecker, Richard N., ed. *Into God's Presence: Prayer in the New Testament.* McMaster New Testament Studies. Grand Rapids: Eerdmans, 2001.

Lopez, Davina C. *Apostle to the Conquered: Reimagining Paul's Mission.* Minneapolis: Fortress, 2008.

Martin, David. *Tongues of Fire: The Explosion of Protestantism in Latin America.* Cambridge, MA: Blackwell, 1993.

Meeks, Wayne A. *The Moral World of the First Christians*. Philadelphia: Westminster, 1986.

Meijer, Fik, and Onno van Nijf. *Trade, Transport, and Society in the Ancient World: A Sourcebook*. London: Routledge, 1992.

Mizusaki, Noriko, and Mayumi Sako, eds. *Poems of War and Peace: Voices from Contemporary Japanese Poets*. Osaka: Chikurinkan, 2007.

Murphy, Frederick J. *Fallen Is Babylon: The Revelation to John*. Harrisburg, PA: Trinity, 1998.

Musurillo, Herbert, trans. *The Acts of the Christian Martyrs*. Oxford: Clarendon, 1972.

Novak, Ralph Martin. *Christianity and the Roman Empire: Background Texts*. Harrisburg, PA: Trinity, 2001.

O'Donovan, Oliver. "The Political Thought of the Book of Revelation." *Tyndale Bulletin* 37 (1986): 61–94.

Peirce, Charles Sanders. *Peirce on Signs: Writings on Semiotic by Charles Sanders Peirce*. Edited by James Hoopes. Chapel Hill: University of North Carolina Press, 1991.

Pescarin, Sofia. *Rome*. Vercelli: White Star, 2000.

Pippin, Tina. *Death and Desire: The Rhetoric of Gender in the Apocalypse of John*. Louisville: Westminster John Knox, 1992.

Price, Simon R. F. *Rituals and Power: The Roman Imperial Cult in Asia Minor*. New York: Cambridge University Press, 1984.

Reddish, Mitchell G. *Revelation*. Smyth & Helwys Bible Commentary. Macon, GA: Smyth & Helwys, 2001.

Rice, Jim. "An Officer and a Pastor." *Sojourners*, April 1994, 12.

Richard, Pablo: *Apocalypse: A People's Commentary on the Book of Revelation*. Maryknoll: Orbis Books, 1995.

Rossing, Barbara R. *The Choice between Two Cities: Whore, Bride, and Empire in the Apocalypse*. Harrisburg, PA: Trinity, 1999.

Rowland, Christopher. *Revelation*. Epworth Commentaries. London: Epworth Press, 1993.

Royalty, Robert M., Jr. *The Streets of Heaven*. Macon, GA: Mercer University Press, 1998.

Ruiz, Jean-Pierre. "Praise and Politics in Revelation 19:1–10." In *Studies in the Book of Revelation*, edited by Steve Moyise, 69–84. Edinburgh: T&T Clark, 2001.

Salisbury, Joyce E. *Perpetua's Passion: The Death and Memory of a Young Roman Woman*. New York: Routledge, 1997.

Sear, David R. *Roman Coins and Their Values*. Vol. 1, *The Republic and the Twelve Caesars, 280 BC–AD 96*. London: Spink, 2000.

Sehested, Ken. "Loyalty Test: The Case of Chaplain Robertson." *Christian Century*, March 2, 1994, 212–14.

Senn, Frank C. *Christian Liturgy: Catholic and Evangelical*. Minneapolis: Fortress, 1997.

Smith, R. R. R. "The Imperial Reliefs from the Sebasteion at Aphrodisias." *Journal of Roman Studies* 77 (1987): 88–138.

Snyder, Graydon F. *Ante Pacem: Archaeological Evidence of Church Life before Constantine*. Rev. ed. Macon, GA: Mercer University Press, 2003.

Stevenson, James. *A New Eusebius: Documents Illustrative of the History of the Church to A.D. 337*. London: SPCK, 1957.

Stringfellow, William. *A Keeper of the Word: Selected Writings of William Stringfellow*. Edited by Bill Wylie Kellermann. Grand Rapids: Eerdmans, 1994.

Swartley, Willard M. *Covenant of Peace: The Missing Peace in New Testament Theology and Ethics*. Grand Rapids: Eerdmans, 2006.

———, ed. *Essays on Peace Theology and Witness*. Occasional Papers 12. Elkhart, IN: Institute of Mennonite Studies, 1988.

Thompson, Leonard L. *The Book of Revelation: Apocalypse and Empire*. New York: Oxford University Press, 1997.

Vermès, Géza. *The Complete Dead Sea Scrolls in English*. 6th rev. ed. Penguin Classics. New York: Penguin Group (USA), 2004.

Wengst, Klaus. *The Pax Romana and the Peace of Jesus Christ*. Translated by John Bowden. Philadelphia: Fortress, 1987.

Wiedemann, Thomas. *Emperors and Gladiators*. New York: Routledge, 1992.

Wink, Walter. *Engaging the Powers: Discernment and Resistance in a World of Domination*. Vol. 3 of *The Powers*. Philadelphia: Fortress, 1992.

Yaguchi, Yorifumi. *The Poetry of Yorifumi Yaguchi: A Japanese Voice in English*. Edited by Wilbur J. Birky. Intercourse, PA: Good Books, 2006.

Yeatts, John R. *Revelation*. Believers Church Bible Commentary. Scottdale, PA: Herald Press, 2003.

Yoder, John Howard. *The Politics of Jesus*. Scottdale, PA: Herald Press, 1972.

———. *The Royal Priesthood: Essays Ecclesiological and Ecumenical*. Edited by Michael G. Cartwright. Grand Rapids: Eerdmans, 1994.

Ancient Works

In citations of English translations from the following ancient works, archaic pronouns and verb forms have been rendered in modern English. British spellings have been changed to American, and pronouns have been made gender inclusive when that, arguably, was the intent of the author.

'Aboth d'Rabbi Nathan. Translated by Eli Cashdan. In The Minor Tractates of the Talmud. 2 vols. 2nd ed. Edited by A. Cohen, 1:1–210. London: Soncino, 1971.

The Apostolic Fathers. Translated by Kirsopp Lake. 2 vols. LCL 24, 25. 1912–13. Cambridge, MA: Harvard University Press, 1985.

Cicero. Tusculan Disputations. Translated by J. E. King. LCL 141. 1927. Cambridge, MA: Harvard University Press, 1960.

Corpus inscriptionum latinarum (CIL). Edited by Theodor Mommsen et al. Berlin-Brandenburg: Deutsche Akademie der Wissenschaften, 1863–.

The Dead Sea Scrolls in English. Translated by G. Vermès. 3rd. rev. ed. 1962. London: Penguin, 1994.

Dio Cassius. Dio's Roman History. Translated by Earnest Cary. 9 vols. LCL 32, 37, 53, 66, 82, 83, 175, 176, 177. 1914–27. Cambridge, MA: Harvard University Press, 1981.

Epictetus. The Discourses as Reported by Arrian, The Manual, and Fragments. Translated by W. A. Oldfather. 2 vols. LCL 131, 218. 1926–28. Cambridge, MA: Harvard University Press, 1969.

Josephus. Jewish Antiquities. Translated by Louis H. Feldman et al. 9 vols. LCL 242, 281, 326, 365, 410, 433, 456, 489, 490. Cambridge, MA: Harvard University Press, 1965.

———. The Jewish War. Translated by H. St. J. Thackeray. 3 vols. LCL 203, 210, 487. 1927–28. Cambridge, MA: Harvard University Press, 1967.

Horace. Satires, Epistles, and Ars poetica. Translated by H. Rushton Fairclough. LCL 194. 1926. Cambridge, MA: Harvard University Press, 1961.

Orientis graecae inscriptiones selectae (OGIS). Edited by W. Dittenberger. 2 vols. Leipzig: S. Hirzel, 1903–1905.

Pliny the Younger. Letters and Panegyricus. Translated by Betty Radice. 2 vols. LCL 55, 59. Cambridge, MA: Harvard University Press, 1969.

Schaff, Philip, and Henry Wace, eds. A Select Library of Nicene and Post-Nicene Fathers of the Christian Church. Second Series. Vol. 14. New York: Charles Schribner's Sons, 1905.

Seneca. Ad Lucilium epistulae morales. Translated by Richard M. Gummere. 3 vols. LCL 75–77. 1917–25. Cambridge, MA: Harvard University Press, 1961–62.

———. Moral Essays. Translated by John W. Basore. 3 vols. LCL 214, 254, 310. 1928–35. Cambridge, MA: Harvard University Press, 1958.

Sibylline Oracles. Translated by J. J. Collins. In *The Old Testament Pseude-pigrapha*, 2 vols. Edited by James H. Charlesworth, 1:317–472. Garden City, NY: Doubleday, 1983.

Strabo. *Geography.* Translated by Horace Leonard Jones. 8 vols. LCL 49, 50, 182, 196, 211, 223, 241, 267. 1923. Cambridge, MA: Harvard University Press, 1988.

Suetonius. Translated and edited by J. C. Rolfe. 2 vols. LCL 31, 38. 1913–14. Cambridge, MA: Harvard University Press, 1997–98.

———. *The Twelve Caesars.* Translated by Robert Graves. Revised by Michael Grant. Harmondsworth: Penguin Books, 1987.

Tacitus. *Agricola.* Translated by M. Hutton. Revised by R. M. Ogilvie. LCL 35. Cambridge, MA: Harvard University Press, 1970.

———. *Annals.* Translated by John Jackson. LCL 322. 1937. Cambridge, MA: Harvard UniversityPress, 1956.

———. *Histories.* Translated by Clifford H. Moore. 2 vols. LCL 111, 249. 1925–31. Cambridge, MA: Harvard University Press, 1981.

Virgil. *Aeneid.* Translated by H. Rushton Fairclough. Rev. ed. 2 vols. LCL 63, 64. 1934. Cambridge, MA: Harvard University Press, 1960.

Wankel, Hermann, et al., eds. *Die Inschriften von Ephesos.* 8 vols. in 9 parts. Bonn: Habelt, 1979–84.

Yonge, Charles Duke, trans. *The Works of Philo.* Peabody, MA: Hendrickson, 1993.

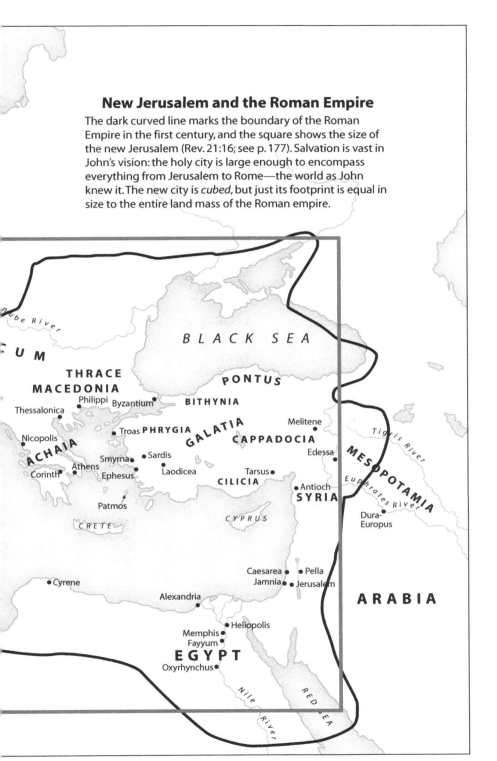

New Jerusalem and the Roman Empire

The dark curved line marks the boundary of the Roman Empire in the first century, and the square shows the size of the new Jerusalem (Rev. 21:16; see p. 177). Salvation is vast in John's vision: the holy city is large enough to encompass everything from Jerusalem to Rome—the world as John knew it. The new city is *cubed*, but just its footprint is equal in size to the entire land mass of the Roman empire.

be River

U M

THRACE
MACEDONIA
Thessalonica
Philippi
Byzantium
BITHYNIA

BLACK SEA

PONTUS

Melitene

Tigris River

Nicopolis
ACHAIA
Troas
PHRYGIA
GALATIA
CAPPADOCIA
Edessa
MESOPOTAMIA
Smyrna
Sardis
Athens
Laodicea
Tarsus
Euphrates River
Corinth
Ephesus
CILICIA
Antioch
SYRIA
Patmos
CYPRUS
Dura-Europus
CRETE

Cyrene

Caesarea
Jamnia
Pella
Jerusalem
ARABIA

Alexandria

Heliopolis
Memphis
Fayyum
EGYPT
Oxyrhynchus

Nile River

RED SEA

Scripture Index

Subject Index